MODERNISM AND MODERNITY

The Nova Scotia Series
Source Materials of the Contemporary Arts
Editor: Benjamin H. D. Buchloh

Volumes 1-8 were edited by Kasper Koenig

MODERNISM
AND
MODERNITY

THE VANCOUVER CONFERENCE PAPERS

Edited by Benjamin H. D. Buchloh, Serge Guilbaut, and David Solkin

THE PRESS OF THE NOVA SCOTIA COLLEGE OF ART AND DESIGN

Canadian Cataloguing in Publication Data
Main entry under title:
Modernism and modernity

(The Nova Scotia series; 14)
Papers presented at a conference held in Vancouver, B.C. in the Spring of 1981.
Includes bibliographical references. ISBN 0-919616-26-7

1. Modernism (Art) — Congresses. 2. Art, Modern — Congresses. 3. Art —
History — Congresses. I. Buchloh, Benjamin H. D. II. Guilbaut, Serge. III.
Solkin, David. IV. Nova Scotia College of Art and Design. V. Series: The Nova
Scotia series: Source materials of the contemporary arts; 14.

N6447.M62 1983   700'.9'03   C83-098842-4

Published by the Press of the Nova Scotia College of Art and Design
5163 Duke Street
Halifax, Nova Scotia
Canada, B3J 3J6 Tel: (902) 422-7381

Copyright 1983 by The Press of NSCAD and by the Authors

All Rights Reserved

Published in 1983
Printed and bound in Halifax, Nova Scotia
Designed by Cathy Quinn
Cover design by Allan Scarth.
Production by Diane Hiscox and Gary Kibbins.
Pressman: Guy Harrison
Published with financial assistance from the Canada Council

CONTENTS

Editor's Note

This is the second volume within the Nova Scotia Series that does not — at least not at first glance — correspond to the original outline of the series' programmatic subtitle: 'Source Materials of the Contemporary Arts.'

At the time the concept of 'Source Materials' must have been understood as referring to the results of an ongoing reflection on the conditions of artistic production within the work of the artists themselves, as the various reflective and critical processes that preceded and accompanied the actual work.

One of the premises of the publication program had been the inherent assumption that these reflections would be part of an autonomous, specialized discourse — that of the artist rather than that of the historian or critic — that did not share the situation of all cultural production in relation to the ideological cultural production in relation to the ideological framework within which it is produced and contained.

As a result of the ongoing process of reflection on the conditions of cultural production it has become increasingly apparent that this position is no longer tenable.

The Vancouver Conference on Modernism (March 12-14, 1981) was in fact one of the more productive steps in that reflection process on the validity of modernism's concepts as well as in the critical investigation of the various claims for its demise (and the latent interests in accelerating that event) as well as an attempt to verify the validity of the concept of post-modernism that has supposedly replaced it.

The decision to include the publication of the lectures that were delivered at the Vancouver Conference on Modernism within the Nova Scotia Series is therefore a decision that intends to reflect and contribute to the critical revision of the conditions of art production and reception. It is hoped that the volume provides 'Source Materials *for* the Contemporary Arts' and all critical cultural production as much as it should be seen in opposition to a contemporary art production that aspires to the conditions of industry.

Benjamin H. D. Buchloh

Serge Guilbaut

The Relevance of Modernism

Modernity is as old as the world . . . almost. Some historians place the birth of the concept in the fifth century, others in the middle ages, others still in the Renaissance, or, better still, in the seventeenth century battle between "Ancients and Moderns". Everyone agrees, however, that it was the nineteenth century which saw the articulation and development of a theory and practice of modernism.

Why, then, a conference on a topic so well known and so heavily knocked about? Very simply, because this old notion of the modern is not immortal; in fact today it is under attack from all sides, even to the point of being pronounced dead . . . or at least moribund.

This death sentence is only the latest installment of a long funerary procession that has formed an integral part of western cultural experience ever since the time of the Enlightenment and the French Revolution. Our culture loves to live in an atmosphere of ongoing crisis, in a frenzy of desire for Apocalypse. Attacks on the modern are nothing new.

But this time, the modernist crisis compels serious attention; a successor has been duly anointed. Not with a very original name, mind you: it seems that Post-Modernism will have to do. Yet this banality precisely defines the radically ironic assault launched against the modern. It is now, apparently, passé. The symbolic death of modernism itself has been announced in the most definitive and precise manner possible by the architect Charles Jencks, the herald of Post-Modernist ideology. According to him, this termination-point occurred at 3:30 p.m. on July 15th, 1972, when St. Louis' Pruitt-Igo housing development — a clean-lined, rational, prize-winning piece of modernist architecture — was blown up with dynamite, at the same time destroying the ghetto which had transformed the modern dream into a pre-historic nightmare. For Jencks, and for many other observers as well, all modernist aspirations seemed to collapse with the annihilation of these functional structures.

The excesses of the modernist logic itself have no doubt been partially responsible for the emergence of Post-Modernism. Another factor has been the recognition of new aspirations of diverse social currents (feminism, gay liberation, etc. . .), as well as what one might call "post-industrial sensitivity" — the product of a cybernetic civilisation, of a society thoroughly dominated by the mass media. What confronts us now is a cultural phenomenon that has at its core the determination to break the vise of modernist exclusions, opening the way to pluralism and regionalism. The exclusivity of modernism has been widely condemned as authoritarian, chauvinistic or even imperialistic — yet one more manifestation of the cultural hegemony exercised by the United States (and perhaps by New York in particular) ever since the end of the Second World War.

Such diatribes — and likewise the declaration that modernism is now dead — should not come as any surprise, once we realize that the theory and practice of modernism have subjected us all along to a hecatomb, a continual ritual murder of the components of occidental culture: death of art, death of the artist, death of the author, death of the critic, of painting, of philosophy, of cinema, of music, etc. Of course, nothing ever really disappears. These are only "des petites morts", little deaths, which have only heightened the pleasure of subsequent resurrections. For the past century or so, such rebirth seems to have played an indispensable part in attempts to rejuvenate our consumer culture. But our current crisis carries further and graver implications, as most of the following texts will insist, focussing on the complex relationship between modernism on the one hand, and everyday life and mass culture on the other.

Though these still warm cadavers may surround us on all sides, the conference participants were not invited to perform a collective autopsy, nor to celebrate a cultural wake. There is, in fact, something yet living within modernism, not least because it continues to provide a basis of reference. Even the very fact of wishing the concept dead shows that it still functions as an anchorage point — or shall we call it a stumbling block? — essential to contemporary consciousness.

This is a privileged moment in history, the moment of passage from modernism to Post-Modernism, a moment of equilibrium and tension between a phase we no longer believe in and a new era already considered with distrust. It was upon this juncture that the conference focussed; to paraphrase the title of a famous symposium held long ago by the *Partisan Review*, what is dead and what is alive in modernism today?

Obviously, there are parts of the modernist ideology which have never fulfilled their contracts, others which no longer fulfill theirs now, and still more which have been so disfigured by successive adaptations to circumstances that they now appear too clearly in all their monstrosity.

Confronted with the enormous complexity of a problem compounded by several hundred years of practice subject to continuous adjustment, the conference was never meant to arrive at a precise definition of either modernism or modernity. Instead we concentrated on one area which seemed to be the keystone of any modernist procedure: its critical/subversive stance, the negative side of a new culture which based its realizations on a coefficient of resistance to the prevailing system.

This element of negativity has been present in modern art since the nineteenth century. Here it is enough to recall painters who cherished the notion of change, the ephemeral, fashion, the vernacular; when they deified what was raw, direct, and singular in contemporary life. This eruption of the present into a culture hitherto protected by the past functioned for a while as a radical disturbance. A simple displacement of emphasis and the introduction of elements from the new technological world were read as an acerbic critique of the dominant social system. The rejection of the past and of the direct quotation, the disdain for an idealized world, the cult of the present in order to liberate the future — all these were also seen as both provocative and threatening.

This was a double-edged critique, however, since it put the modern intellectual in an awkward position confronting a crisis of confidence in his or her own tools of analysis, in his or her own culture. Modernity emphasized the difficulty of knowing, of signifying or of synthesizing the divisions and contradictions of the modern world.

At the same time, to be modern also meant to be capable of disclosing and manipulating to some degree the power embedded within the structure of language, or of visual imagery. In order to free himself, the modern artist, using fragments of the dominant culture and scraps of dominated cultures, re-created a specific world in opposition to the traditional code, without totally severing his connection to the past. Modern artists have also often assumed an ironic stance, sometimes by pastiching important classical works in order to challenge their authority in a particularly pointed way, and to make such a recourse to an outworn world looks especially absurd.

Modern art tried to avoid the programmed sector of everyday life while putting that life on stage; it made an effort to shape new conditions of existence, as well as new conditions of artistic production. In theory, at least, modernism operated as an art of combat, employed by an avant-garde which was often tied, albeit ambiguously, to the idea of revolution. As the sociologist Henri Lefebvre has explained:

Modernity is the shadow of the miscarried revolution, its crumbling and sometimes its caricature.[1]

After 1848, Lefebvre has asserted, the modern artist tried to create "an acceptable fictive world in an unacceptable real world." It is here, in this evasion, that one of modernism's key weaknesses lies and where Jacques Ellul, in his *L'Empire du non-sens,* strikes a telling blow. Modern art, he says, has pinpointed the defeat of man, because despite all appearances to the contrary, such an art simply conforms to the mould prepared for him by a technical society. "Art", he further states, "has become one of the major functions of the integration of man into the technological complex."[2] And this despite the attempts of modernism to avoid co-optation by means of sterilization and radical purification.

To explore this dilemna — our purpose was as simple as that, though it may have been a little too ambitious as well. The decision was made to tap diverse streams of modernist practice, from literature to painting to photography, trying at the same time to keep a tight chronological framework in order to underline our insistence that the problems tackled by modernism were histori-cally defined.

The exchange between Timothy Clark and Clement Green-berg emerged as the centerpiece of the symposium, since it high-lighted the key issue upon which the success or failure of moder-nism could ultimately be determined: its relationship to mass culture. Any serious attempt to consider this question had to in-clude Greenberg, as the individual most responsible for providing a theoretical framework for both the modernist practice in painting and the avant-garde phenomenon. But it was just as important to have Clark present a historical analysis, offered without concessions, of this same theoretical work and of the seminal texts of 1940 in particular. The results underlined the crucial differences between formalism and modernism — a distinction that has often been confused, either unwittingly (by some of Greenberg's followers) or for strategic reasons, by numerous spokesmen for the Post-modern.

Historically, Clement Greenberg's significance rests upon the fact that he analyzed a profound concern shared by many leftist intellectuals during the 1940s: the need for modernist resistance to and negation of the integrating positivism of consumerist society. The uniformity of culture which Kitsch (propagated by capitalism) and programmed art (spawned by propagandistic art and authoritarian regimes) both symbolized — this had to be opposed in order to protect a freedom rejected by both political systems.

This was the moment, after the second World War, when social interaction seemed to cease; when American intellectuals recognized a lack of quality in "art engagé" and chose a median course that often led them, even if against their own wishes, into the realm of pure formalism. Through a concerted effort to break the formalist straitjacket of late modernism, the post-modernist phenomenon has also crushed its living, critical core. The rejection of modernism as elitist has opened the doors to populism, and in so doing has blunted much of what could be political and/or trenchant in the practice of certain contemporary artists. Under the cover of irony, post-modernism has revived something which has been repressed for years, and deservedly so, to a great extent at least: a gigantic operation of reductionism and banalization. All the old academic tricks have come back into fashion. Empy expressionist or impressionist or surrealist carcasses are disinterred every day, safely cut off from the historical moments which once nurtured their production; the old modes nowadays are recycled, lobotomised, transformed into perfect commodities. Paradoxically, the new epoch has been launched in the name of a larger freedom and a stubborn individualism. Thus a new ideology establishes itself on the basis of an unbridled pluralism, conveniently forgetting why it once seemed so important for modernism to protect itself with self-criticism. In a way, it is to remind us of this that the texts of the conference and the debates they provoked have been published.

Surprisingly, the rapid spread of pluralism — the pet project of this new "liberal" world which seeks the "end of ideology"[3] — has encountered very few dissenters among the ranks of contemporary art critics. One exception is Hal Foster, whose excellent article in *Art in America* clearly articulates the naivetés and over-simplifications inherent in post-modernist theory:

> As a term, pluralism signifies no art specifically. Indeed, it grants a kind of equivalence, an art of many sorts is made to seem more or less equal-equally (un)important. Art become an arena of vested interests, of licensed sects: in lieu of culture we have cults. The result is an eccentricity that leads, in art as in politics, to a new conformity: Pluralism as an institution.[4]

Russel Jacoby, in another salient critique, has deflated the concept of subversive narcissism which accompanies pluralism:

> The protest of narcissism within advanced capitalism is shot through with the society it rejects; it affirms and buttresses the commodity market. Its mode is private, its substance the exchange principle of capitalism. If sacrifice recalls pre-capitalist life, narcissism beckons a step closer the stock market of human relations.[5]

The past few years' rejection of the modernist values of selection, history and self-criticism marks the integration and the celebration of its opposites in post-modernism — an ahistoric and narcissistic pluralism. The positive culture of which Marcuse was so afraid seems today to dominate the cultural sphere. That is why a conference like this one on modernism seems ironically but vitally like an arrière-garde battle. A battle full of melancholy and nostalgia for a time when enemies were numerous but definable, as hostile forces defending intransigent, moral and symbolical positions. Is our modernity not, in fact, an era of facility, a slough of molasses into which we fall in a slow and sleepy way, taking it easy, knowing that everything, including "high" culture, has become pre-selected, pre-thought, and pre-processed?

Is Jean Baudrillard right when he defines our period as an era of simulation, of destruction of meaning, and of a generalized process of indifferentiation resulting from a post-modern society in the thrall of the media? No room remains, or at least so it would seem, for traditionally modern values, because the overstock, the overflow of information and of images has destroyed any possibility of signification, while neutralizing and pacifying any attempt to define real differences. The medium itself has become evanescent.

Culture today seems to confront the same predicament that faced Clement Greenberg in 1939, when he wrote "Avant-garde and Kitsch," but with one essential difference. For Greenberg at that time the danger was clearly visible; it came, if I may say so, from the outside, that is to say, from fascism. A solution was possible, even if it did have to take the form of an enormously costly military effort. Similarly, the threat posed by Kitsch originated outside of high culture; here, too, a defence lay to hand, in the shape of the avant garde. But today modern culture is being killed from the inside, through the very structure of post-industrial society. Neither an army nor the avant-garde (now blown apart into pluralism) can effectively contain the dangers involved.

Nor should we expect any form of viable resistance or negation to emerge from art practice as we generally know it today. If our culture is dying of implosion, only explosion offers any real potential for change. In fact, it seems as though resistance to dominant culture must come, if it does at all, either from the fringes of high culture, or, better still, from outside, as Tom Crow has argued in his paper, through short disruptions. This is the age of the guerilla.

Confronted with these difficulties, it would not have been surprising to see melancholy pervade the debates of the symposium, confronted with the strength of so visibly powerful a hegemonic system. But instead what happened was that rage infiltrated the debate. Can this be seen as a sort of beginning, or as a stillbirth, co-opted and spectacularized from the start?

Notes

[1] Henri Lefèbvre, *Introduction à la modernité,* Paris, Editions de Minuit, 1962. p.223.

[2] Jacques Ellul, *L'Empire du Non-Sens,* Paris: P.U.F., 1980, p.277.

[3] See Daniel Bell, *The End of Ideology,* On the Exhaustion of Political Ideas in the Fifties, Collier, 1960. Here it is clear that the end of ideology carries with it an active conservatism.

[4] Hal Foster, "The Problem of Pluralism", *Art in America,* January 1982, p.9-15.

[5] Russell Jacoby, "Narcissism and the Crisis of Capitalism", *Telos,* No. 44, Summer 1980, p.58-65.

Henri Lefebvre

Modernity
and Modernism

Recently, among all the "deaths" recorded or predicted (the death of God, of Man, of the Earth, etc. ..), a new crop of predictions or claims has appeared: the death of the avant-garde, the death of modernity, the postmodern era. The latter expression seems to be part of the annunciation of a new society — post-industrial, informational, the product not of a socio-political revolution but of the "scientific and technical revolution." That situation revivifies an old debate and demands a reassessment of the concept of *modernity.*

a) — Semantics of the term. Its history. In France it first appears in the context of the notorious quarrel between the ancients and the moderns (at the end of the 17th century and beginning of the 18th), and thus is linked with the notion of progress. Since then, there has been no end of controversies between the partisans of progress and modernity and the partisans of tradition, or of regression. In the course of these quarrels the terms "modern" and "modernity" take on various meanings and contradictory connotations, sometimes favorable, sometimes not (cf. discussions of Rousseau, of the romantics, etc. . .). And there are paradoxes: Baudelaire, a post-romantic, praises modernity, while Nietzsche presides over the trial of modernity in modern terms, identifying modernity with decadence or even barbarity, but with a view to pushing forward the Human toward the superhuman. Certain episodes mark the stages of this long debate: the famous Chaplin film that popularises a certain kind of critique of modernity; the journal, "Les Temps Modernes," that maintains an ambiguous stance, etc. . . .

The absolute sovereignty of modernism is ushered in around 1910 by a rupture with the classical and traditional vocabulary: the divine and the human, the city, history, paternity. The reign is consolidated after World War I: cubism, abstract art, the rise of the Bauhaus, etc. . . . That reign lasts until the 60s and 70s; then another reign is ushered in.

b) — *The crisis of modernity.* Something that, strictly speaking, has not changed at all for some centuries but that is accentuated by the present "crisis." This one cannot be confused with all the others because it seems to be total and permanent. Total, in that it throws into question values and norms as much as socio-economic structures. Permanent, in that it is not making for some solution to the crisis, but seems rather to constitute the very mode of existence of "modern" societies. Should we not recognize, in all the sensational annunciations of newness, as much a symptom of the crisis as any prediction based on knowledge? Crisis is a concept that affects all aspects of modernity: art, literature, philosophical truth, everyday life, the priority of the visual in both practice and conscience, etc. . . . Strangely enough, it is always accompanied by a retrogressive — even an archaeological — mode, or by a confusion between the ancient and the modern.

c) — And yet, for all that, technological innovations never cease. We might ask whether technics is not becoming a sort of autonomous, liberated power that no one can master — not even the technocrats, let alone the politicians or the labor movement. So we are witnessing the separation between, on the one hand, modernity as ideology, which has been in any case discredited, and on the other hand, modernity as a partner to a technocracy based on a vast bureaucracy that continues to entrench itself. Modernity? It was a tease. Modernism? It brings only worries and threats disguised by the promise of security.

(translation by Paul Smith)

Henri Lefebvre

Theses on Modernity

a) Our Modernity, whose contours and concepts are now emerging, was born alongside considerable transformations in social praxis in the twentieth century — imperialism, world wars, the Russian Revolution (1905 and 1917), the growth of technics in the processes of accumulation.

In comparison with previous periods, it has most of all brought about a great loss of innocence and a terrible sobering-up. Ideological inebriations, spontaneous or provoked (progress, liberty, democracy, etc.), have all been dispelled, leaving a void to be filled — badly — by dogmatism, by acts of faith, by ideologies upheld by institutions and authorities suffering paroxysms over the decline of ideologies. Thence a general tendency toward cruel lucidity and a cynicism not incompatible with blindness.

b) There has been no essential transformation in man's relations *to himself.* Those relations have changed much less than those of man to an outside world which is dominated by a growing and ever more potent technics. Appropriation by man of his own nature (desire and pleasure), radical transformation of the everyday (presaged in morality and in art), both parts of the original Marxist program of a total praxis, have not come about. The relations designated by the terms "hierarchy," "power," "alienation," have yet to disappear, even though the possibility of their disappearance has been glimpsed.

So there has been a delay in transformatory action, as in radical criticism, in relation to productive forces, and the possibilities harboured there have been turned away from the Marxist goal. The absence of the total revolutionary praxis that, according to Marx, was to abolish alienation is being felt with increasing sharpness. The total revolutionary act, its possibility subtending the whole of Marxist thought like an experimental utopia, has still not taken place. Modernity now embraces a conscience that is at once embittered and confused by the succession of its relative defeats. The world is much changed and it changes more and more, especially — needless to say — on the socialist side, but not in the ways that had been devoutly hoped. Is this temporary? Or final? Modernity cannot answer. Progress no longer has a 'goal,' has no teleology, no orientation and no obvious or perceptible path to follow. Liberty remains an ideal, shaken and confused, abstract yet powerful, even though it is threatened by the knowledge of the utopic character of a simultaneous end to alienation. Hence the resurgence of out-of-date ideologies and attitudes in which we scarcely believe, making the diversity and disorder of Modernity more confused and worried about coherence.

c) The contradictions mount up, but confusedly. In our Modernity they aggravate the contradictions of pre-Modernity (the nineteenth century) without clarifying them at all. Among these contradictions we should, of course, include the contradiction between capitalism and socialism, obscured by analogies between state socialism and state capitalism (analogies which do not actually, as is sometimes suggested, constitute an identity but which none the less bother our conscience and our knowledge).

The cultural archaism of the eastern countries, their controlled pseudo-classicism, the snobbish aestheticism of the bourgeoisie avid for apparent advances (which are to be distinguished from the genuinely new but which include the genuine if they can in order to render it harmless or even useful), the conflict between the vindication of work in the east and justification of leisure in the west (exploited leisure), the concurrence of productivism to the profit of socialist accumulation and productivism for the profit of the bourgeoisie, all carry confusion to its climax.

And there is also a contrast between the confusion and incoherence of the capitalist side and the excessive coherence (superorganisation over the whole of society) on the socialist side.

d) So, two sides to the picture of Modernity. On the one hand, accelerated technical advance (especially on the socialist side), victories over material nature, cumulative processes with rapid growth despite saturation factors, socialisation of society. On the other hand, relative stagnation in man's everyday relations, including his relations to institutions (the state, bureaucracy, the mandarins, etc.).

e) Thus, a displacement of the human (of subjectivity inside, of work and leisure outside) in relation to high technology. Increasing technical alienation, albeit varying according to area, sector and regime. Little enlargement of individual possibility except for certain groups (managers, technicians and technocrats, scholars, artists, astronauts, etc.).

Contraction of the everyday, made more sensitive by the technical dominance of man over nature and by the worldliness of the processes of accumulation and technique. A strangulation at the center of the everyday and the private, in the cultural and anticultural spheres, in the realms of antinature as well as the realms of nostalgic naturalism. The inability to work out a lifestyle, confusedly established upon art and morality and thus destined to failure. Triumph of the antinatural (abstraction and signs) as if it were necessary to pass through such an extremity in order one day to reach the spontaneous (in micro-societies, primarily) —unless the loss is already irremediable.

Collapse of traditional cultures in the path of a shameless usage (commercial, propagandist, political). Great confusion between learning, education and culture — between the accumulation of knowledge and creativity. Massive pedagogical illusions. A tendency to aestheticize profound aspirations. Overvaluation of art (as external spectacle with no real participatory function). Frenetic aestheticism and alibis for aestheticism. The shrivelling of art within its supposed triumphs. Inoffensive novelties and ephemeral events. In fact, the elimination of the spontaneous and the playful — that is, of art's deepest meaning — in favour of a functionalism, especially evident in modern cities (which condense the gamble and the poverty of Modernity).

f) Thence the broad strokes of *a sociology of modern ennui,* insisting on the ambiguity and internal dialectic of "mass-culture." Such a culture lifts the average cultural level, spreading learning, education and, above all, technics. It is informative. It is interesting. *At the same time,* it inundates people with information that is neutralized by its own sheer quantity. It aligns cultural and intellectual consumption with "private" material consumption. It devours. It scraps the accumulation of cultural wealth. It limitlessly exploits symbols, myths, forms, older styles. It transfers the totality of history into discourse, and discourse is then displaced by images. It produces a collapse of culture into biologism and brute naturalism (through sex and violence). Beyond such audacious feints there is a rapid wastage of experience and a shrivelling of the world of expression.

Massive ennui threatens to exhaust themes, shrivel expression, bring about the great pleonasm, the monotony of a spectacle which is only a "private" spectacle, etc.

The propagandist character, superficial and artificial, of optimism (socialist or American).

Nihilism is nearer. Necessity for a radical criticism either to avoid nihilism or to accelerate its realization if that is really where we are.

Urgency for the invention or creation of a style by our constrained groups and micro-societies because of the current impotence of classes and global societies (thus the import and interest, from that angle, of modern cities).

Theses on Modernity

Modernity has two contradictory and indefeasibly linked aspects. It carries alienation to extremes. In addition to all the old alienations it produces a supplement that becomes heavier and heavier — technical alienation. The topsy-turvy world is still the real world. But, at the same time, beyond this maximal alienation, disalienation becomes only more and more pressing. And it too is coming about. Modernity caricatures and trades upon the idea of total Revolution, which has not come about. For better and for worse, badly and clumsily, inside a topsy-turvy world that has not yet been righted, Modernity achieves the job of the Revolution: critique of bourgeois life, critique of alienation, the withering of art, of morality and, generally, of ideologies, etc.

Let us examine these theses more closely.

Rents and tears, dualities, carried to their extremes (private and public, ordinary and sublime, needs and desires, nature and culture, nature and the technical, pleasure and frustration, personal activity and social praxis). Another, more philosophical enumeration: being and thought, ideology and reality, representation and presence, cause and effect, possible and impossible, etc.

Turning to Marx, Engels, Lenin: "Opposition that is abstract and reflective belongs only to the modern world." Let us not understand "reflective opposition" as simply intellectual or subjective reflection; Marx is describing a fact and a concept to which neither sense of the word "reflection" really corresponds. Each term of a duality or an opposition, considered dialectically, reflects the other: each offers the other not just a representation but its own reality refracted through the reality of the other; and it receives through the other a deformed reflection of itself, accentuating difference and distance. This polarised difference is not yet a profound contradiction, still less an antagonism; it can become such, but not necessarily, because it depends on the particular conjuncture whether or not the structure defined in this way splinters or not. Thus the State "reflects" civil society, the needs and interests and relations of the members of non-political society; it constitutes a distinct but not autonomous sphere; it consists in elements that are to one degree or another *representative;* at the same time it projects into the consciousness of the members of society the reflection of what they are — a more or less distorted reflection, of course. In its modern form the political State enshrines certain exigencies that are more or less founded upon or dictated by Reason, and still it "presupposes actualised Reason;" it calls itself rational and yet it falls into a contradiction between "its theoretical definition and its real prerequisites" (Marx to Ruge, Sept. 1843). And it is this that delivers the State to its doom: sooner or later, it shrivels.

And yet it will remain so long as there are bosses, masters, managers; consequently it will last "so long as the topsy-turvy world is the real world" (Marx to Ruge, May 1843).

"The two fundamental conceptions of development (evolution) are: development as decrease and increase, as repetition; and development as a unity of opposites (the division of the One into mutually exclusive opposites and their reciprocal correlation). The first conception is dead, poor and dry; the second is vital" (Lenin, *Materialism and Empirio-criticism*).

"The period that has lasted until today in which every step forward is also relatively a step backward . . . . Everything that civilisation brings forth is double-edged, double-tongued, divided against itself, contradictory . . ." (Engels, *Origins of the Family, Private Property and the State*).

Let us leave aside the exact problem upon which Engels pronounces these neat and general aphorisms (the evolution of the family, marriage, and the situation of women): while talking on the same subject he declares that the irony of history is unfathomable! Engels and Lenin are fully in accord when they reject any simplistic representation of *progress:* a linear, continual evolution, equal in all its parts, advancing on all fronts, everywhere pressing its advantage.

Contradiction is not apparent only at the cutting edge of process, Engels says; it penetrates into its thickness, so to speak. Such conquest, such "progress" can also be a regression up to a certain point. In each case, at each conjuncture, for every situation, analysis alone can point out the gains and the losses; there can be simultaneous gains and losses (what is dialectics after all?)

When official Marxism takes upon itself all the notions of social and ideal progress — ideas abandoned by bourgeois thought — is this not the "dead" conception being restituted and subjected to a skimmed-off dialectics?

If Lenin's writings on the dialectic have any real meaning there must be a rupture and a division of the One into opposites that are mutually exclusive. The struggle of mutually exclusive contradictories (a struggle that deeply suggests mobility) must not, however, cause relative unity to be forgotten. Thus economic and social development, the cumulative process, and modern industrial societies are split into opposites whose struggle dominates our era. But we have no right to place either unity or interaction into parentheses, any more than we can conceive of progress unilaterally (or conceive of process from a "polyscopic" point of view).

In other words, we are not aligning capitalism with socialism and identifying them if we consider them within the unity of a single world process. We are not suppressing difference if we consider that there is no absolute difference: on the one hand absolute "positivity," on the other hand absolute "negativity." Such a view of the conception of the dialectic of history is radically antidialectical.

Technological alienation today is common to both capitalism and socialism. Technocratic danger comes from both sides. *But,* on the socialist side there are discernible social forces and theoretical capacities which might permit us eventually to dominate the technical process, to fight technological alienation, to eliminate the technocracy. (Should this not be part of the function of the Marxist-Leninist party itself? but then, why not say so and tone down the contradictions of socialism?)

Objectivity in these matters is difficult to define, and even more difficult to maintain. In my view it does not exclude the use of irony, nor the taking of a (relative, therefore critical) position. The biggest difficulty arises from the holistic attitude, the total ideology presently adopted by the "parties" in their struggle. Notably, on the Marxist and socialist side the scarcely dialectical principle of "all or nothing" leads to polemics and propaganda. There are no real options. Both criticism and irony, both the relative, approximate nature of the option with its risk of error and failure — in short, its hazardousness — are all suppressed by decree. To submit options to the criterion of an absolute historical, economic and social determinism is to suppress it as such. The hypothesis of a "third way" between capitalist and socialist ideologies is rejected. New and more contradictions. Not only is the very "ideology" that Marx criticised and rejected peculiarly revived, but critical and scientific objectivity — the objectivity of knowledge — is itself made into the third way!

It is a difficult situation for knowledge to be in when the historical situation is such that polemics and propaganda dominate knowledge. It is, too, a difficult situation for the dialectic when both the struggle of contraries and fundamental contradiction threaten to reduce opposing terms to nothing!

> "In our day, everything seems pregnant with its contrary. The victories of technology seem bought by the loss of character. At the same pace as man masters nature, he seems to become enslaved to other men . . . . All our invention and progress seem to result in endowing material forces with intellectual life and in stultifying human life into a material force. We know that to work well the new-fangled forces of society want only to be mastered by new-fangled men. These new men are the workers. They are as much the invention of modern times as machinery itself. In the signs that bewilder the middle-class, the aristocracy and the poor prophets of regression, we recognize our brave friend, the old mole that can work in the earth so fast — the Revolution" (Marx in *The People's Paper,* April 1856).

This text needs to be thought about. To master technics is first of all (but not only) to learn the use of the most refined machines. But such a restrictive interpretation leaves room for the technocrat — this is to master the cumulative process, and who can? Who can direct it toward man's appropriation of nature and of his own nature? The revolutionaries and the revolutionary working class. But isn't the old mole bound to work underground for a long time?

The text does not apply in the same way to "modern" capitalism and socialism. It applies to them both. The topsy-turvy world remains the real world. Fetishes and illusions are just as real as the "real." They are part of it. They are there.

Ideological reflections are not just reflections of the real but are its substance, its substitutes and its alibi. The practical righting of the topsy-turvy world that must accompany the setting on its feet of dialectical theory has not been totally accomplished; but it has been roughly and partially accomplished. Uneven development has taken over.

The consequence: the real movement that suppresses this state of affairs (Marx), that is, communism, no longer has any evidence. Even in socialism man's essence (productive and creative labour, knowledge and technics) remains an imperfectly mastered power and is still one-sided, partially exteriorized and constrictive; it is in opposition to other essential aspects of man — pleasure, rest and leisure, play. Irony is not at an end, but nor is alienation. The longed-for human being, emerging from his labour, is still something else. We can see that the split may be closing, or so we believe; we are most constantly and absolutely assured of the fact by those adherents of the new religiosity — the cult of personality.

Here, on the bourgeois side, the topsy-turvy world is confirmed with impudence and ferocity as the only and only possible real. The fundamental difference in this respect between socialism and capitalism is that in the former the turning of the topsy-turvy world is proposed as a possibility, is being planned; it even tends to be self-righting except, of course, where the righting is assumed to have taken place already.

The contradiction between "worlds," the topsy-turvy real world and the possible righted world, is approaching maximum intensity. In their contradiction these two worlds mix and bear upon each other. The scissions and contradictions (internal/external) provoke the production of mere appearances, ever closer to reality and always more ephemeral — second-rate illusions, ideologies built upon ideologies (aestheticism with regard to authentic works; religiosity penetrating right to the heart of radical criticism; etc.). A unity of false consciousness or of *mauvaise foi* is uncertainly and pregnantly restituted within a divided social consciousness; a unity constructed and deconstructed without being able to surmount its double determinations and proclaim itself real.

Modernity, the shadow of the Revolution, absent here and incomplete there, no longer functions without crises. Contradictions move through it and it constitutes their work in default of a radically revolutionary negativity which, according to the initial Marxist project, would have metamorphosed life itself. More: these crises multiply, grow closer together and become the general rule, the norm. Each sector, each domain takes its turn in crisis or goes through some critical phase or other. Multiple and multifarious, despite all denials, these crises seem to constitute our Modernity.

They are integral to its consciousness, to its image, to its apologetic project. They pass for productive, even when they are denied (and those who most place themselves within the solidity of modernism's substance are exactly those who ought to be re-affirming the fecundity of contradictions, crises, transitions — that is, the official Marxists). Are these crises really and uniformly productive? Nothing prevents us from saying so but nothing obliges us to take the word of those who do say so; but if we reject the absolutist apologists of Modernity nothing obliges us to think that they are totally in the wrong.

The partisan position has for many years now been accusing bourgeois society of sterility, impotence and decadence; but is not such a position just as sterile and impotent as the apologia that it presumes to criticize? It is hardly in doubt but that our Modernity has its elements of decadence and decay; but to say that it can be characterized exclusively by the decline of bourgeois society (of whose decadence it is but a symptom) does seem somewhat dubious. The partisan thesis is bankrupt. It is as difficult to define our Modernity by its decadence alone as it is to accept its snobbery and its unconditional apologies.

If our Modernity travels under the banner of multiple crisis we might suspect that these crises are the small change of the unique and total revolutionary crisis envisaged by Marx and which might have galvanized the radically negative and creative proletariat into one absolute act of history.

So, according to this thesis, one part of the task and of the aim of the total Revolution has been accomplished in the course of Modernity's evolution — albeit in a clumsy, indirect way, in fragments, dissimulation and deviation, often backwards (that is, from within the topsy-turvy world), but always out of phase with the possible Revolution. So we can define our Modernity as the shadow of the Revolution, its dispersal and sometimes its caricature. Consequently, it should be neither rejected out of hand nor enthusiastically proclaimed. This definition seems general (if uneven) and valid for the socialist countries (although not in exactly the same way) as for the bourgeois side. In other words, I am giving full rein to the concept of uneven development: I am stretching it to apply it to everday life, private life, morality, aesthetics, and not just to the modalities of the cumulative process.

Modernity actualizes some of the tasks of the Revolution by dispersing them. Which tasks? First, the critique of bourgeois life in so much as it is abstract, split and torn. This critique is pursued by demonstrating the second-rate abstractions, the aggravated rents and tears, the ever more factitious contentments of bourgeois life. Secondly, the shrivelling up of art, achieving its end through art's own self-mutilation, its own destructiveness, its internal negativity. Then, the impoverishment of philosophy as such, the discrediting of ideologies; then, the elaboration of the idea — the ideology perhaps — of happiness (which degenerates into an ideology of comfort and well-being, always actually begging the question of happiness). Finally the bringing into focus, through errors and successive near misses, of attitudes concerning technics, nature, spontaneity . . . .

So a program can be sketched out, though certainly not filled in on these pages (which would be deceptive if they did not open out onto some further project for research). The completion of this project — that is, the analysis and total exposé of Modernity — would involve the examination of a considerable number of modern works. It would need first of all to classify them methodically and by theme, to some degree taking account of the attitudes demonstrated and the tendencies expressed (left-wing, right-wing, cultural strategies of the right and of the left, etc.) Once this classification by themes and problems was completed, this vast identification parade would clarify and make applicable the concept of Modernity.

An ever thinner membrane, translucid and durable, separates us from the possible. From the other side, always getting nearer but more inaccessible, what is it we see? Not a double. Not a reflection. Much more — me, us, you.

How can we refuse such an option? The old mole, the Revolution, has taken wing and flown. Let us bring it back down to earth — *under* the earth, underground.

The Revolution needs to be re-invented, but first of all to be re-known! Today it is our Promethean courage that tells us that "the Revolution, like love, needs to be re-invented."

(translated by Paul Smith)

Marcelin Pleynet

Modernism — Modernity and the Philosophy of History

The misunderstanding and the conflict implicitly established between artist and critic or art-historian, of which the history of modernity furnishes repeated examples, indicate that since it can be explicitly posed today, the question of the relation between art and its history has haunted the whole of modern cultural production from the start of the nineteenth century and has caused specific contemporary consequences.

If we consider the movement we conventionally call modern art, we can claim that, ever since art's breaking away from the academy at the start of the nineteenth century (a rupture epitomized, for example, in the life, character and work of Courbet), right up to the productions of young artists today, the movement has been constituted by a progressive and increasingly precipitous accumulation of groupings, schools and avant-garde gestures to division and polemical transgression. From romanticism to impressionism, to pointillism, japonism, symbolism, fauvism, cubism, futurism, constructivism, expressionism, orphism, surrealism, l'Ecole de Paris, abstract expressionism, the new realists, pop-art, *arte-povera,* minimalism, land-art, hyper-realism, support-surface, the new figuration, body art, pattern-painting, the new fauves (I'll stop there, having named a few of the more interesting groups), it is easy to see that the accumulation of movements and schools has grown greater as we move from the nineteenth into the twentieth century. It is an accumulation that, even now, the critic and the historian try in some way to avoid by more or less cheerfully regurgitating the divisions and antagonisms of the various avant-gardes: the art critic by particularizing his studies and becoming a sort of specialist, a scribe or the exclusive promoter of a collection of artists grouped under one or another of these denominations; the historian by establishing a chronicle, an itinerary or an evolutionary logic for the works which supposes the exclusive choice of some artistic movements and the rejection (or an ignorance) of others. Needless to say, in time, and because of a sort of saturation of the forms, ideas and styles that produce the accumulation of avant-gardes, it becomes more and more difficult to accord the slightest credit to that sort of critical attitude or to that sort of art-history.

So it still remains unclear what modernity can mean for us today, this modernity that has reigned in confusion over the arts for more than a century. What exactly are these accumulations in and beyond the nineteenth century, these 'modernist' tendencies and objects that have taken up the first three-quarters of the twentieth century? If we look at any particular point in time, we are confronted with noisy and messy groups, plus a plethora of works whose apparently minor and transient nature marks them as uninteresting. If, on the other hand, we look at the ensemble of all those modern artistic manifestations that occupy the nineteenth and twentieth centuries and that abound in multifarious cultural centers and museums of modern or contemporary art, we cannot help but be struck by the sheer vitality of artistic expression in our day, or by the obviously huge amounts of energy that have been put into these works. But it is precisely this vitality, it seems, that the art-world (specialists, critics, historians, museum curators, dealers, buyers) seems to hold of no account, drawing no conclusions from it except in order to carry out their day-to-day speculation. But perhaps it is not that simple; perhaps one might effectively wonder whether it is even possible to take into account this vitality in the gamut of modern or contemporary art movements without getting lost in merely anecdotal meanderings about the groupish forms that compose it. But that is a question that in fact stresses our obligation: we must point out and try to explain as far as possible the abdication and the bankrupt attitudes of the critic and the art-historian. If we can really bring ourselves to imagine that criticism and its function are justified in confining themselves to the temporal designation of artistic data (all the while holding off from judgment and telling us that objective information does in fact exist) we cannot then assess the economy of ideological assumptions that motivates the art historian — assumptions that are often implicitly those of the critic.

If, beyond the glistering accumulation of forms and objects in the modernism we have inherited, we stop to consider the organization and function of the discourses that have served and continue to serve the positioning (partial or global) of all art objects, we notice that the positions of the modern art historians, despite their apparently differing attitudes, all arise from philosophical presuppositions that have the same origin. Indeed, by considering the whole range of cultural itineraries we have inherited, we can claim that the relation between art and the discourse that accompanies it has undergone precious few transformations. And as far as our twenty centuries are concerned (counted and defined only from the birth of Christ, that is to say, from within the space of what is known as the "Christian era"), I would claim that the relation between art and discourse on art is constituted essentially in two forms of organization — the theological and the philosophical. It is possible, I think, to consider the order that Vasari's *Lives* supposes as still formally engaged in a type of theological appreciation of artistic phenomena since "histories" here are still nothing more than "lives", which are incapable of informing any notion of history, however much they try to do so. We have to wait until the eighteenth century and the confluence of Winckelmann and Kant before we can proceed from a history based on the principle of evolution (biological development on the vegetal model, or on the metaphor of the stages of human life) toward a history founded upon a philosophy of nature, which justifies the production of artistic genius by overdetermining it (or by a ruse) — *Critique of Aesthetic Judgment.* Of course, this sort of rationalization (theorization) of art and history does not end there, but we can say that from then on, and in all the forms that it has since taken, metaphysics (Kant) has consistently submitted morality to a psychology (the ruse of nature) and thus evacuated the 'imponderable' from artistic creation by situating the creative subject in a continual state of crisis (and crises soon take on the name "psychological crises" without, however, any alleviation of the problems they manifest). Is it so surprising to discover, on reflection, that the neat ordering of the systems and philosophies of history we inherit is accompanied from the outset — the second half of the eighteenth century, or from romanticism on — by such a great and sometimes dramatic confusion in the artistic world? This submission of art to philosophy will be manifested elsewhere than in just writers like Schiller of Schlegel. The work of Kant, that had for many people seemed to be a non-theological response to that century's disturbances and to the question of the institution of morality, made its mark upon the writers and artists equally. In a letter to Schiller in 1796, Goethe points to "certain artists who represent Kantian ideas through symbolic figuration," and he remarks that "if this is not pure buffoonery, it is at least the most senseless manifestation in art that I can imagine between here and judgment day" (in reference to the works of the painter Carstens).

This institution or invention of a history that is remarkably close to the one we see used today is not, of course, linked solely to the curiosity or snobbism of particular writers and critics. It finds its place in the order of contradictions between the development of scientific and technical thought and a systematic philosophy of all-embracing theology — contradictions of a kind that allow disruption (revolution) and the institutions that follow disruption to claim a new order and set about establishing it. Obviously it is within this general context that artists and writers find themselves confronted by a system (the Kantian system) that construes its legality upon a moral (and psychological) debate. Such a bringing into place of this submission to philosophical rationalism produces everything we already know about the art of the nineteenth and twentieth centuries. It is then that the writer tries to invest the imponderables of gesture and of poetic language by introducing a new literary form that will engage language in the muddle of these psychological "dramas": the novel. The painter began by attempting (throughout the nineteenth century) to psychologize, or rather to systematize nature — not, it is true, so childishly as did Carstens by "representing Kantian ideas through symbolic figuration," but nevertheless symbolically in some way, by, so to speak, ism-izing: romanticism, realism, impressionism . . . . Whatever the system was unable in any case to reduce (and which arose from what I have provisionally called the imponderables of art) went on almost deliriously to investigate psychology (the science, as it were, of moral crises). Psychology found it impossible to give the measure of its charge and so more and more found itself in the position of having to exhibit publicly the very things that no moral legislature could possibly accept. The scandal attached to all modern art movements from the end of the eighteenth century until the present day (the scandal of *Les fleurs du mal,* of *Madame Bovary,* of "Les demoiselles au bord de Seine," of "Olympia," of Balzac and Rodin) is explained only by an inadequacy of the psychological investment that charges the art-work and the system (history) as guarantors of a legal morality. The dimension of the art-work found itself tied to the very fact that it introduced absurdity into the logic of the system, or tied to exactly the quality of the symptoms of inadequacy or inadaptation that it talks about. Unable to place itself anywhere else, modern art sees itself progressively assigned the function either of representing the order of the system according to a selective and rigorously formulated logic, or (and this second function is the one that overwhelmingly dominates the art-world today) of demonstrating marginally, secondarily, almost aculturally the failings of the system — thus, for example, the increasing tendency to confuse the plastic productions of mental patients with those of the artist.

But we will be none the wiser if we content ourselves with this type of analysis, or if we fail to emphasize that the abdication of critics and historians is a product of their refusal to investigate what exactly it is within the system (within history) that ordains the function and position of art and artists: their refusal to question how psychology weighs upon (or weighs up) morality. Indeed, it can be seen in one crisis after another, from the artistic (and psychiatric) exhibition of excess to generalizations about the subjective poverty it produces, that the "system" has inevitably been forced to deal with the nature of exactly that which escapes it — psychology. Through the work of Freud we have become well aware that the discovery of the unconscious gives an entirely new dimension (other than psychological) to the "ludic" characterization of art, and we realize that by restoring Psyche to her illustrious mate (Eros) Freud has gravely wounded the integrity of the system and of history. Quite contrary to what some people seem to think, with the discovery of the unconscious and the Freudian theory of language (Lacan) we have not entered the era of psychology, we have left it. And so it is possible for us now to think how, in art, at the system's heart, causing repetitions and cycles of crisis, something that is not overdetermined but that overdetermines metaphysics, morals, even physics, has been stifled. The multiple forms of modern art can now be ordered, not by chronology or by a systematic itinerary across history, but according to the symptomatic positions they occupy in manifesting a repression which attaches in one degree or another to the very system they should transcend. Considered in this light, the progressive and more or less precipitous (more precipitous of late) and rhythmic accumulation of schools and groups in modern art begins to show us the futility of all systematic assessment of the history of those schools. What is exhibited in the diversity of these forms, taken together, is more exactly an implicit critique of all positions that attempt to establish their chronology. The repression and repetition that they suppose, are these not primarily indicative of a suspension of time and the reiteration of a fixatory trauma through condensation and displacement? In this sense, and again in its diversity, the collection of modern art movements seems to me to determine the complex relations of an always-contemporary resistance to the system, rather than the history of a formal or ideological evolution such as others imagine they espy.

This particular form of resistance has developed to such an extent over the last ten years that it is now more and more difficult to ignore. The sort of implicit contemporaneity indicated by an increasing narrowing of time spans in the succession and accumulation of modern art movements has become quite explicit today with the simultaneous co-existence, often in a single geographical locus, or sometimes even in the work of a single artist, of a plurality of attitudes and styles. This was perhaps first remarked by certain conceptual artists in the form of their more or less sociological refusal of originality and aesthetic quality in the art-work, and might be, once again, more symptom than cause in that these artists, working on a formally anecdotal performance of the "state of art", were reiterating in schemes akin to those of journalism the exhibition of the givens in the crisis witnessed by the nineteenth and (especially) the twentieth century. Welcomed as a new configuration of the avant-garde, this attitude (few examples of which are really of much interest) enjoyed a certain success by playing on its own apparently radical gesture of evacuation. But because of the very ambiguity of the mercantile speculation to which it lent itself, and by adding a new avant-garde form to the lists, this kind of work came finally to justify the chronological system of what is conventionally called the history of art. It seems to me that the contemporary situation entirely escapes this sort of misunderstanding because art now seems to inscribe itself deliberately elsewhere than within the usual conventional games, escaping the characteristic positions of all avant-garde movements.

The accumulation of movements, modes, attitudes and styles found today in Germany as much as in Britain or Italy, as much in Paris as in New York, constitutes a process that is less one of novelty or newness than one of, so to speak, difference; as such it disrupts the speculatory bringing into place (mercantile, critical, historical) of the tradition of avant-gardes and modernisms. If in the first place we try to understand and analyze what is signified in this accumulative co-existence of movements, attitudes, modes and styles, we cannot help but be struck by the nature of the historical function they fill. The ensemble of contemporary production does not seem to me to arise in any way from the leitmotif of the avant-garde (or from what that means in terms of the philosophy of history), nor from any explicit projection at all, but rather from a sense of the art-work's contemporaneity not only with itself but also with exactly the kind of debates, like this one, that found it. It seems to be one of the particularities of this present situation of contemporaneity that the situation itself is in fact assumed; once it is assumed, then everything contradictory and complex about the situation is entertained and explored within a relationship to a history that it is still explicitly dominant but implicitly played-out, unachieved. If we consider young, contemporary artists, either individually or as a diverse collection, they seem to be succeeding on this model of resistance to the system and its characteristic elevations (symptomatic as they are), and are engaging the whole problematic of crisis that has marked modernity. They are denying any semblance of a chronology (which would want to recuperate the present "modernity" as a repetition of the same crisis), forging a contemporaneity, actualizing the more or less huge inadequacies of the dominant mass of novelties, formal propositions and ideological claims — all of which are at stake in this vast game. The work of these contemporary artists usually resists, and makes explicit its resistance to, the pretenders of modernity by playing against the convention that demands that an artist produce the new as if the old new (as if modern "history") had already taken place. It seems to me that what artists are proposing today is a refusal to take place. Contemporary art has no place since it interrogates all systems and proposes as a specific problematic the treatment of the fixatory trauma which has undergone (an historical) repression; art now proposes as the task in hand the whole question of repetition through condensation and displacement. Some artists go so far as to take up the problem at its root and confront the long, sinuous present of modern art with formal disruptions of the theological coherence of past work. In so doing they are explicitly reappropriating all the givens that might throw some light on the approach to that most difficult problem — the history of art. Other artists reinvent and reactivate those aspects that are most significantly attached to the ordering and resolution of the problems they contain. So should we in fact be so surprised to find in the work of young painters today, not only the major references to Picasso or to Matisse, but also evocations of what was called "abstract expressionism" (Pollock to Motherwell), or references to German "expressionism", to Dufy, Monet, Courbet or Bonnard, or to what became known after World War II as the "Ecole de Paris"? This re-evaluation of the whole range of problems that modernity poses is only a beginning, but we can already see that, perhaps for the first time ever since art obstinately short-circuited on its own history, the plastic arts are allowing themselves the opportunity to have done with a "system" that never was, or that was at any rate not theirs. This interpretation is built upon what are perhaps no more than half-suppositions, but we certainly cannot ignore the way in which what we can already positively define as an eclecticism (in the strict sense of the word) is in the process of disrupting all the establishments, habits, conventions, the very mode of being and the ways of thinking that were established by the system of modern art history. Sometime or other (tomorrow, perhaps today) the critic and the historian are going to have to take the time to listen to what is quite clearly being told them.

(translation by Paul Smith)

Paul Hayes Tucker

Monet and the Bourgeois Dream:
Argenteuil and the Modern Landscape

"The aspiration of the population," observed one Parisian author in 1856, "for air, light, the beautiful, and the comfortable could be considered the distinctive characteristic of our epoch."[1] Taken from a guidebook to the suburbs of Paris, this pronouncement was based not only on the transformations taking place in the capital — the demolition of old buildings and the construction of broad tree-lined boulevards — but also the need to escape that urban environment. Having grown between 1830 and 1860 by more than 600,000 "motley, floating, hurried, busy, frightened, provincials and foreigners," as one cynical resident put it, Paris, for many, was an overcrowded, impersonal inferno.[2] It was a place for work and entertainment but not for humane living. That was only available, according to many members of the middle class at least, outside the octroi walls of the capital, in the intermediary zone between city and country, the suburbs.

In the autumn of 1871, nearly half a year after the armistice for the Franco-Prussian war had been signed, Claude Monet brought his family back to Paris ending their self-imposed exile in England and Holland. In December, they left the war-scarred capital and moved to Argenteuil, a picturesque, historic and progressive suburban town only 11 kilometers from the Gare Saint Lazare.

It was the streets and houses of this town, its waving fields and unrivaled basin for boating that Monet rendered in more than 170 canvases during his six-year stay from December 1871 to January 1878. We have rightfully come to see these paintings as constituting a classic phase of Impressionism. Today everyone who knows Monet's work is familiar with their formal qualities as well as their subjects. Yet their significance is seldom considered perhaps because we like them so well as the most classic example of Monet's ability to capture the fleeting effects of nature.[3]

The nineteenth century did not see them so simply. In this paper I would like to examine some of the contemporary issues that Monet's paintings in Argenteuil present. For he was not simply concerned with instantaneity and optical sensation. He was above all trying to be a modern landscape painter.

Like such areas today, the suburbs of Paris in the later 19th century were the great refuge from the city, ideally located close enough to afford easy access but far enough away to permit a quiet comfortable existence. As owner or even renter of a house and garden, people felt closer to nature and to their world reminiscent of past times when the pace of life was slower and human associations were richer and longer lasting.

"We've breathed too much of those exotic perfumes," wrote one critic in 1866. "We want rustic scents now; man — the artist above all — is an Antaius who needs to touch the earth in order to recover the forces lost in the eternal fight with the monstrous Hercules of civilization."[4]

Although for some the suburbs were "un peu trop arrangé," for many in the burgeoning middle class, they were where one could find those lost forces and emotions. Even just a visit on Sunday was an enlivening experience, as popular illustrations from the period suggest. Indeed, Flaubert's Parisian clerks Bouvard and Pécuchet so enjoyed their Sunday walks through Meudon, Belleville and Surenes that they found Monday intolerably dull; with the wisdom of Solomon, therefore, they gave these walks up.[5]

For those with a few francs in the bank or a job that paid a modest wage, living in the suburbs was a goal easily realized. The railroad system continued to expand from its original 19 kilometers of track laid in 1836 to the more than 17,000 in operation in 1866.[6] In addition, developers from mid-century onwards were aggressively buying up small forests and old lots at what many felt were quite reasonable prices. So earnest were their efforts and so great was the demand for these new houses that by 1860 one Parisian journalist could call this development "the new agrarian law of the suburbs."[7]

When Monet moved to Argenteuil, he moved to a town that had not escaped these speculators. On the contrary, the town had done everything to attract them. It had devoted considerable funds to public projects like widening, straightening, and lighting its streets, many of which Monet painted. It had also laid new water pipes and improved its promenades; it had even expanded its health and educational facilities and began supporting more elaborate town fêtes and new boating regattas. All of these efforts actually had begun in 1851. For in that year, the railroad from Paris was extended across the plains of Gennevilliers to the bank opposite the town. Having lobbied for this link to the capital for years, the town fathers knew what it would mean to their community.

"The railroad will increase our gypsum business which will be good for Argenteuil and for the country. It will likewise help the town's wine business. Developed property will gain since Parisians will come more willingly, knowing that living here will not disrupt their daily business in the capital."[8]

This is precisely what happened. Between 1850 and 1870, new houses went up in fields around the town, the population doubled and the number of industries for both work and pleasure grew with every passing year. Argenteuil soon became recognized for its restaurants and boat basin, its chemical plants and crystal factory, its pigeon shoot and most important, its iron works, especially the Usine Joy which built the most renowned iron structure in all France, Les Halles.

What had really sealed Argenteuil's progressive future was the railroad bridge which Monet painted in 1873, a year after he arrived (fig. 1; w. 279). Opened only ten years earlier, the bridge brought the railroad directly into the town and with it, of course, more goods, people and opportunities. During its construction, residents not only recognized the changes that it would bring but also anticipated the structure to be "a veritable monument that will win the admiration of all who come to see it."[9] Their hopes were justified because in size and design, the bridge was an extraordinary achievement, the product of new technology and materials — iron and poured concrete. In addition, the trestle was being built by their own Joly factory.

This and other paintings of the railroad by Monet have long been seen as modern in style, composition, color and subject. And rightfully so. For instead of blending the bridge with the landscape and painting it cautiously with muted tones as Daubigny did with the bridge farther north on the Oise, Monet elevates it high above the water so that in the brilliant light of the afternoon sun, it glistens as it defines a new horizon line. Forceful, dominant, and recognized as a wonder by the two men in the foreground, the bridge is a symbol of Argenteuil's advancement and the industrial progress of the age. The sailboats, symbols of the new industry of leisure, glide out effortlessly from under the concrete piers, their sails billowing by the same wind that blows the smoke from the train, reminding us of the advantages the modern Pegasus could bring.

Monet's picture is perhaps even bolder than traditionally believed for the bridge when completed in 1863 was greeted by the townspeople with surprise and regret. "Instead of a construction of grandiose or bold forms," wrote one editor of the *Journal d'Argenteuil,* "there is only a heavy and primitive work which is not at the level of the progress of science . . . . They made a wall of iron that is impenetrable to the eye, a tunnel without a roof."[10] One resident felt that "they should embellish it with the taste that characterizes our nation . . . . The capitals should be carved, the trestle adorned with cast-iron decorations."[11] Anything, it seems, but to have it be what it was, an industrial structure made from industrial materials.

Monet's picture, therefore, can be understood as an ode to the present, a poetic but forthright presentation of a time and place where the contrasting elements of modern life, city and country, labor and leisure, co-exist in perfect harmony.

If Monet had painted a picture of the bridge a year or so earlier, it would have communicated quite different ideas as the bridge lay in ruins. It had been destroyed during the Franco-Prussian war. A photograph of the structure taken in 1870 or 1871 shows the original lattice-like trestle plunged into the water and the concrete piers standing stained and useless (fig. 2). The sight would have been a painful reminder of the country's humiliating defeat.

The bridge was rebuilt between 1871 and 1872 as can be seen in another photograph taken at the time (Tucker, *Monet at Argenteuil*, p. 58). It was then that the more elegant Second Empire trestle was replaced by one that stretches across Monet's picture more like the tunnel of iron the critic had decried. Having waited for the scaffolding to be taken down, Monet shows the bridge rebuilt in all of its splendor. His picture, therefore, testifies to the powers of the nation and to the fact that Argenteuil could be a kind of utopia.

Much of Monet's work in Argenteuil during the 1870s is concerned with this same theme of utopian harmony, of presenting the contrasts of the age in a way that reveals the positivism of progress and the fulfillment of the era's aspirations for light, air, the beautiful, and the comfortable, as the guidebook author noted.

Tied to his time and committed to rendering the most recent developments of his adopted home town, Monet was responding in his own way to the contemporaneous imperative, "il faut être de son temps," the rallying cry for modernist art and literature since mid-century.

To be of the 1870s, however, was not the same as to be of the 1850s. The positivist historian, Hippolyte Taine, writing in 1864 felt "we have only to open our eyes to see a change going on in the condition of men and consequently their minds, so profound, so universal, and so rapid that no other country has witnessed the like of it."[12]

Although the Franco-Prussian war opened everyone's eyes to the state of affairs in France, the decade of the 70s proved to be a period of extraordinary productivity, as the economist and statistician Michael Mulhall pointed out in 1881. In his *Balance sheet of the world for ten years 1870-1880,* Mulhall asserted "The period of ten years which has just come to a close has been one of marvelous industrial activity, of unprecedented increase in population . . . and an almost unchequered career of prosperity and growing wealth," all of this despite the world-wide depression that began in 1873.[13] France shared in this prosperity as industrial production increased by more than 11 percent and the earnings of the average Frenchman rose by more than 15 percent.[14] One French economist in 1879 felt that "progress would never be as rapid or as marvelous as it has been up until now."[15]

To be a modern landscape painter in this era of rapid change meant, first and foremost, confronting the tangible evidence of that change. Barbizon artists of the 1840s and 50s, faced with the growth of Paris and the rise of industry, chose to retreat into the arms of unspoilt nature, a heroic but last-ditch attempt to recover a rural tradition that was clearly being eroded by progress. The trees spoke to Rousseau, the peasants to Millet. "Monet," observed Theodore Duret in 1878, "feels drawn to embellished nature and to urban scenes . . . . You scarcely ever see cultivated fields in his canvases, you won't find any sheep there, still less any peasants."[16]

An attraction to embellished nature and to the improvements that the town fathers brought to Argenteuil — or that Napoleon III and Baron Haussmann brought to Paris — is a second modern element in Monet's painting, one that was recognized much earlier by Emile Zola. Writing in 1868, Zola placed Monet at the head of a group of artists he called Les Actualistes:

> Among the painters of the first rank I will cite Claude Monet. He has sucked the milk of our age; he has grown and will continue to grow in his adoration of what surrounds him. He loves the horizons of our cities, the grey and white spots that

the houses make on the clear sky; he loves the busy
people in the streets who run about in topcoats;
. . . he loves our women, their umbrellas, their
gloves, their ribbons, their wigs and their face
powder, everything that makes them daughters of
our civilization. In the fields, Claude Monet prefers
an English park to a corner of the forest. He is
pleased to discover man's trace everywhere; he
wants to live among us forever. As a true Parisian,
he brings Paris to the country; he cannot paint a
landscape without including well-dressed men and
women. Nature seems to lose its interest for him as
soon as it does not bear the stamp of our customs
. . . Claude Monet loves with a particular affection
nature that man makes modern . . . . Certainly I
would not admire his works much if he were not a
true painter. I simply want to verify the sympathy
that sweeps him toward modern subjects."[17]

Modern landscapes, therefore, as Zola implies, are those
that show nature altered or enlivened by city people, ties or taste. It
is not surprising that Monet's views of the railroad are so frequently singled out as examples of his modernism; the railroad was
one of the most prominent urban elements in the countryside.

So too were pleasure boats, and they were also just as tied
to Paris. According to Alphonse Karr, the noted social observer,
the first pleasure boaters on the Seine were Parisian artists and
students, "wise epicurians who loved the quiet, free, untrammeled
life far from the maddening crowd of the city."[18] Other authors
asserted workers were the first, escaping in their rowboats from the
demands of their jobs. Regardless of who was correct, the first
boaters in the 1830s and 40s gave the sport such a bad reputation
that even into the following decade, as one author recalled, "you
did not venture to admit that you went out on the water; for going
boating was nothing less than indulging in the most condemned
eccentricity."[19] By the 1860s however, through the efforts of people
like Karr and his circle, boating became not only widely practised
but highly respectable, with organized competitions and private
clubs. And Argenteuil, with its broad river basin became the center
for sailboating in the environs; it even hosted the international
regatta for the universal exposition in 1867.

Boating at Argenteuil, as Monet shows in this picture, was
directly linked to the railroad; so too was industry, as Monet implies. And just as residents of Argenteuil hailed the industrializ-

ation of their town as a positive development, poets and popular illustrators could see factories as welcome symbols of advancement. Monet could as well. One of the first pictures he ever painted was a view of factories, unfortunately now lost. In 1872, he painted no less than five views of the industries outside Rouen, among them *The Train* (w. 213), a scene so filled with chimneys and smoke that it seems closer to Gary, Indiana, or Liverpool, England, than the Impressionists' France of the nineteenth century. In Argenteuil, he frequently includes evidence of the town's industries as in *The Path through the vineyards* (w. 219), also from 1872. Here the Hobbema-like path winds through the grape-ladened stakes of the town's vineyards. In the distance the chimneys of several factories break the horizon paralleling the tower of the parish church. It is as if Monet is showing us the progression of the town from the traditional cultivation of the soil to the mechanized production of goods; and with the path leading so naturally from the foreground to the background it is clear that industry and agriculture form a perfect union.

Monet made this utopian harmony even more evident in another painting from the same year of 1872, *The Promenade along the Seine* (fig. 3; w. 219). The sandy path leads us gently along the waters edge to the petit chateau, warehouses and smokestack in the distance. People stroll along the shore, sailboats bob on the river and across the cloudy sky drifts the smoke of the factories on the right. Nothing disturbs the pervasive tranquility of the scene. Indeed, Monet places the factories with the house under the arch of trees in a manner that recalls Constable's Salisbury Cathedral. Instead of the wonders of god and man, however, Monet is celebrating progress, the new religion where work and pleasure, industry and nature can go hand in hand in the same environment.

It is appropriate that Monet coupled the factories and house, for the desired goal of labor was not just leisure but the opportunity to enjoy that time off in a house of your own. "One of the pronounced characteristics of our present Parisian society," observed Eugène Chapus, the editor of the Parisian journal *Le Sport,* "is that everyone in the middle class wants to have his own little house and garden, his *argenteas mediocritas,* with trees, roses, and dahlias."[20] Popular artists could satirize the suburban family in illustrations (e.g. Tucker, p. 136), but the desire for those petits pavillons was far reaching indeed, touching Bouvard and Pécuchet, the picture-dealer Arnoux from *L'Education Sentimentale,* even Zola who moved to Meudon in 1878 on the profits of

L'Assommoir.[21]

Thus when Monet moved to Argenteuil, he was just like the thousands who preceded him. And when he painted his house and garden, as he did so frequently in the 70s, he was painting the dream that he and his mobile middle class nurtured.

The house and garden, of course, was a private, personal world, a retreat from the complexities of contemporary life. In the eyes of the realist writer or painter, it was also a place that revealed essential traits of the time. First, that quest for peace and beauty, a need that Monet's backyard seemed to fulfill given the idyllic qualities of *The Women in the Garden* of 1872 (w. 202). Second, the desire for light, air and greater contact with nature, again apparently satisfied at Argenteuil. Third, the need for pleasurable pastimes; Flaubert came up with hundreds of projects for Bouvard and Pécuchet and Doré chuckled over the family gardening in Auteuil (Tucker, p. 139). Monet himself seems to have been an equally avid gardener. However, he never shows himself or his family engaged in these activities. When he paints his son Jean, for example, on his mechanical horse (w. 238), he does so with obvious pride, dressing him in his Sunday best, down to his English boater, and posing him in his finest equestrian position. Jean is not the son of a starving artist. On the contrary, he has all the trappings of an aristocrat, recalling the great equestrian portraits by Titian or Velasquez, although Jean's pony is appropriately made of iron.

On the other hand, this association, however unconscious on Monet's part, might seem to suggest that Monet is making things better than they were; only two years earlier, for example, in 1870, he did not have enough money to pay for his hotel room in Trouville yet what does he paint but the summer tourists strolling the boardwalk by the brand new Hotel des Roches Noires (w. 155). He even makes his new wife look like those successful Parisian visitors (w. 158).

This gap between romance and reality, between the beauty of his scenes and the difficulties of his life — has long been part of the Monet mystique. Monet even cultivated it. But for the years he spent at Argenteuil, it simply isn't true. There Monet earned on the average of more than 14,000 francs a year, a substantial sum considering professional men in Paris during the same time made between 7 and 9,000 and workers in Argenteuil a mere 2-3,000.[22]

This makes his apparent enthusiasm for progress and the good life more reasonable; he was doing very well. He even employed a maid at Argenteuil. He ordered wines from Narbonne and

1. Claude Monet, *The Railroad Bridge viewed from the Port,* 1873. Collection Niarchos Family, London.

2. *Anonymous Photograph of the Railroad Bridge at Argenteuil after the Franco-Prussian War,* circa 1871. Collection Musée du Vieil Argenteuil.

3. Claude Monet, *The Promenade along the Seine,* 1872. Private Collection, London.

4. Claude Monet, *Argenteuil, the Bank in Flower,* 1877. Private Collection, Maryland.

5. Claude Monet, *Monet's Family in the Garden-Camille, Jean and the Maid,* 1873. Collection
Hortense Anda Buehrle, Zürich.

8. Pierre-Auguste Renoir, *Monet Painting in his Garden at Argenteuil, 1873.* Collection The
Wadsworth Atheneum, Hartford, Conn.

6. Claude Monet, *A Corner of the Garden with Dahlias,* 1873. Private Collection, New York.

7. Claude Monet, *Gare Saint-Lazare,* 1877. Collection The Fogg Art Museum, Cambridge,
Mass.

Bordeaux and he moved into a new, more expensive house only two years after he arrived.[23]

Despite his success, Monet was not always so secure. His income, for example, varied from month to month. When he had money he spent it, making him frequently short of ready cash. This produced his constant pleas of poverty and some resentment on the part of his friends; Renoir claimed "he was born a lord."[24] Though demanding and supercilious Monet was a sensitive individual as evident in his early letters and his heart-felt responses to nature. He was therefore a man of contrasts which perhaps prompted some of the peculiar qualities in his work. In the portrait of Jean, for example, or better yet, in a view of Camille, Jean and the maid from the following year of 1873 (w. 280), there is both an assertion and a hesitancy, an intimacy and a coolness, a sense of attainment and a countering sense of alienation.

These contrasting qualities, of course, were not just part of Monet's life or personality; they were typical of his times, especially for those who lived in and around Paris. One writer discussing the transformations of the capital felt that he was a bee born in a different hive. "We are in modern Paris rather like foreigners in a spa; we take deep breaths of the air we are given; we look with wonderment and satisfaction at the new streets and houses they are building; we enjoy it all without being attached to anything, just as if this city were not our own and as if tomorrow we were to pack our bags and move on."[25] He admitted he was critical because he felt "less admiration for the future than regret for the past," but even for those who did not suffer from nostalgia, modern life was a dialectic of romance and rawness, empathy and dispassion; it had to be because to survive, no less succeed, you could no longer rely on the old standards of mutual trust and sharing. You lived on your wits and intuition, and you succeeded on your social connections and chance acquaintances. It required calculated manoeuvers, strong personal defenses, harnessed emotions and no small amount of luck. "It created people," as one journalist noted in 1878, "who seem as though they cannot live without someone else and yet are cold, indifferent, and reserved." Maxime DuCamp characterized Parisians as "superficial;" Victor Fournel accused them of being "anxious, nervous, and irritable, the most volatile and capricious people on earth."[26] We need only recall Madame Bovary, however, to recognize this was not exclusive to Paris.

By infusing his work with these qualities, Monet gives his pictures a critical edge that moves them beyond reportage or more anecdotal renderings of similar subjects like P. J. Linder's Salon submission of 1877, *On Holiday* (Tucker, p. 126). "We all know this man," wrote one critic in reference to the Linder's gardener, "with prodigious facility on his part, the entire universe disappears from his mind as soon as he sets foot in the garden. Or better yet he creates it for himself. Everyday there, he creates a little world apart, and this world is just for him . . . filled with emotions of all kinds."[27] Although Monet would like his garden to be similarly evocative, look how luscious and beautiful he makes it, he is all too conscious of the world beyond his walls to close himself off completely. Indeed, in the background of *Camille, Jean and the Maid,* we can see a new house going up; the roof remains to be built. The middle-class desire for a hortus conclusus therefore and the realities of the suburban plot are here laid bare.

The fact that the suburbs are also being changed by urban-ites and city values is also clear in this picture. The manicured garden strongly recalls urban parks or noble compounds, especially in comparison to Linder's more casual place. Camille is clearly an upper bourgeois woman; Linder's gardener, according to one critic, could be from any class which undoubtedly was part of the painting's appeal.

Even when Monet shows his wife at the window of their house (w. 287), he cannot be as uncomplicated as his juste milieu contemporaries, like Linder or Karl Becker. Becker's *Le Matin* (Tucker, p. 137), from the Salon of 1875, provoked one critic to make associations with dawn, love, and the Italian campagna.[28] Monet's picture eludes these romantic associations. On the one hand it is too straightforward. Camille is a passive if not forlorn female, and the house although flower-wrapped is a typical subur-ban structure. On the other hand, Monet's picture is recognizably artful. The window is cropped at the top making the interior of the house seem cavernous. The shrubs and potted plants in the fore-ground almost give off a fragrance. And the honeysuckle that creeps up the side of the window helps to create the illusion of age. It is a kind of suburban version of Manet's *Balcony,* removed and intriguing, part fairy tale, part fact. Where Manet looked to the south to Spain and Goya, Monet turned to the north and to low-lands painters like Nicolaes Maes.

Comparison with Maes' *Woman at the Window* (Tucker, p. 137) makes the unlowly nature of Monet's subject clear. Camille is not a working girl, the house is not a woodsman's cottage and the garden is not a kitchen garden accompanying most middle-class houses even today. Monet's painting, therefore, is not about rustic simplicity but about modern urban life transposed to the country.

Perhaps the most glorious and poignant garden picture of all is Monet's *Luncheon* of 1873 (w. 285), a decorative piece according to Monet, but one that reveals with extraordinary subtlety the facts and fiction of modern bourgeois life in the suburbs.

Nothing appears to be wanting in this scene, filled as it is with beauty, light, and all the desirable class comforts — food, finery, flowers, and substantial house. It breathes the air of contentment, down to the rumpled napkins, crusts of bread, unfinished wine, and untouched peaches.

Yet the more we look at the picture, the more we realize something is missing. There are no connections among the figures; Jean is absorbed in his toys, the women in their walk. No one acknowledges us and most important, no story is being told. Clearly a meal has been consumed but do the two wine glasses and two coffee cups indicate two, three, or four people? If the piece of bread, the coffee cup and the napkin on the left side of the table should be read as a former place setting, what has happened to the chair? And if both of the women have their bonnets on, whose is that up in the tree and what is it doing there?

One thing is certain. The meal is finished. This is extremely important as it explains why Jean and the women are not sitting at the table and why the table is not correct and orderly. It also explains the peculiar emptiness; the pretext for the painting passed when the meal ended. What Monet shows is the remnants of the event, enticing indeed, but none the less the aftermath. To see how final the scene actually is we can juxtapose it to an outdoor banquet picture by Jan Steen (Tucker, p. 148). Monet's picture is almost funereal by comparison. And yet it is full of the potential for Steen's exuberance. Thus while Monet presents all the pleasurable elements sought after by the bourgeoisie with a realism that would convince you of their attainability, and while he shows that they can produce a decided measure of happiness, Monet also makes it clear that happiness and fulfillment are as temporal as the meal itself, that if you move out of your garden and confront the contrasts beyond the walls — the industries, the different classes, the difficulties of work — indeed, if Monet simply looks behind him in this picture, the ideal of the harmonious life in the country can be shown to be a kind of myth. Like the pictures by Steen or still lifes by his contemporaries Kalf or De Heem, *The Luncheon* is a me-

mento mori, not to man and his life on earth, but to modern man and his existence in the suburbs.

Monet was perhaps never again so direct; he too wanted to enjoy all the pleasures of suburban living, a fact that he confirms in another view of his garden from the same summer of 1873 (fig. 4; w. 286). Turning from where he stood to paint *The Luncheon,* he renders the flowers and trees with all the richness of a heightened palette filling the scene with an energy he generally reserved for views of the fields around the town. The profusion of natural growth and the two strollers in the background attest to the rich, revivifying powers of the place.

Monet's garden may have been as attractive as he portrayed it, but a painting by Renoir, which is probably more accurate, shows that it was not as secluded (fig. 5). Standing in the same garden in the same year, looking in the same direction, Renoir shows Monet painting by the blue shuttered house that appears in the center of Monet's view. Being faithful to the site, Renoir also includes the jumble of other houses on the right. Monet judiciously cropped those houses out and he enlarged the trees and undergrowth on the right. Whether the flowers he includes on the left were his own or his neighbor's, usurped by artistic license, is uncertain, but it is clear that he is suppressing some of the evidence of encroaching neighbors and making his garden the suburban ideal.

The energy of his picture, therefore, may derive not only from the season or the moment, but also from the gap between what the garden was and what Monet wanted it to be.

Knowing Monet's work from the decades that follow, it should not be surprising to learn that this suppression of the world beyond the garden walls becomes standard in Monet's garden pictures of 1875 and 1876. In fact, Monet becomes so preoccupied with his garden in 1876, he paints virtually nothing else, no bridges, no boats, no Sunday strollers. It is as if he were retreating into a world of his own making, one that we can see from a view of that year is indeed paradisal (*In the Garden;* w. 386), recalling the 18th century fêtes galantes he so admired.

Are these later garden pictures as modern as the paintings of the railroad or the promenade? In narrow stylistic terms, they could perhaps be considered even more advanced as they are generally bolder in color and more broadly painted, and they frequently emphasize the flatness of the picture plane to a greater extent. In subject, they still show those daughters of our civilization that Zola appreciated.

Yet one might argue that because they do not confront the industries of the town, or the social divisions of the era, they speak about modernism but they are not modern.

This, of course, is true in part; but within the context of their time, they confront an equally significant contemporary fact — Barbizon is a lost ideal; the suburbs are the new haven.

The critic who had claimed that everyone needed to recover the forces of nature lost in the eternal fight against the monster civilization felt that this losing battle had made landscape painting "an article of the first necessity."[29] "We need the fields, the trees, and the shepherds, not those elegant mascarades by Lancret or Vanloo" — or we might add by Monet. Other critics echoed the disdain for those mannered and charming inventors of the 18th century while reporting the excitement of Diaz and Daubigny sales in 1877 and 1878.

On the other hand, the rise of Barbizon art is the familiar stuff of popular taste catching up to the avant-garde. Rousseau, Daubigny, even Corot were not really instated as masters until the 1860s. But why would the 18th century be so despised?

Although more work needs to be done on this question, it seems again tied to class and times. Landscape painting was supposed to be a relief from the dilemmas of the world, a changeless, eternal, and reassuring subject to which everyone could relate. Barbizon art met that need more than the elegant fêtes galantes because as life for the middle class became more complex and their environment more altered by the great force of progress, they only naturally wanted to retreat to the security of the rural past. It reaffirmed their continued existence and their own social and economic position. Barbizon paintings, unlike their 18th century counterparts — or unlike Monet — were more anonymous, the hand of the artist being subordinated to the simple poetry of the scene. Even the earthier colors made them less assertive. In that sense, they conformed to the call to order issued by some critics after the disaster of 1870-71. But since these paintings were radical in their time, the middle class could now safely enjoy the revolution they had caused.

Monet's pictures, and those of his fellow Impressionists, caused an analogous but more violent revolution, as many critics in the 1870s noted. "Their outrageous color, audacious subjects, and liberties in execution could even frighten the horses pulling the omni-buses," observed George Maillard in 1876.[30] "Their vocabulary," another critic noted, "resembled that of *L'Assommoir.*"[31] It was nature seen through a temperament, something that people like Jules Claretie found decidedly missing in the landscape painting at the Salons of the 70s. "Landscapes flood the Salon," he wrote in 1876, "proving once more that the 'métier' rises like a lake and the art disappears like a chapel sitting high on a hill and which little by little is obscured by the mist. As there is no fight going on," he continued, "there is no research, no efforts, and no discoveries."[32]

In Monet's work, there is always a battle. Just like his 20th century counterpart, Matisse, Monet always struggled to find beauty and art in his immediate surroundings. He knew what lay beyond the trees in his garden view. Indeed, in the very same year he painted this canvas, a new iron works opened in Argenteuil, right across the railroad tracks which were directly in front of his house. And while that might make his picture seem overly insular, we must remember that in the following year he could paint the extraordinary views of the Gare Saint-Lazare, the absolute antithesis of his suburban garden.

These views of his backyard and those of the steamfilled station represent the dialectics of modern life. Contemporaries could present them in more anecdotal fashion or they could escape them in the forest of Fontainebleau or in Barbizon — a "true village," wrote one critic in 1876, "with a lively and picturesque appearance. You'll see, it's a long ways from Paris."[33]

Monet never made the trip.

In one final picture, perhaps Monet's last in Argenteuil, *Argenteuil, promenade in flowers,* (fig. 6; w. 453,) he reveals with stunning clarity and beauty, the dilemmas of Argenteuil and the modern suburban existence. Returning to the same site he had painted in 1872, the promenade along the Seine, he shows the same tall trees, turreted house and factory chimneys. This picture, however, is radically different from the earlier version. No path leads us into the scene; in fact, the view is clearly divided between foreground and background with no apparent connection between the two. These are two worlds juxtaposed. The flowers in the foreground, so close they seem tangible, are the twisted realm of nature, the suburban garden, Monet's domain. The background, though bathed in a misty Turneresque light, is the world beyond the walls, with steamboats, smoking factories, pleasure seekers and golden illusions. We are a long ways indeed from Barbizon.

One critic reviewing the Third Impressionist Exhibition in 1877, in which Monet had the most paintings of any participant, summed up what could be considered the essentially modern characteristics of these works:

> "The disturbing ensemble of contradictory qualities which distinguish the Impressionists, the crude application of paint, the down to earth subjects, the appearance of spontaneity, the conscious incoherence, the bold colors, the contempt for form, the childish naiveté that they mix heedlessly with exquisite refinement, all of this is not without analogy to the chaos of contradictory forces that trouble our era."[34]

Notes

W. refers to Daniel Wildenstein's catalogue raisonné of Monet's oeuvre.

[1]B. -R., *Le Guide du promeneur aux barrières et dans les environs de Paris*, Paris, 1856, p. 17.

[2]Benjamin Gastineau, *Sottises et scandales du temps présent*, Pagnerre, 1863, p. 152, as quoted in Joanna Richardson, *La Vie Parisienne*, New York, 1971, p. 215.

[3]Notable exceptions to this are Robert Herbert, "Method and Meaning in Monet," *Art in America*, 67, Sept. 79, pp. 90-108; John House, unpublished doctorate, *Claude Monet: His Aims and Methods c. 1877-1895* (Courtauld, 1976); and Richard Shiff "The End of Impressionism," *Art Quarterly* (new series), Autumn 1978, pp. 338-378.

[4]Hector de Callias, "L'Ecole de Barbizon," *L'Artiste*, 15 December 1866, pp. 57-8.

[5]Gustave Flaubert, *Bouvard and Pécuchet*, trans. by A. J. Krailsheimer, Harmondsworth, p. 29.

[6]Sir Theodore Zeldin, *France 1848-1945*, vol. 2, *Intellect, Taste, and Anxiety*, Oxford, 1977, p. 637.

[7]Eugene Chapus, "La vie à Paris: Le caractère de la société parisienne actuelle; les maisons de la campagne," *Le Sport*, 5 September 1860, pp. 2-3.

[8]Minutes of Argenteuil Municipal Council Meeting, 6 April 1845, in Argenteuil Archives, Registre des délibérations du conseil municipal 1844-1846, 1D18.

[9]F. Lebeuf, "Le Pont du chemin de fer d'Argenteuil," *Journal d'Argenteuil*, 21 September 1862, p. 2.

[10]F. Lebeuf, " Overture de la nouvelle gare d'Argenteuil," *Journal d'Argenteuil*, 7 June 1863, p. 2.

[11]Claude Collas, "Sur le nouveau chemin de fer d'Argenteuil," *Journal d'Argenteuil*, 28 June 1863, p. 2.

[12]Hippolyte Taine, *Lectures on Art*, vol. I, trans. by John Durand, New York, 1875, pp. 162-4.

[13]Michael G. Mulhall, *Balance Sheet of the world for ten years 1870-1880*, London, 1881, pp. 1-3.

[14]*Ibid*, pp. 53-60.

[15]Maurice Block, "La Crise économique," *Revue des deux mondes,* March 1879, pp. 458-9.

[16]Théodore Duret, *Les Peintres Impressionistes,* Paris, 1878, pp. 17-19.

[17]Emile Zola, "Mon Salon: IV. Les Actualistes," *L'Evènement Illustré,* 24 May 1868.

[18]Alphonse Karr, *Le Canotage en France,* Paris, 1858, p. 35.

[19]Philippe Daryle, *Le Yacht histoire de la navigation de plaisance,* Paris, 1890, p. 43.

[20]Chapus, (as in note 7).

[21]Flaubert, (as in note 5); Arnoux "finally fulfilling an old dream, . . . bought himself a country house (in Saint-Cloud)." *Sentimental Education,* trans. by Robert Baldick, Harmondsworth, 1976, p. 89.

[22]Monet recorded his earnings in his account books now in the Musée Marmottan. Daniel Wildenstein tallied them in his catalogue raisonné of the artist's work and I collected them in *Monet at Argenteuil,* London, 1982, chap. 2 note 33.

[23]Wildenstein, *Claude Monet, biographie et catalogue raisonné,* I, 1840-1881, Lausanne-Paris, 1974, p. 87.

[24]Pierre-Auguste Renoir in Jean Renoir, *Renoir, My Father,* translated by Rudolph and Dorothy Weaver, Boston and Toronto, 1962, p. 113.

[25]Edouard Gourdon, *Le Bois de Boulogne,* Bourdilliat, 1861, pp. 85-7 as cited in Richardson (as in note 2) pp. 214-15.

[26]Bachaumont, "La vie à Paris: Paris qui part et Paris qui reste," *Le Sport,* 10 July 1878, p. 2.

Maxime DuCamp, *Paris. Ses organes, sa fonction et sa vie dans la seconde moitié du xixe siècle,* Paris, 1876, vol. VI, p. 401.

Victor Fournel, *Paris nouveau et futur,* Paris, 1865, p. 15 as cited in Richardson (as in note 2).

[27]G. B., "En Villegiature," *L'Illustration,* 13 October 1877, pp. 231-4.

[28]_____ , "Le Matin — gravure d'aprés M. Becker," *L'Illustration* LXV, 27 March 1874, p. 207.

[29]DeCallios (as in note 4). On the disdain for the rococo see for example Bachaumont, "La Vie à Paris: les choses d'art et le goût de jour," *Le Sport,* 7 February 1877, p. 2.

[30]George Maillard, "Exposition impressioniste chez Durand-Ruel," *Le Pays,* 4 April 1876. George Rivière, "L'Impressionisme," *L'Artiste,* 1 May 1876, pp. 347-9, made the direct analogy between the Impressionists' revolution and that of the 1830s, pointing out the former's greater violence and pervasiveness.

[31]Marc de Montifaud, "Le Salon de 1877," *L'Artiste,* 1 May 1877, p. 337.

[32]Jules Claretie, *L'Art et les artistes français contemporains,* Paris, 1876, p. 361.

[33]A. Piedagnel, "Millet chez-lui — souvenirs de Barbizon," *L'Artiste,* XLVII, May 1876, p. 288.

[34]Frédéric Chevalier, "Les Impressionistes," *L'Artiste,* 1 May 1877, p. 331.

Hollis Clayson

Avant-Garde and *Pompier* Images of 19th Century French Prostitution: The Matter of Modernism, Modernity and Social Ideology

In his 1949 essay titled "On the Role of Nature in Modernist Painting," Clement Greenberg wrote:

> The paradox in the evolution of French painting from Courbet to Cézanne is how it was brought to the verge of abstraction in and by its very effort to transcribe visual experience with ever greater fidelity. Such fidelity was supposed, by the Impressionists, to create the values of pictorial art itself. The truth of nature and the truth, or success, of art were held not only to accord with, but to enhance one another.[1]

I use Greenberg's argument, as presented in these few important lines, as the point of departure for this essay. While examining several images of prostitution made in Paris in the late 1870's, I address myself to the strengths and shortcomings of Greenberg's important text while launching a reconsideration of the connections between social and aesthetic ideology in certain *avant-garde* and *pompier* constructions of Parisian prostitution.

Figures 1 and 2 show images which have an obvious equivalence of subject — both showing prostitute and client in a bedroom — and an equally apparent dissimilarity in style: a *pompier* picture, Henry Gervex's *Rolla* of 1878, in Figure 1, and a vanguard image, one of Edgar Degas' brothel monotypes of the late 1870's, in Figure 2. Let us now recall Greenberg's characterization of the Impressionist project and consider its relevance to the ostensible differences between these two images.

According to Greenberg, the Impressionist commitment to the faithful transcription of the objective world coexisted with, was woven into, a truthfulness to the medium of transcription. And "such fidelity was supposed to create the values of pictorial art itself."[2] The point of this reading seems to be that Impressionism, the modernist mode of representing the objective world in the 1870s, ended up being more truthful than other modes in two ways: it was both truer to nature and truer to art, inseparable commitments, inseparable achievements, mutually enhancing. This, despite the fact, as Greenberg reminds us, that the very effort to transcribe visual experience with great fidelity coexisted with the gradual withdrawal of painting from the task of representing the world, largely because of the increasing awareness of what was at stake in painting, in representing the world.

This argument is apposite to a discussion of the differences between the Gervex and the Degas because the Degas, and the series to which it belongs, has been widely interpreted along roughly Greenbergian lines. Largely because the series combines the use of a yielding, materially cooperative printmaking medium; a simplified, vigorous, greasy and loose handling of the ink; fragmented, dislocated, cut-off compositions appearing at first glance close to anti-compositions; and, finally, a highly-charged subject depicted in a disarming and apparently unconventional way, these monotypes have been described in the following terms: objective, forthright, morally indifferent or morally unselfconscious, detached and disengaged.[3] I do not think that this reading, which is the current interpretive orthodoxy, contradicts Greenberg's interpretation in any essential way. It does give weight to the formal peculiarities of Degas' pictorial language, the way in which his fragmentations and disassociations criticize the pictorial and subjective language of an "official" modern life picture such as Gervex's. But there is a crucial presumption which needs reviewing: the presumption that the radical form of Degas' picture conveyed the raw, unvarnished, objective truth about its subject in a way that we presume to be missing from or concealed or cosmeticized in Gervex's canvas because of its look. In other words, the modernist critic would argue that the force and vigor of Degas' critical aesthetic awareness cut through the mystifications and academic conventions upon which a Gervex relied.

From this line of reasoning, the notion follows that the ideological materials of the early modernist representational painter, both despite and because of his effort to transcribe visual experience with fidelity, are essentially purely aesthetic, and therefore his images demystify and tell the visual truth about his slice of the objective world. I think the equation which results is this: the adoption of a radical/critical aesthetic ideology freed the vanguard artist of the 1870's from any social or political or sexual ideologies and let him paint the truth, the modern truth at that. I would argue, on the contrary, that if we situate these two visually different images of prostitution within the terms of certain period realities and within the terms of the reigning prostitutional discourse, we shall discover a large measure of social and sexual ideological agreement.

Prostitution in Paris was regulated by a system called simply *réglementation,* a means of municipal organization and control which was in the hands of a special division of the city police.[4] The system was one of structured forbearance which functioned without the sanction of legislative authority. It was not legitimized, defined or controlled by any laws, federal or municipal. The organization and control of prostitution was handled by the police as a strictly administrative matter. The basis of the system was not the proscription or elimination of prostitution. On the contrary, the regulations accepted prostitution as an inevitable evil, seeking merely to confine it and to control its visibility. In other words, the claim was that this systematic control and confinement prevented any threat to public order, public morality and public health. The system tolerated prostitution while attempting to thoroughly marginalize its female practitioners, and the workings of the system, the registration and surveillance of all prostitutes, were designed to enforce, preserve and contain that marginality.

For decades the number of unregistered prostitutes, called clandestine prostitutes, had been increasing while the number of registered prostitutes had been decreasing.[5] This was clearly a matter of great concern to those responsible for the maintenance of Parisian *réglementation.* Although clandestine prostitution had been on the rise for sometime, new in the *réglementariste* discourse of the 1870s was panic in the face of what they saw as a breakdown of the earlier 19th century *réglementariste* project.[6] So in the writings of the apologists for *réglementation* in the 1870's — whom we can call the *néo-réglementaristes* — the tone is anxious. One senses the almost hallucinatory panic in a statement such as this, written by C. J. Lecour, the *chef* of the *Service des Moeurs,* in 1872:

> One comes round to believing that unregistered prostitutes in Paris form the majority of the personnel of prostitution. They are everywhere, in the brasseries, the cafés-concerts, the theatres and balls. One encounters them in public establishments, in the train stations, even inside the trains. They crowd even the sidewalks, they are in the

windows of the majority of cafés. Until a very late
hour, they circulate, in large numbers, on the most
beautiful boulevards, scandalizing the general
public.[7]

The worry was this: the breakdown of regulated prostitution had a significance beyond the effectiveness of the system itself;
more and more, the escape of prostitution from its long established
confines was interpreted as a sign of a broader social deterioration.
Vice was engulfing society as a whole. Mind you, the *réglementaristes* never celebrated the superior pleasures of the licensed house;
it was its relative safety, both physical and social, which they promoted and insisted upon. Indeed the *néo-réglementariste* discourse
of the period is shot through with worries about society's discovery
of pleasure in extra-conjugal sex and the spread of what they
clearly considered to be the nefarious by-product of spreading
clandestine prostitution: middle-class female adultery.

When *Rolla* — a big painting, 70 × 88″ (now in the Musée
des Beaux-Arts, Bordeaux) — was submitted to the Salon of 1878
by the twenty-four year old Henry Gervex, the artist was *hors
concours.* Nevertheless the canvas was removed from the galleries
at the last moment for reasons of *inconvénance* — moral impropriety.[8] The work was seen and discussed anyway because it hung for
three months at a private dealer's near the Opera. Despite its absence from the Salon, most critics commented on Gervex's painting
in their regular Salon columns.

The painting is based on a section of Alfred de Musset's
poem, titled "Rolla," written in 1833.[9] It chronicles the debauched
decline of a nineteen-year-old bourgeois named Jacques Rolla.
Paris is the scene of his debauchery because, according to Musset,
the capital city was oldest and most rich in vice, and libertinism
came cheap. Also presented is the story of Marion, the innocent
fifteen-year-old who becomes a *prostituée publique,* a worker in an
ignominious and cheap Parisian brothel. Rolla's last night is spent
in her company. The expenditure of his last coins to buy her sexual
services is the culminating episode of his self-destruction, and the
promise of his imminent suicide by poisoning concludes the poem.

Gervex's picture depicts the last morning of Rolla's life,
repose and contemplation at dawn after the evening of venal sex,
before the suicide. The painting, unlike Musset's poem, is set in a
beau quartier in the present tense of the later 1870s.[10] Rolla, standing at the open window, looks thoughtfully but without specific
focus across the room past the girl lying before him. The visual

centerpiece is of course the reclining nude Marion who assumes a posture of languid repose — a body carefully and studiously arranged. The nude is altogether decorous and conventional, with a flawless *poncif* handling of the surface.

The scope of the present article does not allow for a detailed discussion of the *Rolla* criticism. But even though the presentation of the issues raised by the criticism is abbreviated here, the relevance of certain ideologies of prostitution to both the production of and reaction to this painting should be apparent.

The juxtaposition of the impeccable pink nude and the prominently displayed jumble of discarded clothing in the right foreground was the focus of much of the reaction to the picture. It was the modification, the compromising, of a correct and temperate naked body by the still-life of clothing which made the painting "modern" according to these commentators, and, which at the same time, made it offensive according to those who found the canvas unacceptable. In brief, this concern with the moral signification of discarded clothing appears to have been closely bound up with a matter discussed above, alarm over the increase in the ranks of sexually available women on the streets of Paris — clandestine prostitutes and adultresses. One indication of the pervasiveness of this anxiety is the frequency with which one encounters mention of what can be called "the female identification problem." According to a variety of texts, of the qualities immanent in a strange woman's appearance her sexual morality was the most illusive, the most difficult to be sure about. Was the woman honest *(une femme honnête)* or not? This was a problem because honest women and prostitutes looked, or were imagined to look, more alike than ever before.[11] Nevertheless, clothing — its style, its cut, its details — was relied upon as a key sign of honesty or its converse.

This identification problem, *soi-disant,* fueled and reflected the concern that the public spaces of Paris were filling up with prostitutes. This was the privileged obsession of the partisans of a reinvigorated and strengthened *réglementation* who waged a campaign to this end during the early years of the Third Republic. For urban observers of this orientation, the identification problem was not an invigorating, suggestive or enhancing mystery. It was, on the contrary, a cause for considerable alarm. The alarms which sound in certain pieces of *Rolla* criticism are, I suspect, subtended by an agreement with, or at least lipservice paid to, the ideological presuppositions of *néo-réglementarisme.*

In the following critical excerpts, we will find that the clothing is the focus of concern because it is clearly modern and thereby situates sexuality, venal sexuality, as a contemporary issue.

The anonymous review published in *Le Temps* said:

> Here, the accessories spoil everything. The nude is beautiful enough in itself but is mixed in a stew which makes it immediately indecent; next to the bed is piled a stack of petticoats which a black top hat coifs ironically; the cane is not far away. Here is the anecdote which stains, the goad to filthy laughter . . . One would say that here are the devices of vaudeville in the middle of a serious drama.[12]

Roger Ballu, writing for *La Gazette des Beaux-Arts,* objected to *Rolla* in similar terms:

> I'd like to be able to admire unreservedly this body of such delicate tone, of such fresh color in the midst of the whiteness of bed clothes — but, alas! the white materials are those of an undone, ruffled, bed, falling sheets — all the hideous equipment of debauchery. The details are painted with a frank touch and a truth of color of an incontestable merit, but do you know what these details are? A rose satin garter, a starched petticoat fallen in disorder on the ground; a man's hat, insolent and brutal, which perches precipitously upon the dress, thrown and rolled up in the armchair![13]

The avoided piece of clothing is as interesting and revealing as the umbrage taken at the articles enumerated: that inside-out red corset which jars into view next to the starched petticoat. It is a rather careful omission considering its visually prominent position, constituting an almost deliberate and unavoidable aesthetic obstacle to the nude figure's yielding and voluptuous accessibility. Only one critic writing about *Rolla* mentioned the corset and did so in a review which criticized the removal of the painting, pointing to the hypocrisy of the Beaux-Arts administration for objecting to a tableau of modern sexuality while welcoming sexuality of the exotic or historical kinds. "A corset — horrors!" he wrote ironically.[14]

What to say about the critics' obsession with underwear and the omission of a corset in order to rejoin the issue of anxiety over the breakdown of regulated prostitution? It is important in this regard to know that this particular portrayal of the morning after an evening of paid sex seems to have been read as an image of *ad hoc* unregulated clandestine prostitution, due to the details of

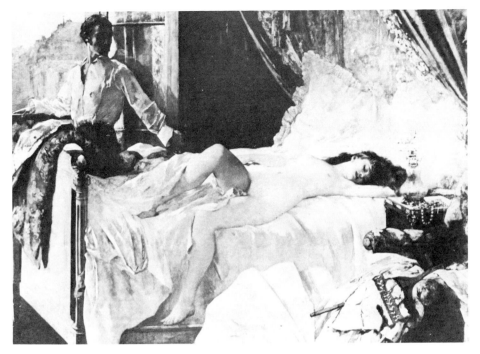

1. Henri Gervex, *Rolla,* 1878. Collection Musee des Beaux Arts, Bordeaux.

2. Edgar Degas, *Waiting for the Client,* circa 1879. Monotype, present location unknown.

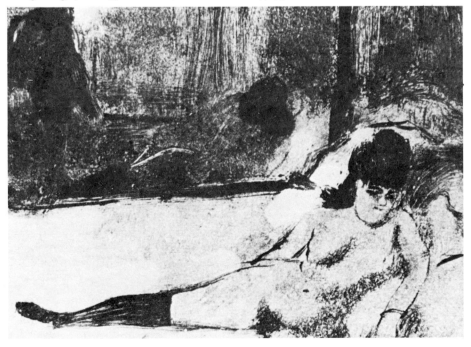

3. Edgar Degas, *In the Salon of a Brothel,* circa 1879. Monotype, Collection Lefèvre Gallery, London.

4. Edgar Degas, *Repose,* circa 1879. Monotype, Collection Musées Nationaux, Donation Picasso, Paris.

5. Jean-Louis Forain, *The Client,* 1878. Present location unknown.

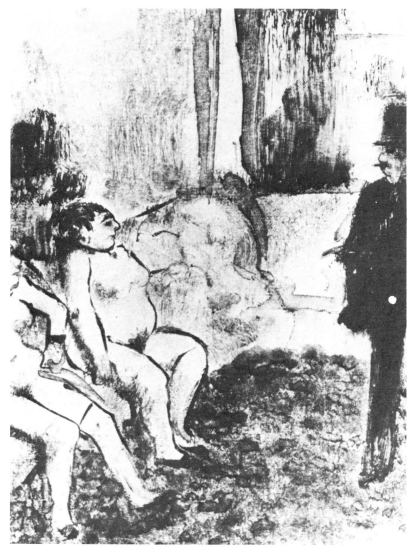

6. Edgar Degas, *The Client,* circa 1879. Monotype, Collection Musées Nationaux, Donation Picasso, Paris.

7. Edgar Degas, *The Serious Client,* circa 1879. Monotype, Collection The Estate of W. Peploe, London.

8. Edgar Degas, *Dancer in her Dressing Room,* circa 1879. Collection Oscar Reinhart, Winterthur.

9. Edgar Degas, *Dancers Backstage,* circa 1890. Collection The National Gallery, Washington, D.C.

setting and clothing. The stilllife of discarded clothes served as the scapegoat for the critics' anger over a portrayal of a correct nude woman in an attitude of sensual gratification, ease, relaxation, pleasure, flanked by the indicators of the precise nature of the sexual transaction, of the prelude to her languid demeanor. More specifically, here an otherwise chaste nude is instantaneously modified and redefined by her surroundings; the abandonment of stays had long been a symbol of female dishonor, of a taking leave of social decencies. This specific corset appears to be a cheap, ready-made one bought in a *grand magasin.* [15] Its red exterior and white interior belong to a corset meant to be seen on rather than off — showy on the outside, plain on the inside. And brightly-colored ready-to-wear corsets were a brand new fashion item in the late 1870's. It is interesting as well that Gervex chose to turn the corset inside-out and show it still laced. This arrangement enforces the disarray of the situation and suggests the haste with which clothes were removed and discarded; the ardor with which love-making was initiated; the sexual abandon of the woman. In fact, it is striking that the conventionality of the nude, its thoroughly unmodernist form, formed no barrier to labelling the picture "modern." The nude figure did not have to convey the painting's erotic message because it has been shifted to the surrounding emblems, that defensive armour which has been so ostentatiously and carelessly laid aside. The body, irrespective really of its style, of its precise features, is more or less automatically eroticized by the abandoned, cheap and showy corset, penetrated by cane, mounted by top hat.

I am suggesting, then, that anxiety about Gervex's construction of the morning after sex between a young bourgeois and an unofficial prostitute from *les classes populaires* was focussed upon the conventionally sensual nude inflected by the still life, because it signified eroticism and sexual gratification in a coupling of a problematic sort. A woman of decent appearance, wearing her Salon nudity like a garment, is revealed by her accessories to be sexually intemperate: a victim, and feared perpetrator, of the rampant contagion of vice. A real fear, after all, was the sexual liberation of decent women.

Degas' monotypes (Figures 3 and 4) use a different language of representation, which is discussed below, and picture a completely different, but not totally unrelated, kind of prostitution. The brothel of Degas' prints coincides in many of its materials, its props, with a specific category of Parisian brothel: the deluxe house, a *maison de luxe* or *grande tolérance.* [16] The type of house to which the settings and costuming of Degas' monotypes most directly correspond occupied the pinnacle of the social, economic and erotic hierarchy of tolerated prostitution in Paris at the time.

Although cloistered prostitution was defined and accepted as necessary for the servicing of base physical need, the *maison de luxe* existed to provide highly specialized erotic services — such as fantasy tableaux, bondage, oral sex, spectator lesbianism and group sex — to the discerning and experienced sexual connoisseur, to stimulate as well as satisfy sexual desire and fantasy.[17]

In a brothel of this category, the client was apparently ushered into a salon to meet the women in a way that would protect him from meeting other customers. Here is a version of the process written in 1884 by a period historian of prostitution, Léo Taxil:

> The serous client makes his entrance. None of the women would address a particular verbal invitation to him: but they all direct to him burning glances, assume exciting poses, smile, and even move their tongues, to make it clearly understood that they can put one thousand voluptuous refinements at the client's disposition.[18]

One finds a closely related representation of the same phenomenon — preparation for the client — in the pages of one of the naturalist prostitution novels, J.-K. Huysmans' *Marthe, histoire d'une fille,* written in 1876. Immediately following a description of a general brouhaha in the brothel salon with the women in all manner of eccentric poses, Huysmans writes:

> Suddenly the bell rang. Silence took over as though by enchantment. Each girl sat up, and those who had been sleeping on the benches woke up with a start rubbing their eyes, forcing themselves for a second to rekindle a flame in their faces, while a passenger mounted the bridge of embarcation.[19]

A similar construction is available in visual form in Jean-Louis Forain's *Le Client* of 1878 (Figure 5). In this gouache over watercolor, the women line up with enthusiasm to pose and offer themselves for selection to the stern judge of a top-hatted client.

The customer who sought sex offering the illusion of ideal bourgeois marital sex would probably not have come to a deluxe licensed brothel. In other words, a man (like Jacques Rolla) looking for polite loving affection with his bought sex, seeking a semblance of romance and continuity in relations, would have likely gone to a clandestine prostitute or to a clandestine house.[20] The deluxe house was for the wealthy and well-practised bourgeois or artistocrat with well-defined erotic tastes, whose lust and fantasy needed the stimulation of a highly professional sexual spa. Here is Léo Taxil again:

> It is worth remarking that the more cheaply priced the prostitute, the less she needs to apply herself to depraved practices. In houses of one to three francs, generally the women know only plain sexual intercourse, pure and simple. On the contrary, in the houses of five francs and above, these unfortunate women are obliged to satisfy the most wild caprices of their visitors; they are moreover adapted to that.[21]

What these social data and various representations allow us to begin to see in Degas' prints are the ways in which they match up with, are involved with describing "the facts" of a deluxe house of prostitution in the late 1870's (furniture, clothing, architecture), while at the same time diverging from a standard account of the characteristic nature and quality of human contact, of sexuality, inside the brothel. Taxil, Huysmans and Forain construct a scenario in which the prostitute is able to simulate — that it is her job to offer the promise of — a subjectivity, a simulacrum of sexual feeling and intimacy; that in the deluxe house the sheerly physical will be inflected by a seductive, professional elegance. Degas disallows this. In his prints, the female body is only physical, is only sexual commodity.

The difference between Degas' picturing of the relationship between client and *filles* at the moment of introduction and selection and that of other accounts of these matters can be seen in Figures 6 and 7, for example. Relegated to the edges of the sheet in both cases, the client's distance from his quarry is insisted upon. In each case, the stiffness and the awkwardness of the moment and the sheer, brute physicality of the women are strongly proposed. In Figure 6, the thickset though obliging women seem the explanation for the man's distance. In Figure 7, the unrefined advance and mocking faces seem to put the client off rather than encourage him to make a selection. As seen in Figures 3 and 4 as well, Degas frequently emphasized the uncontrived and unselfconscious rudimentary physicality of the women even when they were faced with a prospective customer. In Degas' brothel, it is inconsequential whether or not we understand a client to be present to witness the body in Figure 4.

Before considering the ideological significance of Degas' construction of the high-class brothel, let us focus in closely on one of the prints (Figure 3). It pictures an incomplete transaction between two workers and a customer in a ground-floor salon. A man enters the room at left whom we deduce from mere fragments: slices of pant leg, hand, cheek, nose and hat brim. The sliced man sets the immobility of the two women in a specific temporal framework: he hurries in, but they do not shift position; they do not react to his arrival. They do not resist the pull of gravity on their bodies; they maintain their relaxed positions. (The term "pose" would not be appropriate to these bodies). The reclining woman hugs the sofa edge with draped leg; the other sits, hand resting between the thighs of legs cut through at the shins. They appear to attend to their own reveries or to stew in their own blankness, involved neither with one another nor the arriving man. Hence, the picture is devoid of subjective prediction: it does not carry hope for the intimate coalescence of these people.

The production of a suitable accompanying narrative is not entirely relevant here, however. Instead, we need to recognize that the whole format insists that nothing of consequence is going on, or better put, the image does not appear to insist on much of anything: just the material facts of an "average" brothel arrangement, handled broadly, observed from a non-participatory, oblique off-stage angle. It adds up to a virtuoso *semblance* of nonchalance and offhandedness; Degas has found human blankness and narrative inconsequentiality.

A word is required here regarding the point with which this essay began. I argued that the dominant account of Degas' monotypes accepted rather credulously the look of the prints at face value: the semblance of detachment and nonchalance was interpreted to be a frank and honest presentation of the subject of brothel prostitution. It is now possible to suggest the specific ways in which this reading is partially correct, but still falls short.

Degas did find ways to represent the female body, the prostitute's body, as the locus of human debasement. The female bodies in all five prints reproduced here are represented without recourse to the conventions of spectator-oriented eroticism, a convention which Gervex employed wholeheartedly. A recognition of this feature of the monotypes has, on the one hand, produced the Greenbergian version of their meaning (critical frankness) with which we began, and has, on the other, served as the basis for a discovery of

Degas' misogyny.[22]

What is missing is the recognition that in Degas' brothel, sexuality of a conventional sort is absent because it is shown to be lost to the sheer materiality of the world of exchange, the world of money. Degas' narrative of prostitution holds that in this world no feelings are risked, no interiority is achieved or exchanged. As such, Degas' brothel may appear a disheartening place, but, for the clients — men like Degas — it is not a risky place. "Objectivity" does not encompass the meanings of these images, nor certainly does categorical misogyny.

It could be proposed that Degas' prints ignored certain aspects of — or received ideas about — contemporary brothel prostitution, aspects taken into account and relied upon by Taxil, Huysmans and Forain, for example. Their accounts of the prostitutional transaction in Paris at this time reconstitute interiority as the commodity exchanged. Degas' prints do not.

The insistence upon the unmediated physicality of prostitution and of the prostitute does suggest a connection between Degas' representations and the *néo-réglementarisme* of his day. Immaturity, laziness and vulgarity had been cited for decades as the primary characteristics of public prostitutes by the *réglementaristes*,[23] and the insistence upon their possession of these characteristics justified closing the women up inside of licensed brothels. We know, at the same time, that the *maison de luxe* thrived because its women acted differently. This form of prostitution challenged certain of the underpinnings of the *réglementariste* doctrine, since *réglementarisme* never admitted sexual pleasure and erotic stimulation into the terms of toleration. Toleration remained possible as an official policy because of the exclusion of these qualities from the definition of the function of public prostitution. The panic over clandestine prostitution was largely subtended by an equivalence drawn between unregistered prostitution and sexual pleasure — the province of Gervex's picture — and the fear that if the agents of this contagion, uncloistered prostitutes, were not apprehended, appreciation of the possibilities for pleasure outside the marriage bed would unravel the fabric of French society.

In the world of Degas' prints, the last word in sexual glamour, the preserve of the sexual dandy, is converted into a disheartening, unhappy and somewhat humiliating sexual ghetto. As we have already heard, Degas does not propose that sexual stimulation and arousal were to be found in this brothel, and the prints thereby gingerly edge toward parody of the preferred sexual habitat of the upper bourgeois sexual connoisseur.

It seems that Degas' version of life inside the deluxe brothel might have been comforting to the frenzied campaigners for a fortified system of *réglementation.* Because the one form of regulated brothel prostitution which was designed to excite, stimulate and arouse in the most refined and subtle terms is shown by Degas to be a place of uninhibited naked women, ready to meet the standard physical needs, but whose appearance and behavior might have discouraged or extinguished erotic fantasy and sexual appetite.

My modest proposal is that our comprehension of the terms of Gervex's *Rolla* and Degas' monotypes require, or are at least enhanced by, a familiarity with their ideological materials which have certain points of connection, and even appear to complement one another. It clarifies the reaction to Gervex's *pompier* construction of the sensuality of the clandestine prostitute; and it begins to suggest the appropriateness of the subject of the brutal absence of sexual pleasure in the *maison de luxe* for Degas' most sustained private project in the medium of monotype.

For a brief coda, I turn to two of Degas' ballet pictures (Figures 8 and 9). In his picturing of *ad hoc* flirtations such as these, the view of the potential achievement of stimulation and pleasure in extra-conjugal male/female affairs is much different in promising an intimate result. I hope this suggests the further ways in which the modernist and the *pompier* modern life painter can be reincorporated into a shared sphere of social and sexual ideologies, even while considering the different kind of ideological work their images perform or are meant to perform.

Notes

[1]Clement Greenberg, "On the Role of Nature in Modernist Painting," [1949] *Art and Culture,* Boston, Beacon Press, 1961, p.171.

[2]*Ibid.*

[3]See for example: Jean Adhémar and Françoise Cachin, *Degas: the Complete Etchings, Lithographs and Monotypes,* New York, 1975, p.84; Eunice Lipton, "Degas' Bathers: the Case for Realism," *Arts,* May, 1980, p.96; Linda Nochlin, *Realism,* Baltimore, 1971, pp.205-206.

[4]The general outlines of Parisian *réglementation* are available in many sources. The indispensable 19th century account is A. J. B. Parent-Duchatelet, *De la prostitution dans la ville de Paris,* Paris, 1837. See also Dr. Felix Regnault, *L'Evolution de la Prostitution,* Paris, 1906; N. M. Boiron, *La Prostitution dans*

l'Histoire, devant le Droit, devant l'Opinion, Nancy, 1926; Abraham Flexner, *Prostitution in Europe,* 1914 (reprint edition, Montclair, New Jersey, 1969); C. J. Lecour, *La Prostitution à Paris et à Londres,* Paris, 1872; Jean-Jacques Servais and Jean-Pierre Laurend, *Histoire et Dossier de la Prostitution,* Paris, 1965; Alain Corbin, *Les filles de noce: Misère sexuelle et prostitution aux 19ᵉ et 20ᵉ siècles,* Paris, 1978. One should also consult the prostitution dossiers in the Archives de la Préfecture de Police in Paris.

⁵Parent-Duchatelet expressed concern about this matter in the 1830s. (Parent-Duchatelet, *op. cit.,* vol. I, pp.492ff.) Among the many sources reporting this phenomenon are Servais and Laurend, *op. cit.,* pp.207ff; Dr. L. Martineau, *La Prostitution Clandestine,* Paris, 1885; Alfred Delvau, "Le Mont-de-Pitié, La Prostitution, La Misère," *Paris Guide par les principaux écrivains et artistes de la France,* vol. 2, *La Vie,* Paris, 1867, p. 1883; Corbin, *op. cit.,* pp.171ff.

This is also the place to say that most of the research for this essay was done in Paris as part of my research for my Ph.D. dissertation in Art History at U.C.L.A., while the grateful recipient of an Edward A. Dickson Fellowship in the History of Art. Whatever strengths my work on this subject may have, reveal my indebtedness to the example and advice of my advisor, T. J. Clark.

⁶Alain Corbin has provided the most thorough analysis of this phenomenon. See Corbin, *op. cit.,* pp.36ff.

⁷"[. . .] on arrive à constater que les prostituées insoumises [. . .] forment à Paris la majeur partie du personnel de la prostitution. Elles sont partout, dans les brasseries, les cafés-concerts, les théâtres et les bals. On les rencontre dans les établissements publics, les Gares de chemins de fer et même en wagon. Il y en a sur toutes les promenades, aux devantures de la plupart des cafés. Jusqu'à une heure avancée de la nuit, elles circulent, nombreuses, sur les plus beaux boulevards, au grand scandale du public." Lecour, *op. cit.,* pp.144-145.

⁸An incorrect version of *Rolla's* banishment from the Salon has dogged the history of the painting: it has been frequently reported that *Rolla* was refused by the Salon jury. This appears in all of the following: *Equivoques, Peintures françaises du XIXᵉ siècle,* Paris, 1973, *Rolla 1874,* Paris, 1974, p.80; J. Uzanne, *Figures Contemporaines tirées de L'Album Mariani,* Paris, 1896-1908, vol. VI, n.p.; *Le Petit Parisien,* April 16, 1878, p.2; *L'Estafette,* April 14, 1878, p.3; *Le Soleil,* April 15, 1878, p.3.

⁹The poem first appeared in the *Revue des Deux Mondes* on August 15, 1883. See the Editions Gallimard edition of Musset's works, *Premières Poésies, Poésies Nouvelles,* Paris, 1976, p.456.

¹⁰This contention rests on certain of the painting's architectural details. The first pale light of morning flows into the room from newly-Haussmannized Paris. The stylized floral motifs of the iron balustrade and the dome-topped buildings (with part of a billboard visible) on the facing street are characteristic of those recently built in the northwest part of the city center. A critic calling himself Le Sphinx proposed in a piece run in *L'Evènement* that the setting might be the Boulevard des Italiens ("Echos de Paris, Hier, Aujourd'hui, Demain," *L'Evènement,* April 20, 1878, p.1).

¹¹An important consideration here is that during these years Parisian prostitutes were forbidden to wear any distinctive clothing or accessories. In medieval France, for example, various kinds of clothing or bits of decoration were required to be worn by prostitutes out on the public thoroughfare to distinguish them from "honest women." (Parent-Duchatelet, *op. cit.,* vol. I, pp.355-358.) By the 19th century, prostitutes were required to resemble "decent women." This, in order not to attract attention and thereby avoid an outrage to public decency. Parent-Duchatelet expressed the regulationist hope that this uniform dress could accomplish the impossible: "[. . .] qu'elles ne se fassent pas remarquer du reste de la

population, et qu'elles attirent le moins possible les regards. On arrivera au terme de la perfection et du possible en ce genre, en obtenant que les hommes, et en particulier ceux qui les recherchent, puissent les distinguer des femmes honnêtes; mais que celles-ci, et surtout leurs filles, ne puissent pas faire cette distinction, ou ne la fassent du moins qu'avec difficulté." (vol. I, pp.362-363.) On this issue, see Richard Sennett, *The Fall of Public Man: On the Social Psychology of Capitalism,* New York, 1977, pp.164-167.

For splendid early Third Republic examples of popular images which represent a gentleman brought up short by this "problem" see Ovide Desgranges, "De La Madeleine à la Bastille," *Le Petit Journal Pour Rire,* no. 128, 1878, p.2 and the cartoon by Quidam titled "Un Monsieur Qui Suit Les Femmes," in *La Vie Amusante,* no. 99, 1878, p.5.

[12]"Mais ici, ce sont les accessoires qui ont tout gâté. Le nu est assez beau en lui-même pour se passer d'un ragout qui le rend tout à coup indécent; près du lit, s'entasse un tas de jupons empesés que coiffe ironiquement un chapeau noir haute forme, la canne n'est pas loin. Voilà l'anecdote qui fait tache, l'amorce au rire malsain . . . on dirait les artifices de vaudeville au beau milieu d'un drame." "Chronique," *Le Temps,* April 21, 1878, p.2.

My treatment of the *Rolla* incident is fragmentary and condensed owing to the constraints of the original context in which this paper appeared. As a consequence, I may appear to be guilty of using pieces of criticism as so many equal, ungrounded bits of period opinion. In an expanded analysis of the fate of *Rolla* in 1878, there will be room for the necessary examination of the correlations between the aesthetic and political ideologies of the various papers (For an exemplary recent study of this sort, see: Nicos Hadjinicolaou, ' "La Liberté guidant le peuple" de Delacroix devant son premier public,' *Actes de la Recherche en sciences sociales,* no. 28, June 1979). However, my research into this question has shown no consistent pattern of correlation in this regard. This is problematic but not entirely surprising since the 1870s was a decade of constant changes and difficulties for the press. Regarding *Le Temps* in particular, suffice it to say that here we have a case of a dislike for *Rolla's* particular modernity showing up in a paper best described as "républicain conservateur." The paper's circulation in 1880 was 22,764, placing it seventeenth in size of the sixty dailies (Claude Bellanger, Jacques Godechot, Pierre Guiral, Fernand Terrou, *Histoire Générale de la Presse Française, tome 3, 1871 à 1940,* 1969, pp.208 & 234; Raymond Manévy, *La Presse de la IIIᵉ République,* Paris, 1955, p.72; Réné de Livois, *Histoire de la Presse Française, I. Des origines à 1881,* Lausanne, 1965, p.316).

[13]"Je voudrais pouvoir admirer sans réserve ce corps d'un ton si fin, d'une coloration si fraiche au milieu des blancheurs de sa couche; mais, hélas! ces blancheurs représentent un lit défait et foulé, des draps tombants: tout l'appareil hideux de la débauche. Les détails sont peints avec une franchise de touche et une vérité de couleur d'un mérite incontestable, mais savez-vous quels sont des détails? C'est une jarretière de soie rose, un jupon empesé, tombé dans le désordre par terre: c'est un chapeau d'homme insolent et brutal, qui s'étale sur la robe precipitamment jetée et roulée dans ce fauteuil." Roger Ballu, "Le Salon de 1878 — Peintres et Sculpteurs," extrait de *La Gazette des Beaux-Arts,* July & August, 1878, p.42.

[14]It was 'Le Sphinx' *(L'Evènement , op. cit.)* who mentioned the corset. The context of this remark and its interesting aftermath merit a brief mention here. The critic observes that the Beaux-Arts administration which took offense at *Rolla's* impropriety were untroubled by and enthusiastic about "les lupanars de M. Gérôme," for example. The crucial issue, he continues, was the contemporary setting of the painting's story. It is within his mocking list of the offending details that the corset remark appears. To wit: "Mais une jeune fille sur un lit parisien

moderne (quoique de plus pur style Louis XVI), avec un homme en manches de chemise, et, sur un fauteuil, un chapeau noir haut de forme, dernière mode, un parapluie (*bone Deus!*), un corset (horreur!), et sur le tapis, une jupe! . . . Vite, jeune homme, remportez-nous ca!" Only three days later, Le Sphinx ate his words: a retraction was published on April 23, 1878 entitled "Echos de Paris, Hier, Aujourd'hui, Demain. Un Méa Culpa," (L'Evènement, p.1). Detailing the circumstances of the retraction would take us too far afield.

[15]I am grateful to David Kunzle for most of this information on corsets.

[16]I base this association on several consistent features of the monotypes. First of all, the salon of the series is fitted out with plush padded furniture, gilt framed mirrors and chandeliers. These are not, as Eugenia Parry Janis writes, "standard props" *(Degas Monotypes: Essay, Catalogue and Checklist,* Greenwich, Connecticut for Harvard University, 1968, p.xx). On the matter of furnishings, see Gustave Macé, *La Police Parisienne: Gibier de Saint-Lazare,* Paris, 1888, pp.262-263. The fact of a ground floor salon matters here, too, because the *maison populaire* had an *estaminet* occupying the ground floor instead of a salon. See Léo Taxil, *La Prostitution contemporaine,* Paris, 1884, quoted in *Le Crapouillot,* nouvelle série, no. 42, Spring, 1977, p.51. See also Degas' drawings of a *maison populaire* based to some extent on Edmond de Goncourt's novel, *La fille Elisa,* reproduced in Theodore Reff, "The Artist and the Writer," *Degas: The Artist's Mind,* The Metropolitan Museum of Art, 1976, pp.172-173. The dress of the clients aligns with the status of a *maison de luxe,* and nudity among the pensioners of a *grand tolérance* was apparently a common enough practice. (See Corbin, *op. cit.,* p.90 and Mr. Jean (Ancien Inspecteur Principal de la Sureté), *Le bas-fonds du crime et de la prostitution,* Paris, n.d. [c. 1900], pp.58-59.)

[17]Corbin, *op. cit.,* pp.182ff.

[18]"Le miché sérieux fait son entrée. Aucune femme ne doit lui adresser une invitation verbale particulière; mais toutes lui envoient des regards brulants, se dandinent, prennent des positions excitantes, sourient, et même agitent la langue, pour faire comprendre clairement qu'elles ont à la disposition du client mille raffinements de volupté." Léo Taxil, *op. cit.*

[19]"Soudain un coup de timbre retentit. Le silence se fit comme par enchantement. Chacune s'assit, et celles qui dormassaient sur les banquettes se réveillèrent en sursaut et se frottèrent les yeux, s'efforçant de rallumer pour une seconde la flamme de leur regard, alors qu'un passage montait sur le pont pour embarquer."J. -K. Huysmans, *Marthe, histoire d'une fille* [Brussels, 1876; Paris, 1879] Paris, 10/18 edition, 1975, p.50.

[20]See Corbin, pp.296-300.

[21]"Il est à remarquer que plus la fille publique est à bon marché, moins elle se livre aux pratiques dépravées. Dans les maisons de trois à un franc, les femmes ne connaissent en général que le coït pur et simple. Au contraire, à cinq francs et au-dessus, ces malheureuses sont obligées de satisfaire les caprices les plus insensés de leurs visiteurs; elles sont du reste dressées à cela." Léo Taxil, *op. cit.,* p.52.

[22]For misogynist interpretations, see: J. -K. Huysmans, "Degas," *Certains* [1886], 10/18 edition, Paris, 1975, pp.295-297; and Denis Rouart, *E. Degas Monotypes,* Paris, 1948, pp.9-10. Jean Adhémar proposes that Degas parodies the women (Adhémar and Cachin, op. cit., p.82). Norma Broude's attempt to undo the allegations of misogyny in Degas' work runs completely aground on the brothel monotypes largely because of the flaws in her psychobiographical method (Broude, "Degas's 'Misogyny'," *Art Bulletin,* March, 1977, p.105).

[23]See, for example, Parent-Duchatelet, *op. cit.,* vol. I. pp.138-142 and ·Macé, *op. cit.,* pp.258-259.

John Wilson Foster

Romantic Revival, Modernist Prescription:
An Irish Case-Study

I

The difficulties in detecting the first stirrings of what became the Modernist movement in literature are increased, not diminished, by those scandalous suggestions (scandalous because so
brazen and various) that the movement sprang adult from the
womb. I need hardly remind students of literature of those precise
dates on which the world was supposed to have changed. Yeats
elected 1900; Woolf 1910, on or about December; Lawrence 1915;
Willa Cather 1922. Writers surely offer such dates in mock-
historical accuracy, to confound the cultural historians, and the
intention may itself be a Modernist ploy. Modernism was meant by
many writers, after all, to travesty cultural movements, to be a
movement to end movements, in whose floruit was waged, suitably,
the war to end wars.

Contemporary critics, shed of irony, suggest Modernist beginnings as splendidly precise as the writers'. One strong candidate
is 1880. In that same year, on an island largely shielded from
Europe, Standish James O'Grady published Volume Two of his
History of Ireland. Although this high nonsensical work was a good
deal laughed at by the Anglophile historians of Trinity College,
Dublin, it more inarguably set in motion the Irish Literary Revival
than did, say, Brandes' essays of 1883 or the post-Impressionist
Exhibition Modernism. That Revival gave to European literature
writers whose names were they erased from its history would seriously impoverish it.

The Irish Literary Revival was, as it happens, co-terminous
with Modernism's innings — shall we say 1880 until, as Kermode
suggests for Modernism, 1925, with the years of high accomplish-
ment in each case the latter fifteen?[1]

This seems an odd coincidence in the light of the Revival's

dedication to the restoration to Ireland of its so-called Heroic Period (variously dated from the Iron Age to the Middle Ages) and to the championing of the primitive present, alleged vestige of that Heroic Period. In being so dedicated, the Revival was a belated Irish expression of Romanticism, which makes the coincidence odder, though it is diminished somewhat (but in such a way as to complicate the picture) by the fact that several Revival writers express a note of modernity in their work, for instance that irony and scepticism we find coursing through the Revival — we hear the note in Synge, O'Casey and the middle Yeats, though it may have been sounded first by George Moore who brings it to one triumphant conclusion with the eloquent malice of *Hail and Farewell* (1911-1914). In Joyce, though not in Moore, who in any case was born too early, irony and scepticism became cultural artifice and lucid indifference, a terminus that by a far different route Yeats also reached. Joyce, it seems, is incontrovertibly a Modernist, even in his earlier, more naturalistic and realistic years. After him came Flann O'Brien and Samuel Beckett, second, or third, generation Modernists who nevertheless wrote in the distant wash and wake of the Revival.

Yeats, as usual, writing where literature is at tension, is the crux. One Yeats placed the Unionist landowner O'Grady among the Olympians and acknowledged him as cultural ethnarch, father of the Revival whom he, Yeats, succeeded. Another Yeats wrote admiringly of the deracinated last romantics, of whom he accounted himself one, inheritors of a mood which, in his own words, "Edgar Poe found in a wine-cup, and [which] passed into France and took possession of Baudelaire, and from Baudelaire passed to England and the Pre-Raphaelites, and then again returned to France, and still wanders the world, enlarging its power as it goes, awaiting the time when it shall be, perhaps, alone, or, with other moods, master over a great new religion, and an awakener of the fanatical wars that hovered in the gray surges, and forget the wine-cup where it was born."[2]

Perhaps I can try to show the identity of these two Yeates while attempting to explain the coincidence of Irish Revivalism and international Modernism with larger claims of a fitful native Modernism than have been so far advanced for Ireland. Ireland is not charted in Bradbury and McFarlane's recent geography of Modernism, nor Dublin enrolled among its cities, yet Joyce and Yeats are weightily indexed. But I do not want my claims to run in one direction only. Using the Irish case, I would like to weaken, or at least adjust, the claims of international Modernism upon us, in Ireland at any rate, and in the light of Irish cultural reality, having — perversely — claimed the Irish Revival as itself more generously Modernist than previously thought. The conjunction of Revivalism and Modernism may throw light on the latter and sceptical shadow on its orthodoxy.

II

No paradox or incongruity need exist, of course, if we make capacious enough our definition of Modernism, if, for example, we offer this: "In short" — in short! — "Modernism was in most countries an extraordinary compound of the futuristic and the nihilistic, the revolutionary and the conservative, the naturalistic and the symbolistic, the romantic and the classical. It was a celebration of a technological age and a condemnation of it; an excited acceptance of the belief that the old régimes of culture were over, and a deep despairing in the face of that fear; a mixture of convictions that the new forms were escapes from historicism and the pressures of the time with convictions that they were precisely the living expressions of these things."[3] The "formal desperation" which has been seen as a Modernist characteristic seems to have infected its diagnosis whose epidemic of binary oppositions is its own symptom of despair. One wonders if the bewildering diversity of so-called Modernist works does not make Modernism, like Romanticism, a vagrant and essentially contested concept.

Be that as it may, it would be difficult to regard as Modernist, in its slackest definition, certain important features of the Irish Revival: the preoccupation with heroism ("whatever is not heroic is not Irish," AE declared), the call for patriotic sacrifice, the obstinate nativism, though its primitivism, its sense of a beginning and of an ending (that is, its apocalyptic view of history) would give less trouble. The backward look of Modernism has been pointed out by some critics, though they prefer to speak of synchronicity, of synthesized contemporaneity and antiquity. This was certainly the aim of the Irish Revivalists, though perhaps only Joyce — no ostensible Revivalist — and Yeats turned manifesto into achieved art. In reviving, the Irish did not think of themselves as bringing out, dusting off, and winding up — one definition of Revival — but as living again, as fully as ineradicable time would permit. For O'Grady and the cultural nationalists he fathered, what had happened between the bardic rendition of the Heroic Period and the imminent recovery of the Heroic Period at the close of the 19th century was a bad dream or a case of suspended animation; it had not in a sense happened at all. The well of Irish legendry had been capped by Christianity and successive philistine invasions and was now being re-opened by a generation that claimed to be the bards' legitimate and even, where the imagination was concerned, immediate successors.

One thinks of that significant tendency of Modernism to vault over 19th century Realism, Naturalism and Romanticism, to vault over even Renaissance humanism in search of the countering artifice of eternity, that lucid indifference. It is at its most conscious a kind of internal contest and it is waged with greatest understanding in the pages of an Irishman, in *Dubliners* (1914), in *A Portrait of the Artist As a Young Man* (1916) and *Ulysses* (1922). We make much of the Medieval bent of Joyce's mind, a mind happiest it seems working in terms of analogue, structure, law, rhetoric, authority. Stephen Dedalus believes his monkish learning may be a handicap, "held no higher by the age he lived in than the subtle and curious jargons of heraldry and falconry."[4] Like Joyce's, his monkish learning is, of course, a strength, but only I believe when it addressed, painfully, what Joyce in "The Universal Learning Influence of the Renaissance" identified as the chief legacies of that cultural watershed — compassion and realism.[5] Solve Joyce's treatment of pity, charity and compassion — a chief conceptual arena in his work — and you have solved much of him — his point of view, his dialectic, the relation of his constructs to the world in which we live and die.

I do not mean to underestimate the Medievalism — or Modernism — of Joyce's mind. His Medievalism was a Christian one which he displaced into secularism, and in doing so moved back as well as forward, back to the pagan structures of Irish art. Ostensibly he dismissed, actually he absorbed the Medieval Irish sagas and heroic romances upon whose translation and adaptation the Irish Literary Revival rested. Despite their fitful, startling realism, the splendid stories of the Cuchulain, Fenian, Mythological and Historical Cycles must ultimately be understood in terms of narrative structure and code. The stories proceed by formula and convention, by rhetorical commonplaces, set-pieces, genealogies, etymologies, inventories, word-games, runs, teichoscopies, rhapsodies, lays, kennings (the latter being an esoteric form of speech concocted by bards and thought by some to be a — rather Joycean — form of erudite slang). The Irish sagas are cultural encyclopedias. Speech in them is not so much self-expression as incantation, song, spell, prophecy. Prophecy provides a prior arrangement of the narrative and a mnemonic cue for composer and reciter, and the result is a form of narrative foreclosure very different from the modern, realistic — but not Modernist — conception of fiction. It is not surprising that in such narratives the will and individuality of the characters are thematically at the mercy of outside forces. The relationship between these forces can perhaps best be described by the physicist's phrase, 'sympathetic resonance', of which the arch-waves of Erin that invariably roar in response to battle-strokes delivered against Conchubar's shield (in the Cuchulain Cycle) are merely the most vivid example that comes to mind. The sympathetic resonance takes place at a high frequency of motif, seme and formula. The result is that the world of the hero tales is a unified field that not even the brutal factionalism or the heroic solitude and enterprise, that theme and character often illustrate, can fragment. Or, to put it in homelier fashion, as James Stephens did when discussing the violence of the tales: it's a give-and-take world, and there is no great harm in it.

Readers of Levi-Strauss, Barthes and Joyce would be at ease in this old narrative dispensation. Many Revivalists were not so at ease and they shamelessly altered the old stories, not for Modernist but for romantic nationalist reasons. Ironically it was Joyce the counter Revivalist — who was most faithful to the old stories. Where the romantic Revivalists edited out the comic grotesqueries, for example, Joyce swooped on them as matter for parody (think of the portrait of the Citizen in *Ulysses);* where the romantic Revivalists humanized and historicized the old stories, Joyce retained their spirit and structure, their tenebrous indifference. James Stephens — in whom Joyce sensed a kindred spirit and whom he invited to complete *Finnegans Wake* (1939) in the event of his own death — was possibly the closest in temperament of all Revivalists to the old writers. *Irish Fairy Tales* (1920) is a mis-nomered masterpiece that rewrites the ancient Fenian and Mythological tales, but its swift intersecting planes of narrative slicing across expected continuities suggest the influence of Cubism in which we know Stephens was interested. When Stephens attempted to combine the old stories with psychological realism, as in his novels *Deirdre* (1923) and *In the Land of Youth* (1924), the result was calamitous. At his best, Stephens exhibits those Medieval and perennial qualities of Irish mentality and art in which authority, eschatology and correspondence cuckoo philosophy and science out of

the nest, in which chronophobia flourishes, and supererogation —
of which Joyce is a laureate — makes expressive plurality inescapable, part of the territory, no mere Modernist prescription.

Irish mentality and art happily — or unhappily — accord
with 20th century European artistic mentality, in part because
Joyce, Yeats and the Revivalists helped to shape the European 20th
century. (Though it did not coincide with the 19th century artistic
mentality, as Matthew Arnold's essay on Celtic literature will tell
you at a glance.[6] It was then, understandably, a sportive and dangerous thing, to be reduced to, and kept as, a "note" and carefully
administered in small but essential doses to English writers, a tonic
in medical and musical senses, you might say.) But in part it is pure
coincidence. The archaic inventiveness of Joyce and other Catholic
(or in the case of Stephens, poor) Irish writers is given impetus by a
sense of linguistic orphanhood, one more among the orphanhoods
on which Joyce eloquently brooded. Confronted by Joyce's stylistic and linguistic plurality — a Modernist characteristic — Hugh
Kenner attributes it to Joyce's pyrrhonism, a fundamental scepticism that leads him to adopt a variety of disguises in place of any
central or stable certainty.[7] But the whole truth involves the Irish
comic tradition and, beyond that, the deep, often subliminal sense
of linguistic deprivation many Irish writers feel. The native mode of
expression has been lost, a foreign tongue has been grafted on to
the remnant of the old. The Irish writer's linguistic *brio* may be a
disguised double act of revenge — an attempt to enliven the foreign
tongue with the energy of the native (a revenge of impurity) and to
colonise in turn, if not the English, then tracts of English literature,
as in fact the Irish have done this century. The Irish writer has an
enviable linguistic freedom. One, he is, at the very least in the Hugh
MacDiarmid sense, bilingual. Two, if the English language is not
his, he owes no obligation to rules and regulations that in England,
moreover, have been allied to that class structure to which the
Irishman is foreigner or victim. But the freedom can be hazardous
because it can lead to irresponsibility, monomania, diseased
subjectivity.

III

The Ascendancy had imposed that class structure on Ireland, but inefficiently, among other reasons because there was no
vigorous bourgeoisie to complete a hierarchy. The absence of a
vigorous bourgeoisie probably explains in part the absence of a

vigorous realist tradition (indeed a reputable novel tradition) in Irish literature, and this may have facilitated the Revival triumph of Romanticism, its return to Medieval literature, and its fitful Modernism. The Irish Literary Revival was largely a flight from reality, especially on the part of Protestant intellectuals whose life and heritage had rarely been depicted with seriousness and realism. The Protestant Revival — and most important Revivalists were Protestant — was an unearned class apostasy. The Revivalists called into question the two class cultures to which they belonged: that of landlordism and the gentry, and that of the mercantile middle class. Only the latter did they reject outright. They rejected the landlord class only for what they considered it had become, while nursing hopes for a return to what they thought it had been, a cultivated nobility. Their prescription was an imaginary feudalism made up of a gallant aristocracy, a fey peasantry, and a troubadourish or patronized artistry. This flight from reality helps to make of Yeats the qualified Modernist (and the great poet) he is, but one might with some perplexity regret the flight while honouring the achievement it enabled.

The Revivalists' desire to be ancestrally Irish obliged them to evade the reality of Anglicized Ireland, a reality their own class had entrenched. This amounted to a denial of self at the level of class. In a sense the denial proved an impossibility. The Irish Literary Revival, dominated by the Anglo-Irish, was what Foucault has called a "fellowship of discourse" whose function it is "to preserve or to reproduce discourse, but in order that it should circulate within a closed community, according to strict regulations, without those in possession being dispossessed by this very distribution."[8] From the raw materials of a peasant folklore and a bardic literature in another language, the Anglo-Irish *littérateurs* amassed what Foucault terms "the property of discourse." Even when the theme of Revival literature, like that of political nationalism, was selflessness, the assumed and collectively egotistic function of the Revivalists was that of culture-givers. When Standish James O'Grady forfeited leadership of the Revival by failing to follow his cultural premises to their political conclusion (he remaining a Unionist) and their literary conclusion (he maintaining that the heroic romances ought not to be dramatized), Yeats became his successor, inviting writers to change direction, indefatigably prefacing and introducing the works of the chosen, bestowing his approval here, withholding it there (as in the case of James Cousins and the middle O'Casey). Successively O'Grady and Yeats led a clerisy whose ultimate social base was manorial, in which dissident voices as articulate as their own were remarkably few.

This clerisy is at once uniquely Irish (or Anglo-Irish) and the figure in a recurring European cultural pattern; either way it is relevant to any claim that Yeats and other Protestant Revivalists were Modernists. Consider the case of John Synge. Synge was much influenced by the Breton writer, Anatole le Braz whom he read the year before he travelled to the Aran Islands. Le Braz celebrates in his works a rather Medieval peasantry very like the Aran Islanders, a legend-loving, credulous yet humorous people, steeped in Catholicism and an elder paganism. A refrain in *Au Pays des Pardons* (1894) — a book whose influence is visible in *Riders to the Sea* (1904) and *The Aran Islands* (1907) — is Le Braz' fear of the extinction, at the hands of merchants, tourists, trains, machines and other symptoms of bourgeois civilization, faced by age-old customs, beliefs and communities. Yet in the interstices of civilized interference endures a way of life so old and unchanging that it creates in the writer "that feeling of being in a new-made land, a world scarce wakened out of chaos." In Breton society are both changelessness and change, beginning and end. Le Braz disapproves of modernization as strongly as Synge. One student of Breton nationalism has claimed that it was in order to shield Brittany from the modernizing influences of French culture that members of the Breton clerico-aristocratic right were converted to the regionalist ideas that strengthened ethnic minority nationalism in Brittany around the time Le Braz was most involved in the affairs of his native region.[9] Unlike Le Braz, such Bretons were exclusively French-speaking, yet it was remarked as early as 1919 that "their lack of the language paradoxically heightens their sense of being threatened in their Bretonness."[10] A claim could be made that many exclusively Anglophone Irish Revivalists similarly were political or cultural nationalists chiefly because, and to the extent that they were, enemies of capitalism and bourgeois industrialism, and not because of undiluted nationalist impulses. Several of the Revivalists, including Yeats and O'Grady were, when they were political at all, right-wing and aristocratic in sympathy. (One might wish to note the rightward bias in the political thinking of several major Modernist writers whose Modernism ironically inverts their anti-modernization.)

We would, of course, have to exclude Synge from generalizations about aristrocratic-rightwing tendencies in Irish Revivalism (and he did learn Gaelic), but the connection in his life and work between cultural nationalism and anti-modernization remains intact. It is a connection that was reinforced through the influence of Le Braz, though of course Synge met Irish cultural nationalists before he read the Breton. (Le Braz, as it happened, played a role in the Breton Revival not unlike that of Douglas Hyde in its Irish counterpart. The recovery of the old language and of the region's submerged history and racial pride, and, for some, the maintenance of Catholicism, were all important in the Breton Revival as they were in the Irish, but some Revivalists went further and encouraged separatism. Le Braz was the first director of the *Union Régionaliste Bretonne,* an avowedly nonpartisan and nonsectarian alliance between intellectuals and members of Brittany's upper classes begun in 1898 "to develop by the revival of Breton sentiment all forms of Breton activity."[11] The following year — the year Synge himself visited Brittany — Le Braz resigned as director when some members at the second annual URB congress attacked the Third Republic, just as Douglas Hyde resigned the presidency and his membership of the Gaelic League because of its espousal of Irish nationalism.)

Besides the overt resemblances between Breton and Irish nationalism, there was a comparable millenarianism directed by intellectual prophets. (These and other millenarianisms would surely have to be taken into account when we examine the "apocalyptic, crisis-centred views of history" said to be a feature of the Modernist age.[12]) What Jack Reece, drawing upon other social philosophers, has deduced from Breton millenarianism could, I think, be said to some degree of the Anglo-Irish millenarianism of the Irish Revival. Reece sets the Breton phenomenon within a recurring European pattern that has led Anthony D. Smith to theorize that a leading historical function of nationalism has been to resolve "the crisis of the intelligentsia." Such a crisis, says Reece "arises out of the threat to the social dependencies of a traditional order that is being undermined by modernizing currents. Among these dependencies the intellectuals, by virtue of their superior educational attainments and their broad cultural experience, are particularly cognizant of the peril in which they are placed by the conjunction of the old and the new. Indeed, their vulnerability is perhaps greater than that of any other dependent group. Long the most articulate exponents of the ideological world view that gave the traditional order its theoretical legitimacy, they had received substantial moral and material rewards from those whose interests they served. Such intellectuals thus find themselves doubly threa-

tened: from above by the collapsing debris of the old order and
from below by the builders of the new one, who are determined to
sweep away all those whose fortunes are tied to the traditional
holders of power. According to Karl Mannheim, the social thinker
to whom Smith is most heavily in debt, these intellectuals may
extricate themselves from their dangerous situation by following
either of two courses of action. They may seek affiliation with one
of the various groups that are struggling to dominate the emergent
social order or, through scrutiny of their social moorings, they may
seek to rise above their particular class interests and forge a new
mission for themselves as the detached guardians of the moral and
material objectives of the people as a whole."[13] In the case of the
Irish intellectuals, mostly Protestant, the collapse of the old order
— be it the Ascendancy whose heyday was the century before the
Act of Union or the landlord class dangerously corrupt by the late
19th century — exceeded in import the danger from builders of a
new order, many of whom had indeed been in recent history Protestants. As for the two methods of extrication from the predicament, both were attempted by the versatile leaders of the Revival.
Yeats's and AE's and Synge's admiration for aristocrat, peasant
and artist, for example, embodied several social options, and only
from the petty bourgeois class that emerged later did they withhold
all admiration and support. Unifying the various social adaptations
and ploys was, of course, the desire of the chief Revivalists to be the
detached guardians of the moral objectives of the Irish people as a
whole. Joyce, it might be said, did not feel the same need to extricate himself since he owed no more than dubious emotional allegiance to the old order and was in any case a middle-class Catholic;
besides, he aligned himself with no social group and therefore felt
far less the resonances of group and class peril (though his racial
allegiance he felt strongly on occasion).

IV

One way in which the Protestant Revivalists sought to rise
above their class interests was by exploring the mystical and the
occult. Mystical rites were required preparation for envisioning
Heroic Ireland, but it is probable that they simultaneously satisfied
the cruder need of some Protestants for ritual discipline, a need
normally satisfied for the less demanding by Free Masonry and for
the more orthodox by Anglicanism. (Not irrelevantly, Yeats noted

that Irish country people "often attribute magical powers to Orangemen and to Freemasons."[14]) With Catholics, Anglo-Irish Protestants shared a detestation of puritanism, for which unscriptural ceremony is corrupt, a disdain Yeats expresses in "The Curse of the Fires and of the Shadows," one of the stories in *The Secret Rose* (1897). At any rate, the fact is that the most famous leaders of Irish literary transcendentalism were Protestant — Yeats, AE, John Eglinton, James Stephens, James and Margaret Cousins, Charles Johnston. According to Gretta Cousins, Charlotte Despard, an Englishwoman, "was one of the rare Catholics who were Theosophists." That the most responsive and intellectual members of a declining ruling social class would turn to a mysticism ritually organized by rank (one co-opting the hierarchical society of Heroic Ireland) does not seem surprising: it was in part a withdrawal through unconscious pique into esotericism, in part — and this could be ventured, *mutatis mutandis,* of the whole Anglo-Irish Revival — an attempt to regain leadership (intellectual and cultural where moral and social leadership had faltered) by concealing new symbols of power in cabbalistic language and gesture. Perhaps too the mystical advocates of self-transcendence found peculiarly receptive listeners among Anglo-Irish Protestants. Stephens, AE, Yeats, Synge — all were preoccupied with the transience of the self and the natural order and with the need to escape both. It is possible that the themes of self-escape and self-denial reflected the uncertainty of the Anglo-Irish in any new Ireland, perhaps a degree of guilt, even self-hatred.

Yeat's interest in the occult was bound up with his early symbolism, which takes fictional form in the so-called apocalyptic stories of the 1890s, "Rosa Alchemica," "The Adoration of the Magi" and "The Tables of the Law," in the stories of *The Secret Rose* and in the *Stories of Red Hanrahan* (1905). In these fictions we are in the mood whose beginning Yeats ascribed to Poe. Yeats's symbolist heroes court unreality, a Paterian and exclusive world of beauty and spirituality, and risk being "thrown fatally out of key with reality," incurring "penalties which are not to be taken lightly."[15] If there is anything to Edmund Wilson's distinction — the romantic hero is at war with society while the symbolist hero is in flight from it (a distinction difficult to maintain in Ireland where unreal and quixotic insurrections have been commonplace; the Easter Rising is one such and has symbolist overtones) — and if there is anything to the claim that symbolism is a component of Modernism, then symbolism might well be the key to the apparent paradox of Modernism's uneasy relationship with modernization. It is possible that we have two kinds of symbolism in mind however, when *Ulysses,* written by a man indifferent to modernization, is described as "the most characteristic Symbolist novel."[16]

I adduce the mysticism, symbolism, millenarianism and anti-modernization of the Irish Revivalists as evidence of a cultural unreality and self-transformation. Shape-changing is of course an archaic phenomenon in the Celtic literature the Revivalists championed. It is a Druid craft and necessity; which is to say it is the poetic craft and necessity. In the old literature, the Druids, poetry and Ireland herself all survive the centuries by adaptive transformation. Yeats, like Stephens and Joyce, assumes it as theme and form, little guessing perhaps that the entire Revival was a remarkable exercise in shape-changing. In its multitude of guises, flights and masks, it is what defines the Revival. Little wonder that the versatile writers of the Revival can invade Modernism, which has been seen by some in terms of displacement, accommodation, plurality, surrogation.

We find shape-changing supremely in folklore. In returning to the Irish folktale and saga, the Revivalist fiction writers were, in the absence of a native novel tradition, returning by necessity to the foundations of narrative, ignoring an advanced narrative realism that barely existed for them in helpful or hindering form. Once again, here was a happy coincidence, since 20th century pioneers such as Picasso, Stravinsky and Eliot were, as we have been told, inquiring into the nature and foundations of their mediums. Yeats's interest in folklore was largely romantic, though he half-heartedly imitated the structure of folktale in his early fictions; folkore was the art of a diminishing peasantry: a spade is poetry, he said, the machine is prose and a *parvenu.* Folklore was also the diminishing record of the Irish belief in the supernatural. He scorned scholars who approached folklore scientifically and compiled motifs like grocery lists. We now know (from Hyde and his successors) that many Irish folktales are international narrative forms largely independent of local and expressive concerns and have been generated according to a mainly internal 'genetic' programme of type and motif. Propp has distinguished 'text' from 'tale'.[17] What the teller gives us is a text but this may include more than one tale or render a tale imperfectly.

In the transmission of traditional narratives (many of which were collected and published as part of the Revival), the storyteller's freedom of expression is limited and regulated. Motifs, runs and other migratory formulas are not his invention and their deployment should comply with the laws of folk narrative (which might through Anderson's Law of Self-correction put right any egregious error).[18] The ability of Gaelic storytellers to memorize after one hearing novella-length tales and keep them in the memory for years until asked to recite them suggests not only that the tellers had phenomenal memories but also that the tales were self-memorizing in the sense that one link suggested the next, not only by association or contiguity but by a delimitation of sequential possibilities that grew increasingly severe as the tale progressed. To tell a story is to re-count it, to pay out the chain of motifs.

One is reminded, of course, of talk of the autonomy of the Modernist fictive structure, of the autotelic species of literature, of which the international folktale is surely one. I find Fletcher and Bradbury's distinction between pre-Modernist and Modernist self-consciousness of form (the earlier works draw attention to the autonomy of the narrator, Modernist works to the autonomy of the text) inadequate as a definition of Modernist narrative reflexiveness, since the folktale frequently draws attention to itself. "One of the great themes of the Modernist novel has been . . . the theme of the art of the novel itself," they say;[19] but one thinks of those Irish tales in which the pursuit of a story *is* the story; the story must be found and completed before the enveloping story can itself be completed. One thinks, too, of that folktale character, the man who has no story and who had better find one before the tale is through.

So while staking Modernist claims to the narrative introversion of the Irish folktale as it is mimicked by Irish writers, notably Stephens who was powerfully interested in the dynamics of story-telling, I am wondering if the Modernist autonomy of text is new except perhaps in its high incidence — which may, of course, be sufficiently definitive — within the tradition of the novel.

V

There is method in my heterodoxy. The Irish critic must bridle his enthusiasm for Irish Modernism with the reflection that no reputable body of realist fiction appeared in Ireland until the Revival had spent itself. The European chronology was therefore reversed. When it did appear, realism (in the hands of Frank O'Connor, Sean O'Faolain and others) was dwarfed by the Revival and could not fulfil itself because it was in truth romantic feedback and frustration, a diseased retractive subjectivity in disguise. This has been a serious matter in a country where realism, literary, political, psychological, is in desperately short supply, where fantasy impinges cruelly, maimingly on reality. So much in Ireland militates against realism: the rurality, the unsophistication, the lack of a vigorous middle class, the political instability. "We [Irish] cannot become philosophic like the English," Yeats approvingly quoted an Irish poet, "our lives are too exciting."[20] We Irish can barely afford such excitement nowadays.

Yeats saw no excitement in the only Ireland O'Faolain regarded as real: the Catholic, English-speaking, democratic, petit-bourgeois world created by Daniel O'Connell in the 19th century; this Ireland was a wave of Yeats's "filthy modern tide." He did not take under his notice the Ulster Protestant equivalent. Yet these are only two Irelands that exist today, and their horns are locked. They are the basic, inescapable data, the forces of life over there, the disordered surfaces of living upon which literary naturalism and realism in the hands of a great writer needs to go to work.

It is for tactical reasons, then, that I stress Joyce's realism and naturalism, his laureateship of O'Connellite Ireland. I do so, knowing that the Irish genius has not thus far been for a final realism. In *Dubliners, A Portrait* and *Ulysses,* the contest between symbolism and realism recurs, and even if the upshot is synthesis, I choose to emphasize the symbolism's rejection. Joyce thought "The Adoration of Magi" and "The Tables of the Law" were "work worthy of the great Russian masters," and indeed they are powerful stories of a kind. Joyce has Stephen Hero repeat them by heart as he passes through the throng of Yeats's impure multitude. Young Joyce reads Joachim of Flora in Marsh's Library, seeking to re-enact the transport of the narrator of "The Tables of the Law" who is shown a subversive book of Joachim's by Owen Aherne. *Stephen Hero, Dubliners, A Portrait, Ulysses* all reveal the temptations that esotericism, monasticism, prophecy and secret sinfulness represent for many of Joyce's major characters. In all, the temptations are resisted or surmounted. In *Ulysses,* Stephen decides not to visit his Uncle Richie Goulding's house, and thinks: "Houses of decay, mine, his and all. You told the Clongowes gentry you had an uncle a judge and an uncle a general in the Army. Come out of them, Stephen. Beauty is not there. Nor in the stagnant bay of Marsh's Library where you read the fading prophecies of Joachim Abbas." As an alternative to the Symbolist tempters, we are given the impure Bloom "the prophet of sanity, realism, and a secular decency unsupported by dogma," as one critic puts it, "and he passes his ministry on to Stephen."[21]

Joyce is a great Modernist, encompassing. The period symbolism I have been talking about is part of his work; even when it is thematically and stylistically rejected, it remains inerasable in the simultaneous text each literary work is. Nevertheless, I prefer to regard his work as narrative dialectic, as endlessly amenable and extrusive, as ultimate realism rather than ultimate symbolism, though both are necessary stages in the dialectic to whose synthesis they may each claim superior contribution. Having said that, I remind myself of the biographical irony. Yeats did not flee Ireland; he remained to fight. Joyce sequestered himself in Europe, blinding himself with monkish tenacity.

Notes

[1]Frank Kermode, cited by Malcolm Bradbury and James McFarlane, "The Name and Nature of Modernism" in *Modernism 1890-1930,* eds. Bradbury and McFarlane (Harmondsworth: Penguin Books, 1976), p.32.

[2]The *Savoy,* April 1896, quoted by Robert O'Driscoll, *"The Tables of the Law:* A Critical Text," *Yeats Studies,* 1 (1971), p.90.

[3]Bradbury and McFarlane, "The Name and Nature of Modernism" in *Modernism 1890-1930,* p.46.

[4]*A Portrait of the Artist as a Young Man* (Harmondsworth: Penguin Books, 1960), p.179.

[5]"The Universal Literary Influence of the Renaissance" in Louis Berrone, ed., *James Joyce in Padua* (New York: Random House, 1977), pp.19-23.

[6]*On the Study of Celtic Literature* (1867).

[7]*Joyce's Voices* (Berkeley: University of California Press, 1978).

[8]Michel Foucault, *The Archaeology of Knowledge* (New York: Harper and Row, 1976), p.225.

[9]Jack E. Reece, *The Bretons Against France: Ethnic Minority Nationalism in Twentieth-Century Brittany* (Chapel Hill: University of North Carolina Press, 1977), p.52.

[10]Maurice Marchal, quoted by Reece, p.29.

[11]Quoted from the URB charter by Reece, p.54.

[12]Bradbury and McFarlane in *Modernism 1890-1930,* p.20.

[13]Reece, pp.39-40.

[14]"Witches and Wizards and Irish Folk-Lore" in Lady Gregory, *Visions and Beliefs in the West of Ireland* (Gerrards Cross: Colin Smythe, 1970), p.302.

[15]Edmund Wilson, *Axel's Castle: A Study in the Imaginative Literature of 1870 to 1930* (New York: Charles Scribner's Sons, 1931), p.34.

[16]Melvin J. Friedman, "The Symbolist Novel: Huysman to Malraux" in *Modernism 1890-1930,* p.456. By other contributors to this collection of essays (John Fletcher and Malcolm Bradbury, "The Introverted Novel"), *Ulysses* is called "the Modernist novel *par excellence,"* p.405.

[17]Vladimir Propp, *Morphology of the Folktale* (Bloomington: Indiana University Research Center in Anthropology, Folklore, and Linguistics, 1958).

[18]Stith Thompson, *The Folktale* (Berkeley: University of California Press, 1977), p.437.

[19]Fletcher and Bradbury, "The Introverted Novel" in *Modernism 1890-1930,* p.396.

[20]Introduction to *The Oxford Book of Modern Verse,* rpt. in *W. B. Yeats: Selected Criticism,* ed. A. Norman Jeffares (London: Pan Books, 1976), p.219.

[21]Joseph C. Voelker, "'Proteus' and the *Vaticinia* of Marsh's Library: Joyce's Subjunctive Selves," *Eire-Ireland,* XIV, No. 4 (1979), p.139.

Benjamin H. D. Buchloh

Figures of Authority, Ciphers of Regression

Notes on the Return of Representation in European Painting

> The crisis consists precisely in the fact that the old
> is dying and the new cannot be born; in this interreg-
> num a great variety of morbid symptoms appears.
> — Antonio Gramsci, *Prison Notebooks*

How is it that we are nearly forced to believe that the return
to traditional modes of representation in painting around 1915,
two years after the Readymade and the Black Square, was a shift of
great historical or aesthetic import? And how did this shift come to
be understood as an autonomous achievement of the masters, who
were in fact the servants of an audience craving for the restoration
of the visual codes of recognizability, for the reinstatement of figuration? If the perceptual conventions of mimetic representation —
the visual and spatial ordering systems that had defined pictorial
production since the Renaissance and had in turn been systematically broken down since the middle of the nineteenth century —
were reestablished, if the credibility of iconic referentiality was reaffirmed, and if the hierarchy of figure-ground relationships on the
picture plane was again presented as an "ontological" condition,
what other ordering systems outside of aesthetic discourse had to
have already been put in place in order to imbue the new visual
configurations with historical authenticity? In what order do these
chains of restorative phenomena really occur and how are they
linked? Is there a simple causal connection, a mechanical reaction,
by which growing political oppression necessarily and irreversibly
generates traditional representation? Does the brutal increase of
restrictions in socio-economic and political life unavoidably result
in the bleak anonymity and passivity of the compulsively mimetic
modes that we witness, for example, in European painting of the

mid-1920s and early 1930s?

It would certainly appear that the attitudes of the Neue Sachlichkeit and Pittura Metafisica cleared the way for a final takeover by such outright authoritarian styles of representation as Fascist painting in Germany and Italy and socialist realism in Stalinist Russia. When Georg Lukács discussed the rise and fall of expressionism in his "Problems of Realism," he seemed to be aware of the relationship of these phenomena, without, however, clarifying the actual system of interaction between protofascism and reactionary art practices: "The realism of the Neue Sachlichkeit is so obviously apologetic and leads so clearly away from any poetic reproduction of reality that it can easily merge with the Fascist legacy."[1] Paradoxically, however, both traditional Marxism and standard liberalism exempt artists from their responsibilities as sociopolitical individuals: Marxism through its reflection model, with its historical determinism; liberalism through its notion of the artist's unlimited and uninhibited freedom to produce and express. Thus both political views extend to artists the privilege of assuming their determinate necessity to produce unconscious representations of the ideological world.

But would it not be more appropriate to conceive of these radical shifts of the period between the wars, with such decisive selections of production procedures, iconographic references, and perceptual conventions, as calculated? Should we not assume that every artist making these decisions would be aware of their ramifications and consequences, of the sides they would be taking in the process of aesthetic identification and ideological representation?

The question for us now is to what extent the rediscovery and recapitulation of these modes of figurative representation in present-day European painting reflect and dismantle the ideological impact of growing authoritarianism; or to what extent they simply indulge and reap the benefits of this increasingly apparent political practice; or, worse yet, to what extent they cynically generate a cultural climate of authoritarianism to familiarize us with the political realities to come.

In order to analyze the contemporary phenomenon, it may be useful to realize that the collapse of the modernist idiom is not without precedent. The bankruptcy of capitalist economics and politics in the twentieth century has been consistently anticipated and accompanied by a certain rhythm of aesthetic manifestations. First there is the construction of artistic movements with great potential for the critical dismantling of the dominant ideology. This is then negated by those movements' own artists, who act to internalize oppression, at first in haunting visions of incapacitating and infantilizing melancholy and then, at a later stage, in the outright adulation of manifestations of reactionary power. In the present excitement over "postmodernism" and the "end of the avant-garde," it should not be forgotten that the collapse of the modernist paradigm is as much a cyclical phenomenon in the history of twentieth-century art as is the crisis of capitalist economics in twentieth-century political history: overproduction, managed unemployment, the need for expanding markets and profits and the resultant war-mongering as the secret promise of a final solution for late capitalism's problems. It seems necessary to insist upon seeing present developments in the larger context of these historical repetitions, in their nature as response and reaction to particular conditions that exist outside the confines of aesthetic discourse.

If the current debate does not place these phenomena in historical context, if it does not see through the eagerness with which we are assured from all sides that the avant-garde has completed its mission and has been accorded a position of comfort within a pluralism of meanings and aesthetic masquerades, then it will become complicit in the creation of a climate of desperation and passivity. The ideology of postmodernism seems to forget the subtle and manifest political oppression which is necessary to save the existing power structure. Only in such a climate are the symbolic modes of concrete anticipation transformed into allegorical modes of internalized retrospection. If one realizes that melancholy is at the origin of the allegorical mode, one should also realize that this melancholy is enforced by prohibition and repression. What is taken as one of the key works for postmodernist aesthetics and the central reference for any contemporary theory of the return to allegory in aesthetic production and reception, Walter Benjamin's *The Origin of German Tragic Drama,* was written during the dawn of rising fascism in Germany. Its author was well aware of the work's allusion to contemporary artistic and political events, as is confirmed by Benjamin's friend Asja Lacis:

> He said that he did not consider this thesis simply as an academic investigation but that it had very direct interrelationships with acute problems of contemporary literature. He insisted explicitly on the fact that in his thesis he defined the dramaturgy of the baroque as an analogy to expressionism in its quest for a formal language. Therefore I have,

so he said, dealt so extensively with the artistic
problems of allegory, emblems, and rituals.[2]

Or, as George Steiner describes it in his introduction to the
English edition of Benjamin's study:

> As during the crises of the Thirty Years' War and
> its aftermath, so in Weimar Germany the extremi-
> ties of political tension and economic misery are
> reflected in art and critical discussion. Having
> drawn the analogy, Benjamin closes with hints to-
> wards a recursive theory of culture: eras of decline
> resemble each other not only in their vices but also
> in their strange climate of rhetorical and aesthetic
> vehemence. . . . Thus a study of the baroque is no
> mere antiquarian archival hobby: it mirrors, it an-
> ticipates and helps grasp the dark present.[3]

Repression and Representation

It is generally agreed that the first major breakdown of the
modernist idiom in twentieth-century painting occurs at the beginning of the First World War, signaled by the end of cubism and
futurism and the abandonment of critical ideals by the very artists
who had initiated those movements. Facing the deadlock of their
own academicization and the actual exhaustion of the historical
significance of their work, Picasso, Derain, Carrà, and Severini
— to name a few of the most prominent figures — were among the
first to call for a return to the traditional values of high art. Creating the myth of a new classicism to disguise their condition, they
insisted upon the continuation of easel painting, a mode of production that they had shortly before pushed to its very limits, but
which now proved to be a valuable commodity which was therefore to be revalidated. From this situation there originated their
incapacity or stubborn refusal to face the epistemological consequences of their own work. Already by 1913 their ideas had been
developed further by younger artists working in cultural contexts
which offered broader historical, social, and political options to
dismantle the cultural tenets of the European bourgeoisie. This is
particularly the case with Duchamp in America and Malevich and
the constructivists in Russia. But, even in Paris, such artists as
Francis Picabia recognized the imminent demise of cubism. Upon
his return from his first journey to New York in 1913, he wrote,
"But, as you know, I have surpassed this stage of development and
I do not define myself at all as a cubist anymore. I have come to

realize that one cannot always make cubes express the thoughts of the brain and the feelings of the psyche."[4] And in his "Manifeste de l'Ecole Amorphiste," published in a special issue of *Camera Work* in 1913 he was even more explicit: "One has said of Picasso that he studies objects in the way a surgeon dissects a cadaver. We do not want these bothersome cadavers anymore which are called objects."[5]

Even in 1923 these polemics continued among various factions of the Parisian avant-garde. On the occasion of the first performance of Tristan Tzara's "Coeur à Gaz" at the Soirée du Coeur à Barbe, a fistfight broke out in the audience when one of the artists present jumped onto the stage and shouted, "Picasso is dead on the field of battle."[6] But even artists who had been allied with the cubist movement realized by the end of the second decade that it was exhausted, without, however, necessarily advocating a return to the past. Blaise Cendrars, for example, in his text "Pourquoi le cube s'effrite?" published in 1919, announced the end of the relevance of the cubist language. On the other hand, in the very same year a number of ideological justifications appeared for the regression that had begun around 1914-15. Among the many documents of the new attitude of authoritarian classicism are a pamphlet by the cubist dealer Léonce Rosenberg, *Cubisme et Tradition,* published in 1920, and Maurice Raynal's, "Quelques intentions du cubisme," written in 1919 and published in 1924, which stated, "I continue to believe that knowledge of the Masters, right understanding of their works, and respect for tradition might provide strong support."[7] If properly read, this statement, in its attempt to legitimize the academicization of an aging and ailing cubist culture, already reveals the inherent authoritarian tendency of the myth of a new classicism. Then as now, the key terms of this ideological backlash are the idealization of the perennial monuments of art history and its masters, the attempt to establish a new aesthetic orthodoxy, and the demand for respect for the cultural tradition. It is endemic to the syndrome of authoritarianism that it appeal to and affirm the "eternal" or ancient systems of order (the law of the tribe, the authority of history, the paternal principle of the master, etc.). This unfathomable past history then serves as a screen upon which the configurations of a failed historical presence can be projected. In 1915, when Picasso signals his return to a representational language by portraying the cubist poet Max Jacob, recently converted to Catholicism, in the guise of a Breton peasant, drawn in the manner of Ingres, we get a first impression of the degree of eclecticism that is necessary to create the stylistic and historical pose of classical simplicity and equilibrium, with its claim to provide access to the origins and essentials of universal human experience. Subsequently this historicist eclecticism becomes an artistic principle, and then, as in Jean Cocteau's "Rappel à l'Ordre" of 1926, it is declared the new avant-garde program.

In Picasso's work the number and heterogeneity of stylistic modes quoted and appropriated from the fund of art history increases in 1917: not only Ingres' classical portraits but, as a result of Picasso's journey to Italy in the company of Cocteau, the iconography of the Italian commedia dell'arte and the frescoes of Herculaneum (not to mention the sculpture of the Parthenon frieze and the white figure vases at the Louvre, the peasant drawings of Millet, the late nudes of Renoir, the pointillism of Seurat, as Blunt, Green, and other Picasso scholars have pointed out). And, of course, there is the self-quotation of synthetic cubist elements, which lend themselves so easily to the high sensuousness of Picasso's decorative style of the early twenties.

Again it is Maurice Raynal who naively provides the clue to an analysis of these works when he describes Picasso's 1921 *Three Musicians* as "rather like magnificent shop windows of cubist inventions and discoveries."[8] The free-floating availability of these cubist elements and their interchangeability indicate how the new language of painting — now wrenched from its original symbolic function — has become reified as "style" and thus no longer fulfills any purpose but to refer to itself as an aesthetic commodity within a disfunctional discourse. It therefore enters those categories of artistic production that by their very nature either work against the impulse to dissolve reification or are oblivious to that impulse: the categories of decoration, fashion, and objets d'art.

This transformation of art from the practice of the material and dialectical transgression of ideology to the static affirmation of the conditions of reification and their psychosexual origins in repression have been described as the source of a shift towards the allegorical mode by Leo Bersani:

> It is the extension of the concrete into memory and fantasy. But with the negation of desire, we have an immobile and immobilizing type of abstraction. Instead of imitating a process of endless substitutions (desire's ceaseless "travelling" among different images), abstraction is now a transcendence of the desiring process itself. And we move toward an

art of allegory.[9]

This becomes even more evident in the iconography of Pittura Metafisica, which de Chirico and the former futurist Carrà initiated around 1913. The conversion of the futurists, parallel to that of the cubists, involved not only a renewed veneration of the cultural tradition of the past — as opposed to their original fervent antipathy to the past — but also a new iconography of haunting, pointlessly assembled quotidian objects painted with meticulous devotion to representational conventions. De Chirico describes his paintings as stages decorated for imminent but unknown and threatening acts, and insists on the demons that are inherent in the objects of representation: "The metaphysical work of art seems to be joyous. Yet one has the impression that something is going to happen in this joyous world."[10] De Chirico speaks of the tragedy of joy, which is nothing other than the calm before the storm, and the canvas now becomes the stage upon which the future disaster can be enacted. As the Italian historian Umberto Silva pointed out, "De Chirico is the personification of Croce's Italian disease: not quite fascism yet, but the fear of its dawn."[11]

As was the case in Picasso's conversion, the futurists now fully repudiated their earlier nonrepresentational modes and procedures of fragmentation and pictorial molecularization. They further rejected the collage techniques by which they had forced the simultaneous presence of heterogeneous materials and procedures within the painted surface, and through which they had underlined the interaction of aesthetic phenomena with their social and political context. It is surely no accident that one of Severini's first paintings to manifest his return to history is a work called *Maternity*, which represents a mother suckling an infant in the traditional pose of the Madonna. Even more conspicuous perhaps is the case of Carrà, who had been one of the most important futurists due to his development of nonmimetic pictorial signs, his systematic transgression of verbal and visual codes through the insertion of verbal fragments within painting, and his mechanization of pictorial production processes and their juxtaposition with pictorialized remnants of mechanical production processes. Carrà turned at that time to representational depictions of biblical scenes in the manner of Tuscan painting.

Art, Past and Master

To the very same extent that the rediscovery of history serves the authoritarian purpose of justifying the failure of modernism, the atavistic notion of the master artist is reintroduced to continue a culture oriented to an esoteric elite, thus guaranteeing the elite's right to continued cultural and political leadership. The language of the artists themselves (or rather these particular artists, for there is an opposite definition of artistic production and culture simultaneously developing in the Soviet Union) blatantly reveals the intricate connection between aesthetic mastery and authoritarian domination. Three examples from three different decades may serve to illustrate this aesthetic stance:

> Hysteria and dilettantism are damned to the burial urns. I believe that everybody is fed up now with dilettantism: whether it be in politics, literature, or painting. — Giorgio de Chirico, 1919.[12]

> Socialism has only been invented for the mediocre and the weak. Can you imagine socialism or communism in Love or in Art? One would burst into laughter — if one were not threatened by the consequences. — Francis Picabia, 1927.[13]

and finally, Picasso's notorious statement from 1935:

> There ought to be an absolute dictatorship . . . a dictatorship of painters . . . a dictatorship of one painter . . . to suppress all those who have betrayed us, to suppress the cheaters, to suppress the tricks, to suppress mannerisms, to suppress charms, to suppress history, to suppress a heap of other things.[14]

Like senile old rulers who refuse to step down, the stubbornness and spite of the old painters increase in direct proportion to the innate sense of the invalidity of their claims to save a cultural practice that had lost its viability. When, in the early twenties, the former German dadaist Christian Schad attempts a definition of the Neue Sachlichkeit by portraying members of the Weimar hautemonde and demimonde in the manner of Renaissance portraits; when, in 1933, Kasimir Malevich portrays himself and his wife in Renaissance costumes, then obviously the same mechanism of authoritarian alienation is at work. In a text from 1926 Schad delivers a complete account of the syndrome's most conspicuous features:

> Oh, it is so easy to turn one's back on Raphael.
> Because it is so difficult to be a good painter. And
> only a good painter is able to paint well. Nobody
> will ever be a good painter if he is only capable of
> painting well. One has to be born a good painter
> . . . . Italy opened my eyes about my artistic voli-
> tion and capacity . . . . In Italy the art is ancient
> and ancient art is often newer than the new art.[15]

The idealization of the painter's craft, the hypostasis of a
past culture that serves as a fictitious realm of successful solutions
and achievements that have become unattainable in the present, the
glorification of the Other culture — in this case Italy — all of these
features — currently discussed and put into practice once again
— recur through the first three decades of twentieth-century modernism. They seek to halt that modernism and to deny its historical
necessity as well as to deny the dynamic flux of social life and
history through an extreme form of authoritarian alienation from
these processes. It is important to see how these symptoms are
rationalized by the artists at the time of their appearance, how they
are later legitimized by art historians, and how they are finally
integrated into an ideology of culture.

The concepts of "aesthetic paradox" and "novelty," essential features of avant-garde practice, serve as explanations for these
contradictions. Here, for example, is Christopher Green's justification for Cocteau's and Picasso's neoclassicism:

> For Cocteau a return to narrative clarity and to
> form in the novel did not mean a denial of pa-
> radox, and in the same way neither did a return to
> representation in painting. Indeed it seems possible
> that it was at least partially out of a sense of pa-
> radox that Picasso turned against the antirepresen-
> tational dogma associated with Cubism to revive
> Ingres in 1915 . . . . Cocteau suggests that where
> audacity had become convention — as in the Pari-
> sian avant-garde — the resurrection of the old
> modes could create a special kind of novelty: that
> looking backwards the artist could even more
> dramatically look forward. There is no direct evi-
> dence that Picasso consciously aimed to create
> such a paradox, but the fact remains . . . that by
> turning back he did achieve novelty and that his
> perverse development of Synthetic Cubism and re-
> presentational styles alongside one another be-
> tween 1917 and 1921 was calculated to throw the

paradox implicit in his progressive move backwards into the highest possible relief.[16]

The degree of congruity between Cocteau's antimodernist
stance (or should we say cliché of ahistorical thought?) and the
arguments against avant-garde practice in the art press's current
discussion of postmodernism is striking. The stereotype of the
avant-garde's audacity having become convention is, of course,
used primarily by those who want to disguise their new conservatism as its own kind of audacity (Cocteau at the time of "Rappel à
l'Ordre" had just turned to Catholicism). They deny the fact that
conventionalization itself is a maneuver to silence any form of
critical negation, and they wish to share in the benefits that bourgeois culture bestows on those who support false consciousness as
it is embodied in cultural conventions. With regard to historical
eclecticism, the congruity between the neoclassicists of the 1920s
and the contemporary figuration is even more astounding. Intellectual acrobatics are needed to make the ideological stance look like
an organic historical necessity, as opposed to a construct determined by extreme social and political factors. Whatever we are to
understand by a "progressive move backwards" or a "paradox as
novelty," and however Green's observation of Picasso's "perverse
development" indicates his limited awareness of the contradictions
resulting from the art historian's need to accommodate a cultural
notion of the master who necessarily moves from achievement to
achievement, it becomes even more evident that the art historian's
manoeuvers cannot explain the contradictions when we read:

> His [Picasso's] work between 1917 and 1921, rang-
> ing as it did from a gay Synthetic Cubism to a
> sober Classicism repeatedly confirmed the irrele-
> vance for him of having a style and the relevance
> for him of Cocteau's idea of "style." The bright
> color planes of Cubism are right for the carnival
> brilliance of the 1918 *Arlequin,* the sheer figurative
> weight of Roman fresco painting and of Ingres'
> *Madame Moitessier* were right for the monumental
> stability of *La Femme assise lisant;* the implication
> was that any style, old or new, could be adapted to
> Picasso's needs, could be made subject to his will.[17]

Style, the very gem of reified art-historical thinking, the
fiction that there could be a pictorial mode or a discursive   practice
that might function autonomously — traditionally rejected by artists — is now applied by the artists to imbue these exhausted

1. De Chirico, The Disquieting Muses, 1916. Collection Pietro Feroldi, Brescia.

2. Gino Severini, *Spherical Expansion of Light* (Centrifugal), 1914. Collection Riccardo Jucker, Milan.

3. Gino Severini, *Maternity,* 1916. Collection Museo dell'Academia Etrusca Cortone.

4. Carlo Carra, *Patriotic Celebration,* 1914. Collection Mattioli, Milan.

5. Carlo Carra, *The Daughters of Loth,* 1919. Private Collection, Bolzano.

6. Christian Schad, *Portrait of a Woman,* 1920. Collection Christian Schad, Keilberg.

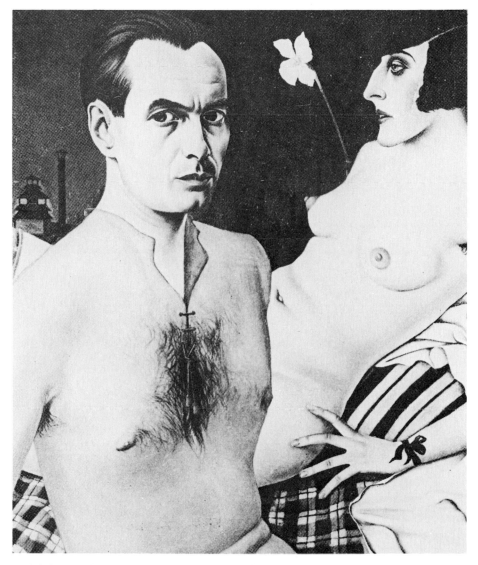

7. Christian Schad, *Self-Portrait,* 1927. Collection Wolf Uecker, Hamburg.

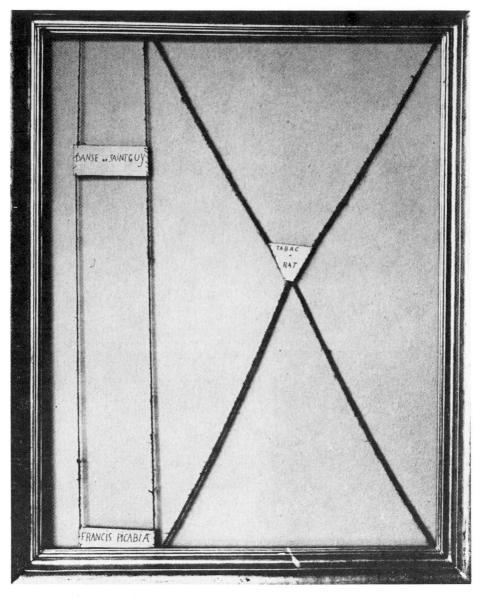

8. Francis Picabia, *Tabac Rat or Dance of Saint Guy,* 1919-1921. Present whereabouts unknown.

9. Francis Picabia, *Printemps (Portrait of M. et Mme. Romain)*, 1942. Private Collection, Paris.

10. Kasimir Malevich, *The Black Cross,* 1915. Musée National d'Art Moderne, Centre Georges Pompidou, Paris.

11. Kasimir Malevich, *Self-Portrait,* 1933. Collection State Museum, Leningrad.

13. Alexander Rodchenko, *Oval Hanging Construction,* 1920. Collection George Costakis, Athens/New York.

12. Gino Severini, *The Two Polichinelle,* 1922. Collection Gemeentemuseum, The Hague.

14. Alexander Rodchenko, Romance (Circa Scene), 1935. Private Collection, Moscow.

modes with historical meaning. "All the wasms have become isms," is a vulgar contemporary variation on the theme of historicism put forward by the self-styled spokesman of postmodernist architecture, Charles Jencks.

Style then becomes the ideological equivalent of the commodity: its universal exchangeability, its freefloating availability indicating a historical moment of closure and stasis. When the only option left to aesthetic discourse is the maintenance of its own distribution system and the circulation of its commodity forms, it is not surprising that all "audacities have become convention" and that paintings start looking like shop windows decorated with fragments and quotations of history.

None of the manifold features of this eclecticism should be seen as random; they confirm one another in an intricate network of historical meaning, which may, however, be read differently from the intentions of the authors or the interests of their audience and the art historians who constitute their cultural reception. This transformation of the subversive function of aesthetic production to plain affirmation necessarily manifests itself in every detail of production. The discovery of "history" as a treasure trove into which one might dip for the appropriation of abandoned elements of style is but one obvious step. The secret attraction of the iconography of Italian theater for Picasso and others at that time becomes more comprehensible in such a perspective. The Harlequins, Pierrots, Bajazzos, and Pulcinelles invading the work of Picasso, Beckmann, Severini, Derain, and others in the early twenties (and, in the mid-thirties, even the work of the former constructivist/productivist Rodchenko in Russia) can be identified as ciphers of an enforced regression. They serve as emblems for the melancholic infantilism of the avant-garde artist who has come to realize his historical failure. The clown functions as a social archetype of the artist as an essentially powerless, docile, and entertaining figure performing his acts of subversion and mockery from an undialectical fixation on utopian thought.[18]

This carnival of eclecticism, this theatrical spectacle, this window dressing of self-quotation become transparent as a masquerade of alienation from history, a return of the repressed in cultural costume. It is essential to the functioning of historicism and its static view of history that it assemble the various fragments of historical recollection and incantation according to the degree of projection and identification that these images of the past will provide for the needs of the present. Quite unlike the modernist collage, in which various fragments and materials of experience are laid bare, revealed as fissures, voids, unresolvable contradictions, irreconcilable particularizations, pure heterogeneity, the historicist image pursues the opposite aim: that of synthesis, of the illusory creation of a unity and totality which *conceals* its historical determination and conditioned particularity.[19] This appearance of a unified pictorial representation, homogeneous in mode, material, and style, is treacherous, supplying as it does aesthetic pleasure as false consciousness, or vice versa. If the modernist work provides the viewer with perceptual clues to all its material, procedural, formal, and ideological qualities as part of its modernist program, which therefore gives the viewer an experience of increased *presence* and autonomy of the self, then the historicist work pretends to a successful resolution of the modernist dilemma of aesthetic self-negation, particularization, and restriction to detail, through *absence,* leading to the seductive domination of the viewer by the experience of alienation and perversion that ideology imposes on the subject.

The Returns of the New

> The meaning structure of art seems to have been undergoing reorganization while the market merely faltered briefly and then regained its stride. The '70s may turn out to have been a revanchist period in which controlling influences within audience and market elites regrouped to reestablish the stratification of the audience and its objects, thereby reasserting, for example, the preeminence of painting as artifactual meaning bearer and as tangible investment.
>
> — Martha Rosler, "Lookers, Buyers, Dealers, Makers: Thoughts on Audience"

Perceptual and cognitive models and their modes of artistic production function in a manner similar to the libidinal apparatus that generates, employs, and receives them. Historically, they lead a life independent of their original contexts and develop specific dynamics: they can be easily reinvested with different meanings and adapted to ideological purposes. Once exhausted and made obsolete by subsequent models, these production modes can generate the same nostalgia as does iconic representation for an obsolete code. Emptied of their historical function and meaning, they do not disappear but rather drift in history as empty vessels waiting to be filled with reactionary interests in need of cultural legitimation. Like other objects of cultural history, aesthetic production modes can be wrenched from their contexts and functions, to be used to display the wealth and power of the social group that has appropriated them.

To invest these obsolete modes with meaning and historical impact requires, however, that they be presented as *radical* and *new*. The secret awareness of their obsolescence is belied by the obsession with which these regressive phenomena are announced as innovation. "The New Spirit of Painting," "The New Fauves," "Naive Nouveau," "Il Nuove Nuove," "The Italian New Wave" are some of the labels attached to recent exhibitions of retrograde contemporary art (as though the prefix *neo* did not indicate the restoration of preexisting forms). It is significant in this regard that the German neoexpressionists who have recently received such wide recognition in Europe (presumably to be followed by a similar acclaim in North America) have been operating on the fringes of the German art world for almost twenty years. Their "newness" consists precisely in their current historical availability, not in any actual innovation of artistic practice.

The historical specificity of iconographic codes is generally more apparent than that of production procedures and materials. It had seemed until recently, for example, that the representation of saints and clowns, of female nudes and landscapes, was entirely proscribed as an authentic expression of individual or collective experience. This proscription did not extend, though, to less conspicuous aspects of pictorial and sculptural production. Excited brushwork and heavy impasto paint application, high contrast colors and dark contours are still perceived as "painterly" and "expressive" twenty years after Stella's, Ryman's, and Richter's works demonstrated that the painted sign is not transparent, but is a coded structure which cannot be an unmediated "expression." Through its repetition the physiognomy of this painterly gesture so "full of spontaneity" becomes, in any case, an empty mechanics. There is only pure desperation in the recently reiterated claim of "energism," which betrays a secret foreboding of the instant reification that awaits such a naive notion of the liberating potential of apolitical and undialectical aesthetic practices.

But the intentions of the artists and their apologists remain to be understood, because contrary to their claim to psychic universality they in fact "express" only the needs of a very circumscribed social group. If "expressivity" and "sensuousness" have again become criteria of aesthetic evaluation, if we are once again confronted with depictions of the sublime and the grotesque — complementary experiential states of modernism's high culture products — then that notion of sublimation which defines the individual's work as determined by alienation, deprivation, and loss is reaffirmed. This process is simply described by Lillian Robinson and Lise Vogel:

> Suffering is portrayed as a personal struggle, experienced by the individual in isolation. Alienation becomes a heroic disease for which there is no social remedy. Irony masks resignation to a situation one cannot alter or control. The human situation is seen as static, with certain external forms varying but the eternal anguish remaining. Every political system is perceived to set some small group into power, so that changing the group will not affect our "real" (that is private) lives . . . . Thus simply expressed, the elements of bourgeois ideology have a clear role in maintaining the status quo. Arising out of a system that functions through corporate competition for profits, the ideas of the bourgeoisie imply the ultimate powerlessness of the individual, the futility of public action and the necessity of despair.[20]

Modernist high culture canonized aesthetic constructs with the appellation "sublime" when the artists in question had proven their capacity to maintain utopian thought in spite of the conditions of reification, and when, instead of actively attempting to change those conditions, they simply shifted subversive intentions into the aesthetic domain. The attitude of individual powerlessness and despair is already reaffirmed in the resignation implicit in a return to the traditional tools of the craft of painting and in the cynical acceptance of its historical limitations and its materially, perceptually, and cognitively primitivist forms of signification.

Such paintings, experienced by a certain audience as sensuous, expressive, and energetic, perform and glorify the ritual of instant excitation and perpetually postponed gratification that is the bourgeois mode of experience. This bourgeois model of sublimation — which has, of course, been countered by an avant-garde tradition of negation, a radical denial of that model's perpetrations of the extreme division of labor and specialization of sexual role behavior — finds its appropriate manifestation in the repeated revitalization of obsolete representational and expressive pictorial practices. It is not accidental that Balthus — champion of the bourgeois taste for high titillation with his scopophilic pictures of sleeping or otherwise unaware adolescent female nudes — has recently received renewed acclaim and is regarded as one of the patriarchal figures of the "new" figuration. Nor is it accidental that not *one* of the German neoexpressionists or the Italian Arte Ciphra painters is female. At a time when cultural production in every field is becoming increasingly aware of, if not actively countering, the oppression of traditional role distinctions based on the construction of sexual difference, contemporary art (or at least that segment of it that is currently receiving prominent museum and market exposure) returns to concepts of psychosexual organization that date from the origins of bourgeois character formation. The bourgeois concept of the avant-garde as the domain of heroic male sublimation functions as the ideological complement and cultural legitimation of social repression. Laura Mulvey has analyzed this phenomenon in the context of the "visual pleasure" of cinematic experience:

> Woman then stands in patriarchal culture as signifier for the male other, bound by a symbolic order in which man can live out his phantasies and obsessions through linguistic command by imposing them on the silent image of woman still tied to her place as bearer of meaning, not maker of meaning.[21]

and Max Kozloff puts it explicitly in the context of the visual arts:

> Further scouting might produce more evidence that virility is often equated with the probing of space or the masterful brushing of a surface. The metaphor of sculptural extension or battling with the canvas is easily sexualized because it conflates two desirable goals associated with the energy of creation. With Expressionist theory, German and American, we are never far removed from its special aura . . . . The imagery of modern art, of course, is rich with overtones of masculine aggression and depersonalization of woman.[22]

The abandonment of painting as sexual metaphor that occurred around 1915 implied not only formal and aesthetic changes but also a critique of traditional models of sublimation. This is most evident in Duchamp's interest in androgyny and in the constructivists' wish to abolish the production mode of individual master in favor of one oriented to collective and utilitarian practice. In contradistinction, those painting practices which operate under the naive assumption that gestural delineation, high contrast color, and heavy impasto are immediate (unmediated, noncoded) representations of the artist's desire propagate the traditional role model; and they do so far more effectively than the painting practices which systematically investigate their own procedures. The former's attraction and success, its role and impact with regard to notions of high culture and the hierarchy of the visual arts, are governed by its complicity with these models of psychosexual organization. Carol Duncan has described how psychosexual and ideological concepts interrelate, how they are concealed and mediated in early twentieth-century expressionist painting:

> According to their paintings, the liberation of the artist means the domination of others; his freedom requires their unfreedom. Far from contesting the established social order, the male-female relationship that these paintings imply — the drastic reduction of women to objects of specialized male interest — embodies on a sexual level the basic class relationship of capitalist society. In fact such images are splendid metaphors for what the wealthy collectors who eventually acquired them did to those beneath them in the social as well as the sexual hierarchy. However, if the artist is willing to regard women as merely a means to his own ends, if he exploits them to achieve his boast of virility, he, in his turn, must merchandise and sell himself — an illusion of himself and his intimate life — on the open, competitive avant-garde market. He must promote (or get dealers and critic friends to promote) the value of his special credo, the authenticity of his special vision, and — most importantly — the genuineness of his antibourgeois antagonism. Ultimately, he must be dependent on and serve the pleasure of this very bourgeois world or enlightened segments of it that his art and life seem to contest.[23]

Inasmuch as this sexual and artistic role is itself reified, *peinture* — the fetishized mode of artistic production — can assume the function of an aesthetic equivalent and provide a corresponding cultural identification for the viewer. Not surprisingly, then, both German neoexpressionists and Italian Arte Ciphra painters draw heavily upon the stock of painterly styles that predate the two major shifts in twentieth-century art history: fauvism, expressionism, and Pittura Metafisica before Duchamp and constructivism; surrealist automatism and abstract expressionism before Rauschenberg and Manzoni — the two essential instances in modern art when the production process of painting was radically questioned for its claim to organic unity, aura, and presence, and replaced by heterogeneity, mechanical procedures and seriality.

The contemporary regressions of "postmodernist" painting and architecture are similar in their iconic eclecticism to the neoclassicism of Picasso, Carrà, and others. A variety of production procedures and aesthetic categories, as well as the perceptual conventions that generated them, are now wrested from their original historical contexts and reassembled into a spectacle of availability. They postulate an experience of history as private property; their function is that of *decorum*. The gaudy frivolity with which these works underscore their awareness of the ephemeral function they perform cannot conceal the material and ideological interests they serve; nor can their aggressivity and bravura disguise the exhaustion of the cultural practices they try to maintain.

The works of the contemporary Italians explicitly revive, through quotation, historical production processes, iconographic references, and aesthetic categories. Their techniques range from fresco painting (Clemente) to casting sculpture in bronze (Chia), from highly stylized primitivist drawing to gestural abstraction. Iconographic references range from representations of saints (Salvo) to modish quotations from Russian constructivism (Chia). With equal versatility they orchestrate a program of disfunctional plastic categories, often integrated into a scenario of aesthetic surplus: freestanding figurative sculpture combined with an installation of aquatint etchings, architectural murals with small-scale easel paintings, relief constructions with iconic objects.

The German neoexpressionists are equally protean in their unearthing of atavistic production modes, including even primitivist hewn wood polychrome sculpture, paraphrasing the expressionist paraphrase of "primitive" art (Immendorff). The rediscovery of ancient teutonic graphic techniques such as woodcuts and linocuts flourishes (Baselitz, Kiefer), as does their iconography: the nude, the still life, the landscape, and what these artists conceive of as allegory.

Concomitant with the fetishization of painting in the cult of *peinture* is a fetishization of the perceptual experience of the work as *auratic.* The contrivance of aura is crucial for these works in order that they fulfill their function as the luxury products of a fictitious high culture. In the tangibility of the auratic, figured through crafted surface textures, aura and commodity coalesce. Only such synthetic uniqueness can satisfy the contempt that bourgeois character holds for the "vulgarities" of social existence; and only this "aura" can generate "aesthetic pleasure" in the narcissistic character disorder that results from this contempt. Meyer Schapiro saw this symbiotic relationship between certain artists and their patrons in 1935: "The artist's frequently asserted antagonism to organized society does not bring him into conflict with his patrons, since they share his contempt for the public and are indifferent to practical social life."[24]

The aesthetic attraction of these eclectic painting practices originates in a nostalgia for that moment in the past when the painting modes to which they refer had historical authenticity. But the specter of derivativeness hovers over every contemporary attempt to resurrect figuration, representation, and traditional modes of production. This is not so much because they actually derive from particular precedents, but because their attempt to reestablish forlorn aesthetic positions immediately situates them in historical secondariness. That is the price of instant acclaim achieved by affirming the status quo under the guise of innovation. The primary function of such cultural re-presentations is the confirmation of the hieratics of ideological domination.

Notes

*I have limited my investigations here to European phenomena, even though I am aware that a comparable movement is presently emerging in North America. The reasons for such a limitation are best described by Georg Lukács: "We will restrict our observations to Germany, even though we know that expressionism was an international phenomenon. As much as we understand that its roots are to be found everywhere in imperialism, we know as well that the uneven development in the various countries had to generate various manifestations. Only after a concrete study of the development of expressionism has been made can we come to an overview without remaining in the abstract." ("Grösse und Verfall des Expressionismus" [1934], in *Probleme des Realismus,* vol. I, *Gesammelte Werke,* vol. IV, Berlin, 1971, p.111).

[1]Lukács, p.147.
[2]Asja Lacis, *Revolutionär im Beruf,* ed. Hildegard Brenner, Munich, 1971,

p.44.

[3]George Steiner, "Introduction," in Walter Benjamin, *The Origin of German Tragic Drama,* London, 1977, p.24.

[4]Francis Picabia, "Comment je vois New York," in *Francis Picabia,* Paris, Musée National d'Art Moderne, 1976, p.66.

[5]Francis Picabia, "Manifeste de l'Ecole Amorphiste," *ibid.,* p.68.

[6]See William Rubin, *Picasso,* New York, Museum of Modern Art, 1980, p.224. The awareness of Picasso's decline eventually developed even among art historians who had been previously committed to his work: "Picasso belongs to the past . . . . His downfall is one of the most upsetting problems of our era" (Germain Bazin, quoted in Rubin, p.277.)

[7]Maurice Raynal, "Quelques intentions du cubisme," *Bulletin de l'effort moderne,* no. 4 (1924), p. 4.

[8]*Ibid.*

[9]Leo Bersani, *Baudelaire and Freud,* Berkeley, 1977, p.98.

[10]Giorgio de Chirico, "Über die metaphysische Kunst," in *Wir Metaphysiker,* Berlin, n.d., p.45.

[11]Umberto Silva, *Kunst und Ideologie des Faschismus,* Frankfurt, 1975, p.18.

[12]Giorgio de Chirico, *Valori Plastici,* Nos. 3-4, Rome, 1919. This phenomenon finds its earliest explicit manifestation in de Chirico's declaration "Pictor sum classicus," with which he concludes emphatically his call for a return to the law of history and classic order, a manifesto called "The Return to the Craft" published in *Valori Plastici* in 1919. Like Carlo Carrà in his "Pittura Metafisica," also published in 1919, de Chirico not only requests the return to the "classic" tradition and the "masters" of that tradition (Uccello, Giotto, Piero della Francesca), but to the specific *nationality* of that tradition. This is the most obvious of the three historical fictions in that authoritarian construct of a return to the past, since the nation-state as a socio-economic and political ordering system did not exist at the time of these masters' production.

It is only logical to find Carrà's name subsequently among the artists who signed the "Manifesto of Fascist Painting" in 1933 which reads as follows: "Fascist Art rejects research and experiments . . . . The style of Fascist art has to orient itself towards antiquity."

It seems that with increasing authoritarianism in the present the projection into the past has to be removed further and further away — from Renaissance to antiquity in this case. More explicitly we find this substitution of present history by mnemosynic fictions of past history in an essay by Alberto Savinio, published in *Valori Plastici* in 1921: "Memory generates our thoughts and our hopes . . . we are forever the devoted and faithful sons of Memory. Memory is our past; it is also the past of all other men, of all men who have preceded us. And since memory is the ordered recollection of our thoughts and those of the others, memory is our religion: *religio."*

When the French art historian Jean Clair tries to understand these phenomena outside of their historical and political context, his terminology, which is supposed to explain these contradictions and save them for a new reactionary anti-modernist art history writing, has to employ the same clichés of authoritarianism, the fatherland, and the paternal heritage: "[These painters] come to collect their paternal heritage, they do not even dream of rejecting it . . . . Neoclassicism is lived as a meditation on the exile, far from the lost fatherland which is also that of painting, the lost fatherland of paintings" (Jean Clair, "Metafisica et Unheimlichkeit," in *Les Réalismes 1919-1939,* Paris, Musée National d'Art Moderne, 1981, p.32).

[13]"Francis Picabia contre Dada ou le Retour à la Raison," in *Comoedia,*

March 14, 1927, p.1. "The Return to Reason" and "The Return to Order" not only espoused almost identical programs of authoritarian neoclassicism, but also shared the same supposed enemies and targets of attack. Dada was, of course, one of them, so it seems useful in this context to recall the attitudes of the literary neoclassicist T. S. Eliot towards dada: "Mr. Aldington treated Mr. Joyce as a prophet of chaos and wailed at the flood of Dadaism which his prescient eye saw bursting forth at the tap of the magician's rod . . . . A very great book may have a very bad influence indeed . . . . A man of genius is responsible to his peers, not to a studio full of uneducated and undisciplined coxcombs." (T. S. Eliot, "Ulysses, Order and Myth," *The Dial,* vol. LXXV [1923], pp.480-483).

[14]Pablo Picasso, in conversation with Christian Zervos, in *Cahiers d'Art,* vol. X, no. 1 (1935), p. 173.

[15]Christian Schad, statements in exhibition catalogue, Galerie Würthle, Vienna, 1927. See also a nearly identical statement by the former expressionist Otto Dix: "The new element of painting for me resides in the intensification of forms of expression which *in nuce* exist already as given in the works of *old masters"* (in *Das Objekt ist das Primäre,* Berlin, 1927). Compare this with the statement by George Grosz, a peer of Schad and Dix: "The return to French classicist painting, to Poussin, Ingres, and Corot, is an insidious fashion of *Biedermeier.* It seems that the political reaction is therefore followed by an intellectual reaction." (in *Das Kunstblatt,* 1922, as a reply to Paul Westheim's inquiry "Towards a New Naturalism?").

[16]Christopher Green, *Léger and the Avantgarde,* London, 1976, p.218.

[17]*Ibid.*

[18]When Max Beckmann in the twenties referred to himself as the "alienated clown and the mysterious king" he expressed precisely the unconscious dilemma of the artist's fluctuation between authoritarian rule and melancholy, as George Steiner puts it in his introduction to *The Origin of German Tragic Drama:* "Prince and Puppet are impelled by the same frozen violence" (p.18). Renato Poggioli described this dilemma without coming to an adequate understanding: "Aware that bourgeois society looks at him only as a charlatan the artist deliberately and ostentatiously assumes the role of the comic actor. From this stems the myth of the artist as *pagliaccio* and mountebank. Between the alternating extremes of self-criticism and self-pity, the artist comes to see himself as a comic victim and sometimes as a tragic victim, although the latter seems to be predominant." (Renato Poggioli, "The Artist in the Modern World," in *The Spirit of the Letter,* Cambridge, 1965, p.327).

This new icon of the clown is only matched in frequency in the paintings of that period by the representation of the *manichino,* the wooden puppet, the reified body, originating from both shopwindow decoration and from the props of the classical artist's studio. If the first icon appears in the context of the carnival and the circus as the masquerades of alienation from present history, the second appears on the stage set of reification. With due historical transformation we can observe parallel phenomena in the iconography of the "New Painting." As described in the following example: "The comic and the self-effacing aspects . . . loom very large (and very small in the work of many recent artists). Miniaturization, stick figures, dimpled dollies, micro freaks and the humanoid progeny of Krazy Kat are all part of an every increasing Lilliputian population; the doll house syndrome is very much with us" (Klaus Kertess, "Figuring It Out," *Artforum,* November 1980, p.30). Or, a more adequate critical understanding of these phenomena: "In another of a long string of ironic (?) refusals of virtuosity and 'sensitivity,' painters have recently adopted a reduced brutish figuration (seemingly chosen from a lexicon of the drastically damaged mentally) whose nihilism strikes not at any society in particular but at 'civilization' — a familiar desperate move." (Martha Rosler, unpublished notes on quotation).

[19]These "concealed collages" in paintings represent a false unification. Fredric Jameson describes this analogous attempt at unification in literature: ". . . the mirage of the continuity of personal identity, the organizing unity of the psyche or the personality, the concept of society itself, and not least, the notion of the organic unity of the work of art" *(Fables of Aggression,* Berkeley, 1980, p.8). The term "painted collages" was used by Max Ernst in his "Au-delà de la Peinture" in 1936 to describe the painting of Magritte and Dali. Of course Ernst was not able to provide a historical differentiation between the original collage techniques and their implications and the attempt of renewed painterly unification of fragmentation, fissures, and discontinuity of the plastic language. Since then several authors have described the phenomenon of the "painted collage" in the neoclassicist paintings and their peculiar unreal spatiality, a surface and pictorial space that seem to be made of glass or ice. See, for example, Wieland Schmied, "Pittura Metafisica et Nouvelle Objectivité, in *Les Realismes 1919-1939,* p.22. This is of course the spatial configuration of the static melancholic experience which is fixated on the authoritarian images of the alien and the ancient and that recognizes itself in the shimmering surface of classicist painting that seems to contain life in a shrine.

[20]Lillian Robinson and Lise Vogel, "Modernism and History," *New Literary History,* vol. III, no. 1, p.196.

[21]Laura Mulvey, "Visual Pleasure and Narrative Cinema," *Screen,* vol. XVI, no. 3 (1975), p. 7.

[22]Max Kozloff. "The Authoritarian Personality in Modern Art," *Artforum.* vol. XXI, no. 8 (May 1974). p. 40.

[23]Carol Duncan, "Virility and Domination in Early Twentieth Century Painting," *Artforum,* vol. XII. no. 9 (June 1974), p. 38.

[24]Meyer Schapiro, quoted in Kozloff.

After Benjamin Buchloh

Audience:
You seem to associate Soviet Socialist Realism with Fascist art. I think that interesting, but I don't really see that connection. You made reference to two sets of entirely different economic and social situations, and I would like to hear you clarify that point.

Benjamin Buchloh:
I think I made it specifically clear at the one point where I connect the two phenomena — that I talked about art production under authoritarianism. I connect the two phenomena on the level of actual political organization. I did not equate Fascism and Stalinism as interchangeable or equal phenomena, but I related them under the heading of authoritarianism.

The other connection that I did in fact establish would suggest that it is very evident from the material that I have shown, is that we cannot deny a tendency — a similar tendency —that occurs in both western and eastern Europe at the time, in the work of such artists as Malevich and Rodchenko, for example, and the work of the other artists that I have shown, which — however one would have eventually to distinguish them — can be clearly related on the level of an explicit programmatic return to figurative representation. Whether or not those modes of representation, in a more detailed analysis, would turn out to be quite different from each other is left open, but we could see quite clearly that in the modes of representation not only do we witness a change to that particular practice, but we also see a clear iconographical selection and we see a very clear attitude, at least in Malevich's case, to history. So on those two levels, as well, the comparison works, it's an absolutely convincing comparison.

I am not implying that the Soviet Union under Stalin and Fascism in Italy and Germany were politically identical or comparable systems. That was not at all the implication. I was simply pointing to the parallelism of a return to representational practices under authoritarian political conditions and I think you would agree with me that, in comparison to the Soviet Union up to 1925, the cultural conditions changed drastically under Stalin — i.e. the conditions which define the production of art. I did not say that the political conditions, economic conditions under Stalin were identical or similar to the political or economic conditions under Mussolini or Hitler in Germany. I have not made a political comparison.

I have made a structural comparison between two aesthetic phenomena that happened at the same time. I have not given a conclusion, which I confess at this point in time, I am not willing to give. I am not willing to say, for such and such reason does figuration appear under Stalin, and for such and such reason does it appear in the fascist states. That was clearly indicated in the beginning as a speculative question.

Audience:
You are talking about classical modes of representation. It seemed that most of the pictures you showed dated from about 1917 to 1923, or thereabouts. I was surprised that you didn't really mention at all the fact of World War I. Does that not enter into some of the analyses?

Benjamin Buchloh:
Yes. There is one phrase that I recall that states the first collapse in modernist art in the 20th century, could be located with the beginning of World War I, 1914, with Picasso's return to Ingresque drawings. I did not go into any detail. What I was implying, however, and I think that's the insinuation in your question, was of course that the phenomenon of authoritarianism is not historically limited to the late 20's. Authoritarianism in as much as it is an essential dimension of imperialism pervades 20th-century history. It's not only that we find it in its manifestations in the late twenties. Obviously you would call the imperialist war, the First World War, a political event that released the authoritarian forces that were inherent in the organization of society at that point in time.

Again one would have to be very careful about an immediate connection, saying neoclassicism is a necessary mechanical reflection of imperialist authoritarianism. All of these questions, as I said in the introduction to the paper, are wide open, and I do not claim to be able at this point in time to answer them, but I certainly try to collect some of the materials in that context — or see them in that context.

Audience:
So then you are taking the position that, in fact, it might be misleading to try to refer specifically to this change to classicism as a phenomenon of the war. In fact that there is the underlying fact of authoritarianism and that this . . .

Benjamin Buchloh:

Yes. In as much as the First World War was equally determined by
the reaffirmed imperialist policy of the nation state — that is a
situation which is structurally comparable. And as much as we
witnessed the same phenomena in 1981, you see as these patterns
re-occur with the historical modifications and changes that they are
inherently cyclical phenomena, that they are not located specifically in one moment only, which would be 1928 or 1933. But they
do reappear in different formations and they are structurally very
similar. Of course we would have to specify them.

And again, I am not saying post-modernist architecture —
Johnson's proposal for the AT&T building in New York would be
a perfect example — I am not saying that is explicit fascist architecture. Of course not, but it certainly has its precursor/predecessor in
similar historicist returns in the decades of 1915-25.

Audience:

Maybe you could just say something about the work of people like
Clemente and Chia because your referencing there is not high art,
it's naive, and it's distinctly post-modern, if you want to use that
term. A lot of your discussion is about high art referencing, and
architecture not painting.

Benjamin Buchloh:

I would say in Chia's and Clemente's case the reference to naïveté,
to false naïveté, first of all is by now to be considered one of the key
ingredients of high art references all through the 20th century. And
nobody can claim any original or authentic access to naiveté any
more, I suppose.

Secondly, there is a wide range of historical high art references in
both Chia and Clemente, or in the Italian and the German and the
American work that we are talking about. For example, I have
heard or read texts where the Italians do particularly claim Sironi
(who was one of the Italian painters that I did not mention, but
who was certainly crucial in that transition that I described) and de
Chirico and the late de Chirico in particular, as some of the historical reference-figures that they would like to claim as their ances-
tors. The Italians also jumble aesthetic plastic categories together
— for instance, they appropriate drawing modes that come as
much out of Surrealism as they do out of Abstract Expressionism.
The whole practice seems to be a very conscious and deliberate
reference system.

In a way perhaps, that was very well described today, however from a different point of view and with a different intention, by Marcelin Pleynet, when he said what contemporary art practice does seem to contain and refer to all of the various stages, procedures, categories that have been developed all through its history. I think that would be true for the contemporary American work as much as it is true for the Italian work that you were mentioning.

Allan Sekula

The Traffic in Photographs

I. Introduction: Between Aestheticism and Scientism

How can we work towards an active, critical understanding of the prevailing conventions of representation, particularly those surrounding photography?[1] The discourse that surrounds photography speaks paradoxically of discipline and freedom, of rigorous truths and unleashed pleasures. Here then, at least by virtue of a need to contain the tensions inherent in this paradox, is the site of a certain shell game, a certain dance, even a certain politics. In effect, we are invited to dance between photographic truths and photographic pleasures with very little awareness of the floorboards and muscles that make this seemingly effortless movement possible.

By discourse, then, I mean the forceful play of tacit beliefs and formal conventions that situates us, as social beings, in various responsive and responsible attitudes to the semiotic workings of photography. In itself constrained, determined by, and contributing to "larger" cultural, political, and economic forces, this discourse both legitimates and directs the multiple flows of the traffic in photographs. It quietly manages and constrains our abilities to produce and consume photographic imagery, while often encouraging, especially in its most publicized and glamorous contemporary variants, an apparently limitless semiotic freedom, a timeless dimension of aesthetic appreciation. Encoded in academic and "popular" texts, in books, newspapers, magazines, in institutional and commercial displays, in the design of photographic equipment, in schooling, in everyday social rituals, and — through the workings of these contexts — within photographs themselves, this discourse exerts a force that is simultaneously material and symbolic, inextricably linking language and power. Above all, in momentar-

ily isolating this historically specific ideology and practice of representation we shouldn't forget that it gives concrete form to —
thus lending both truth and pleasure to — other discursively borne
ideologies: of "the family," of "sexuality," of "consumption" and
"production," of "government," of "technology," of "nature," of
"communications," of "history," and so on. Herein lies a major
aspect of the affiliation of photography with power. And as in all
culture that grows from a system of oppressions, the discourses
that carry the greater force in everyday life are those that emanate
from power, that give voice to an institutional authority. For us,
today, these affirmative and supervisory voices speak primarily for
capital, and subordinately for the state. This essay is a practical
search for internal inconsistencies, and thus for some of the weaknesses in this linkage of language and power.

Photography is haunted by two chattering ghosts: that of
bourgeois science and that of bourgeois art. The first goes on about
the truth of appearances, about the world reduced to a positive
ensemble of facts, to a constellation of knowable and possessable
objects. The second specter has the historical mission of apologiz-
ing for and redeeming the atrocities committed by the subservient
— and more than spectral — hand of science. This second specter
offers us a reconstructed *subject* in the luminous person of the
artist. Thus, from 1839, onward, affirmative commentaries on photography have engaged in a comic, shuffling dance between technological determinism and auteurism, between faith in the objective
powers of the machine and a belief in the subjective, imaginative
capabilities of the artist. In persistently arguing for the harmonious
coexistence of optical truths and visual pleasures, in yoking a positivist scientism with a romantic metaphysics, photographic discourse has attempted to bridge the philosophical and institutional
separation of scientific and artistic practices that has characterized
bourgeois society since the late eighteenth century. The defenders of
photography have both confirmed and rebelled against the Kantian cleavage of epistemology and aesthetics; some argue for truth,
some for pleasure, and most for both, usually out of opposite sides
of the mouth. (And a third voice, usually affiliated with liberalism,
sporadically argues for an ethical dimension to photographic
meaning. This argument attempts to fuse the separated spheres of
fact and value, to graft a usually reformist morality onto
empiricism.)

This philosophical shell game is evidence of a sustained
crisis at the very center of bourgeois culture, a crisis rooted in the

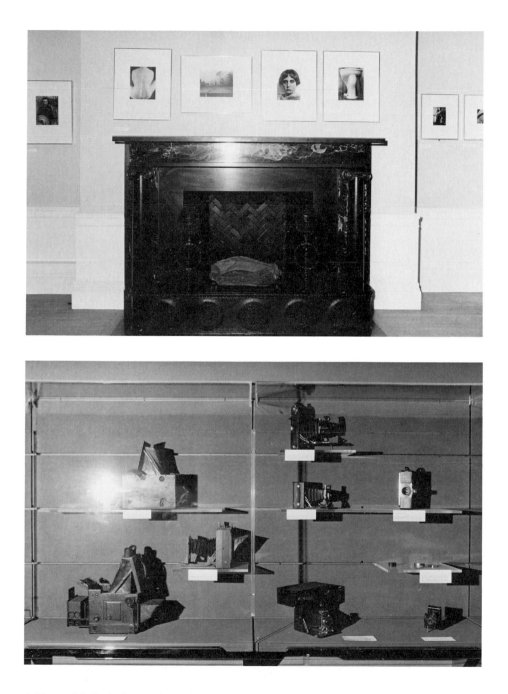

1. Figures 1-2: At the International Museum of Photography at George Eastman House in Rochester, New York — the only museum devoted entirely to photography and cinema — two historiographic tendencies are evident. The viewer is offered both a technological history and an art history; the cult of the machine and the cult of the artist are celebrated under one ecumenical roof. Photographs by Allan Sekula, 1978.

emergence of science and technology as seemingly autonomous productive forces. Bourgeois culture has had to contend with the threat and the promise of the machine, which it continues both to resist and embrace.[2] The fragmentary and mechanically derived photographic image is central to this attitude of crisis and ambivalence; the embracing issue is the nature of work and creativity under capitalism. Above all else, the ideological force of photographic art in modern society may lie in the apparent reconciliation of human creative energies with a scientifically guided process of mechanization, suggesting that despite the modern industrial division of labor, and specifically despite the industrialization of cultural work, despite the historical obsolescence, marginalization, and degradation of artisanal and manual modes of representation, the category of the artist lives on in the exercise of a *purely mental, imaginative* command over the camera.[3]

But during the second half of the nineteenth century, a fundamental tension developed between uses of photography that fulfill a bourgeois conception of the *self* and uses that seek to establish and delimit the terrain of the *other*. Thus every work of photographic art has its lurking, objectifying inverse in the archives of the police. To the extent that bourgeois society depends on the systematic defense of property relations, to the extent that the legal basis of the self lies in property rights, every proper portrait of a "man of genius" made by a "man of genius" has its counterpart in a mug shot. Both attempts are motivated by an uneasy belief in the category of the individual. Thus also, every romantic landscape finds its deadly echo in the aerial view of a targeted terrain. And to the extent that modern sexuality has been invented and channeled by organized medicine, every eroticized view of the body bears a covert relation to the clinical depiction of anatomy.

With the rise of the modern social sciences, a regularized flow of symbolic and material power is engineered between fully-human subject and less-than-fully-human object along vectors of race, sex, and class. The social-scientistic appropriation of photography led to a genre I would call *instrumental realism,* representational projects devoted to new techniques of social diagnosis and control, to the systematic naming, categorization, and isolation of an otherness thought to be determined by biology and manifested through the "language" of the body itself. Early anthropological, criminological, and psychiatric photography, as well as motion study photography used somewhat later in the scientific analysis and management of the labor process, constitutes an ambitious attempt to link optical empiricism with abstract, statistical truth, to move from the specificity of the body to abstract, mathematical laws of human nature. Thus photography was hitched to the locomotive of positivism.

Consider for a moment the symbolist cult of metaphor, so central to the rhetoric of emergent avant-garde art photography in the United States in the first quarter of this century. In its attempt to establish the free-floating metaphorical play, or equivalence, of signifiers, this symbolist-influenced photography was fundamentally reactive, the outcome of a desire to seize a small area of creative autonomy from a tainted, instrumentalized medium, a medium that had demonstrated repeatedly its complicity with the forces of industrialism. Thus the free play of metaphorical associations was implicitly contrasted to the slavish metonymy of both instrumental realism and the sentimental realism of late nineteenth-century family photography. With symbolism, the ultimate goal of abstraction also looms, but in metaphysical and spiritualist rather than positivist guise. But both modern science and modernist art tend to end up worshipping in floating cathedrals of formal, abstract, mathematical relations and "laws." Perhaps the fundamental question to be asked is this: can traditional photographic representation, whether symbolist or realist in its dominant formal rhetoric, transcend the pervasive logic of the commodity form, the exchange abstraction that haunts the culture of capitalism? Despite its origins in a radical refusal of instrumental meaning, symbolism appears to have been absorbed by mass culture, enlisted in the spectacle that gives imaginary flesh to the abstract regime of commodity exchange.[4]

No theory of photography can fail to deal with the hidden unity of these extremes of photographic practice without lapsing into mere cultural promotion, into the intellectual background music that welcomes photography into the shopping mall of a bureaucratically administered high culture that has, in the late capitalist period, become increasingly indistinguishable from mass culture in its structural dependence on forms of publicity and stardom. The goals of a critical theory of photography ought, ultimately, to involve the practical, to help point the way to a radical, reinvented cultural practice. Other more powerful challenges to the order of monopoly capitalism need to be discovered and invented, resistances that unite culture and politics. Neo-symbolist revolts are not enough, nor is a purely instrumental conception of politics. This essay is an attempt to pose questions that I take to be only preliminary, but necessary, steps in that direction.

II. Universal Language

It goes almost without saying that photography emerged and proliferated as a mode of communication within the larger context of a developing capitalist *world order*. No previous economy constituted a world order in the same sense. Inherently expansionist, capitalism seeks ultimately to unify the globe in a single economic system of commodity production and exchange. Even tribal and feudal economies at the periphery of the capitalist system are drastically transformed by the pressures exerted from the aggressive centers of finance and trade. These forces cause local economies and cultures to lose much of their self-sufficiency, their manner of being tied by necessity and tradition to a specific local ecology. This process of global colonization, initially demanding the outright conquest and extermination or pacification of native peoples, began in earnest in the sixteenth century, a period of expanding mercantile capitalism. In the late twentieth century this process continues in a fashion more intensive than extensive, as modern capitalism encounters national political insurrections throughout the colonized world and attempts to fortify its position against a crisis that is simultaneously political, economic, and ecological, a crisis that is internal as well as external. Despite these changes, a common logic of capital accumulation links, for example, the European slave trade in west Africa in the seventeenth and eighteenth centuries to the late twentieth-century electronics sweatshops operated by American multinationals in Singapore and Malaysia. And today, established as well as recently insurgent socialist economies are increasingly forced to adjust to the pressures of a global system of currency dominated by these large multi-national enterprises of the West.[5]

What are we to make, then, of the oft-repeated claim that photography constitutes a "universal language?" Almost from 1839 to the present, this honorific has been expansively and repetitively voiced by photographers, intellectuals, journals, cultural impresarios, and advertising copy writers. Need I even cite examples? The very ubiquity of this cliché has lent it a commonsensical armor that deflects serious critical questions. The "universal language" myth seems so central, so full of social implications, that I'd like to trace it as it surfaced and resurfaced at three different historical conjunctures.

An initial qualification seems important here. The claim for semantic universality depends on a more fundamental conceit: the belief that photography constitutes a language in its own right. Photography, however, is *not* an independent or autonomous language system, but depends on larger discursive conditions, invariably including those established by the system of verbal-written language. Photographic meaning is always hybrid construction, the outcome of an interplay of iconic, graphic, and narrative conventions. Despite a certain fugitive moment of semantic and formal autonomy — the Holy Grail of most modernist analytic criticism — the photograph is invariably accompanied by, and situated within, an overt or covert *text*. Even at the level of the artificially "isolated" image, photographic signification is exercised in terms of pictorial conventions that are never "purely" photographic. After all, the dominant spatial code in the Western pictorial tradition is still that of linear perspective, institutionalized in the fifteenth and sixteenth centuries. Having made this point, only in passing and only too briefly, suppose we examine what is necessarily the dependent clause, a clause anchored in the dubious conception of a "photographic language."

My first example consists of two texts that constituted part of the initial euphoric chorus that welcomed and promoted the invention of photography in 1839. In reading these, we'll move backwards, as it were, from the frontiers of photography's early proliferation to the ceremonial site of invention, tracing a kind of reverse geographical movement within the same period of emergence.

Early in 1840, a glowing newspaper account of the daguerreotype (mistranslated understandably enough as the "daguerreolite") was published in Cincinnati, Ohio. Cincinnati, a busy center for river-borne shipping in what was then the western United States, would soon support one of the more ornate and culturally pretentious of American photographic portrait establishments, Ball's Daguerrian Gallery of the West.[6] Here is a fragment of what was undoubtedly the first local announcement of the novel invention which was soon to blossom into the very embodiment of Culture: "Its perfection is unapproachable by human hand and its truth raises it above all language, painting or poetry. It is the first universal language addressing itself to all who possess vision, and in characters alike understood in the courts of civilization and the hut of the savage. The pictorial language of Mexico, the hieroglyphics of Egypt are now superseded by reality."[7]

I find it striking that this account glides from the initial trumpeting of a triumph over "all language," presumably including all previous European cultural achievements, to the celebration of a victorious encounter with "primitive" and archeologically remote pictographic conventions, rendering these already extinct languages rather redundantly "obsolete." This optimistic hymn to progress conceals a fear of the past. For the unconscious that resides within this text, dead languages and cultures may well be pregnant with the threat of rebirth. Like zombies, they must be killed again and embalmed by a "more perfect union" of sign and referent, a union that delivers "reality" itself without the mediation of hand or tongue. This new mechnical language, by its very closeness to nature, will speak in civilizing tones to previously unteachable "savages." Behind the rhetoric of technologically derived egalitarianism lurks a vision of the relentless imposition of a new pedagogical power.

Consider also a related passage from one of the central ideological documents of the early history of photography, the report on the daguerreotype given by the physicist and left-republican representative François Arago to his colleagues in the French Chamber of Deputies. This report was published along with the texts of related speeches by the chemist Gay-Lussac and the interior minister Dûchatel in the numerous editions in many languages of Daguerre's instruction manual. As is well known, Arago argued for the award of a state pension to Daguerre for his "work of genius;" this purchase would then be offered "generously to the entire world." Not without a certain amount of maneuvering (involving the covert shunting aside of photographic research by Hippolyte Bayard and the more overt down-playing of Nicéphore Nièpce's contribution to the Nièpce-Daguerre collaboration), Arago established the originality of Daguerre's invention.[8] Arago also emphasized the extraordinary efficiency of the invention — its capacity to accelerate the process of representation — and the demonstrable utility of the new medium for both art and science. Thus the report's principal ideological service was to fuse the authority of the state with that of the individual author — the individuated *subject* of invention.

While genius and the parliamentary-monarchic state bureaucracy of Louis-Philippe are brought together within the larger ideological context of a unified technical and cultural progressivism, the report also touches on France's colonial enterprises and

2. Figure 3: The International Museum of Photography at George Eastman House enshrines a third history as well, a history of entrepreneurial and industrial genius. Here the biography of George Eastman — who is described by museum publicity as the "father of popular photography" — is the central narrative. Photograph by Allan Sekula, 1978.

specifically upon the archival chores of the "zealous and famous scholars and artists attached to the army of the Orient."[9] Here is the earliest written fantasy of a collision between photography and hieroglyphics, a fantasy that resurfaced six months later in Ohio:

> While these pictures are exhibited to you, everyone will imagine the extraordinary advantages which could have been derived from so exact and rapid a means of reproduction during the expedition to Egypt; everybody will realize that had we had photography in 1798 we would possess today faithful pictorial records of that which the learned world is forever deprived by the greed of the Arabs and the vandalism of certain travelers.
>
> To copy the millions of hieroglyphics which cover even the exterior of the great monuments of Thebes, Memphis, Karnak, and others would require decades of time and legions of draughtsmen. By daguerreotype one person would suffice to accomplish this immense work successfully . . . . These designs will excel the works of the most accomplished painters, in fidelity of detail and true reproduction of atmosphere. Since the invention follows the laws of geometry, it will be possible to re-establish with the aid of a small number of given factors the exact size of the highest points of the most inaccessible stuctures.[10]

In this rather marked example of what Edward Said has termed "Orientalist" discourse, a "learned" Occident colonizes an East that has either always lacked or has lost all memory of learning.[11] A seemingly neutral, mathematical objectivism retrieves, measures, and preserves the artifacts of an Orient that has "greedily" squandered its own heritage. In a sense, Arago's argument here is overdetermined: France, a most civilized nation, a nation aware of its historical mission, must not fail to preserve and nurture its own inventions. In effect, Arago's speech conflates photography-as-an-end and photography-as-a-means. This shouldn't be at all surprising, given the powerful tendency of bourgeois thought to collapse all teleology into the sheer, ponderous immanence of technological development. Rational progress becomes a matter of the increasingly quantitative refinement of technical means; the only positive transformations are those that stem from orderly technical innovations — hence Arago's emphasis on the conquest of vandalism, greed, and ignorance through speed and the laws of geometry.

In a very different historical context — that of the last crisis-ridden years of Weimar Germany — a text appeared that is reminiscent of both Arago's refined promotion and the hyperbolic newspaper prophecy from Ohio. August Sander, that rigorously and comprehensively sociologistic portraitist of the German people, delivered a radio talk in 1931 entitled "Photography as a Universal Language." The talk, the fifth in a series by Sander, stresses that a liberal, enlightened, and even socially critical pedagogy might be achieved by the proper use of photographic means. Thus Sander's emphasis is less on the pictorial archive anticipated by Arago in 1839 than on a global mode of communication that would hurdle barriers of illiteracy and language difference. But at the same time, Sander echoes the scientistic notions of photographic truth that made their initial authoritative appearance in Arago's report:

> Today with photography we can communicate our thoughts, conceptions, and realities, to all the people on the earth; if we add the date of the year we have the power to fix the history of the world . . . .
> Even the most isolated Bushman could understand a photograph of the heavens — whether it showed the sun or the moon or the constellations. In biology, in the animal and plant world, the photograph as picture language can communicate without the help of sound. But the field in which photography has so great a power of expression that language can never approach it, is physiognomy . . . .[12]

Perhaps it is understandable that in his enthusiasm for photographic enlightenment Sander led his unseen radio audience to believe that a Copernican cosmology and a mechanically rendered Albertian perspective might constitute transhistorical and transcultural discourses: photography could deliver the heliocentric and perspectival truths of the Renaissance to any human viewer.

Further, Sander describes photography as the truth vehicle for an eclectic array of disciplines, not only astronomy but history, biology, zoology, botany, and physiognomy (and clearly the list is not meant to be exhaustive). Two paragraphs later, his text seeks to name the source of the encyclopedic power to convey virtually all the world's knowledges: "No language on earth speaks as comprehensively as photography, always providing that we follow the chemical and optic and physical path to demonstrable truth, and understand physiognomy. Of course you have to have decided whether you will serve culture or the marketplace."[13] In opposing photographic truth to commercial values, and in regarding photography as "a special discipline with special laws and its own special language,"[14] Sander is assuming an uncompromisingly modernist stance. This position is not without its contradictions. Thus, on the one hand Sander claims that photography constitutes a "language" that is both autonomous and universal; on the other, photography is subsumed within the logical order of the natural sciences. The "laws" that are "special" to photography turn out to be those of chemistry and optics. From this subordinate position photography functions as the vehicle for a scientific pedagogy. For Arago, photography is a means of aggressively acquiring the world's truth; for Sander, photography benignly disseminates these truths to a global audience. Although the emphasis in the first instance is on acquisition, and in the second on distribution, both projects are fundamentally rooted in a shared epistemology. This epistemology combines a faith in the universality of the natural sciences and a belief in the transparency of representation.

For Sander, physiognomy was perhaps the highest of the human sciences, which are in turn merely extensions of natural scientific method. Physiognomic empiricism serves as the basis for what Alfred Döblin, in his preface to Sander's *Antlitz der Zeit,* described as a project methodologically analogous to medical science, thereby collapsing history and sociology into social-anatomy:

> You have in front of you a kind of cultural history, better, sociology of the last 30 years. How to write sociology without writing, but presenting photographs instead, photographs of faces and not national costumes, this is what the photographer accomplished with his eyes, his mind, his observations, his knowledge and last but not least his considerable photographic ability. Only through studying comparative anatomy can we come to an understanding of nature and the history of the internal organs. In the same way this photographer has practiced comparative anatomy and therefore found a scientific point of view beyond the conventional photographer.[15]

The echoes of nineteenth-century positivism and its Enlightenment antecedents are deafening here, as they are in Sander's own implicit hierarchy of knowledge. The grim master-voice is that of August Comte's systematic and profoundly influential effort to invent sociology (or "social physics," as he initially labeled the new discipline) on the model of the physical sciences, in his *Cours de philosophie positive* of 1830-42.[16]

Physiognomy predates and partially anticipates positivism. A number of social scientific disciplines absorbed physiognomic method as a means of implementing positivist theory during the nineteenth century. This practice continued into the twentieth century and, despite a certain decline in scientific legitimacy, took on an especially charged aspect in the social environment of Weimar Germany. Sander shared the then still common belief — which dated back at least as far as Johann Caspar Lavater's *Physiognomische Fragmente* of 1775-78 — that the body, especially the face and head, bore the outward *signs* of inner character. Lavater himself had first suggested that this "original language of Nature, written on the face of Man" could be deciphered by a rigorous physiognomic *science*.[17] The "science" proceeded by means of an analytic isolation of the anatomic features of the head and face — forehead, eyes, ears, nose, chin, and so on — and the assignment of a significance to each. "Character" was judged through a concatenation of these readings.

Of course Sander never proffered so vigorous a mode of physiognomical interpretation for his photographs. He never suggested that each fragment of facial anatomy be isolated through the kind of pictorial surgery sketched by Lavater and practised by his myriad disciples. I suspect Sander wanted to envelop his project in the legitimating aura of science without violating the aesthetic coherence and semantic ambiguity of the traditional portrait form. Despite his scientistic rhetoric, his portraits never achieve the "precision" and "exactitude" so desired by physiognomists of all stripes. Sander's commitment was, in effect, to a sociologically extended variant of formal portraiture. His scientism is revealed in the ensemble, in the attempt to delineate a social anatomy. More than anything else, physiognomy served as a telling *metaphor* for this project.

The historical trajectories of physiognomy, and of the related practices of phrenology and anthropometrics, are extremely complicated and are consistently interwoven with the history of photographic portraiture. And as was the case with photography, these disciplines gave rise to the same contradictory but connected rationales. These techniques for reading the body's signs seemed to promise both egalitarian and authoritarian results. At the one extreme, the more liberal apologetic promoted the cultivation of a common human understanding of the language of the body: all of humanity was to be both subject and object of this new egalitarian discourse. At the other extreme — and this was certainly the dominant tendency in actual social practice — a specialized way of knowledge was openly harnessed to the new strategies of social channeling and control that characterized the mental asylum, the penitentiary, and eventually the factory employment office. Unlike the egalitarian mode, these latter projects drew an unmistakable line between the professional reader of the body's signs — the psychiatrist, physiologist, criminologist, or industrial psychologist — and the "diseased," "deviant," or "biologically inferior" object of cure, reform, or discipline.

August Sander stood to the liberal side of positivism in his faith in a universal pedagogy. Yet like positivists in general, he was insensitive to the *epistemological* differences between peoples and cultures. Difference would seem to exist only on the surface; all peoples share the same modes of perception and cognition, as well as the same natural bodily codes of expression. For nineteenth-century positivism, anthropological difference became quantitative rather than qualitative. This reduction opened the door to one of the principal justifications of social Darwinism. Inferiority could presumably be measured and located on a continuous calibrated scale. Armed with calipers, scalpel, and camera, scientists sought to prove the absence of a governing intellect in criminals, the insane, women, workers, and nonwhite people.[18] Here again, one lineage stretches back beyond positivism and social Darwinism to the benign figure of Lavater, who proclaimed both the "universality of physiognomic discernments" and defined a "human nature" fundamentally constituted by a variable mixture of "animal, moral, and intellectual life."[19]

But Sander, in contrast to his nineteenth-century predecessors, refused to link his belief in physiognomic science to biological determinism. He organized his portraiture in terms of a social, rather than a racial, typology. As Anne Halley has noted in a perceptive essay on the photographer, herein lay the most immediate difference between Sander's physiognomic project and that of Nazi race "theorists" like Hans F. K. Günther who deployed physiognomic readings of photographic portraits to establish both the biological superiority of the Nordic "race" and the categorical otherness of the Jews.[20] The very universalism of Sander's argument for photographic and physiognomic truth may well have been an indirect and somewhat naive attempt to respond to the racial particularism of the Nazis, which "scientifically" legitimated genocide and imperialism.

The conflict between Sander and National-Socialist *Rassentheorie,* which culminated in the Nazi destruction of the plates for *Antlitz der Zeit* in 1934, is well remembered and celebrated by liberal historians of photography. One is tempted to emphasize a contrast between Sander's "good" physiognomic science and the "bad" physiognomic science of Günther and his ilk, without challenging the positivist underpinnings of both projects. That is, what is less apparent is that Sander, in his "scientific" liberalism, shared aspects of the same general positivist outlook that was incorporated into the fascist project of domination. But in this, Sander was little different from other social democrats of his time. The larger questions that loom here concern the continuities between fascist, liberal capitalist, social democratic, and bureaucratic socialist governments as modes of administration that subject social life to the authority of an institutionalized scientific expertise.[21]

The politics of social democracy, to which Sander subscribed, demand that government be legitimated on the basis of formal representation. Despite the sense of impending collapse, of crisis-level unemployment, and imminent world war conveyed by Sander in his radio speech of 1931, he sustains a curiously inflected faith in the *representativeness* of bourgeois parliamentary government: "The historical image will become even clearer if we join together pictures typical of the many different groups that make up human society. For instance, we might consider a nation's parliament. If we began with the Right Wing and moved across the individual types to the farthest Left, we would already have a partial physiognomic image of the nation."[22] Just as a picture stands for its referent, so parliament stands for a nation. In effect, Sander regards parliament as a picture in itself, a synecdochic sample of the national whole. This conflation of the mythologies of pictorial and political representation may well be fundamental to the public discourse of liberalism. Sander, unlike Bertolt Brecht or the left-wing photomontagist John Heartfield, believed that political relations were evident on the surface of things.[23] Political revelation was a matter of careful sampling for Sander, his project shares the logic of the opinion poll. In this, Sander stands in the mainstream of liberal thinking on the nature of journalism and social documentation; he shares both the epistemology and the politics that accompany bourgeois realism. The deceptively clear waters of this mainstream flow from the confluence of two deep ideological currents. One current defends science as the privileged *representation* of the real, as the ultimate source of social truth. The other current defends parliamentary politics as the *representation* of a pluralistic popular desire, as the ultimate source of social good.

Despite Sander's tendency to collapse politics into a physiognomic typology, he never loses sight of the political arena as one of conflict and struggle. And yet, viewed as a whole, Sander's compendium of portraits from the Weimar period and earlier possess a haunting — and ideologically limiting — synchronicity for the contemporary viewer. One witnesses a kind of false stasis, the appearance of a tense structural equilibrium of social forces. Today, Sander's project suggests a neatly arranged chessboard that was about to be dashed to the floor by brown-shirted thugs. But despite Sander's and Döblin's claims to the contrary, this project was not then and is not now an adequate reading of German social history.

What of an even more ambitious photographic project, one that managed not only to freeze social life but also to render it invisible? I'm thinking here of that celebrated event in American postwar culture, the exhibition *The Family of Man.* Almost thirty years after Sander's radio talk, the photographer Edward Steichen, who was director of the photography department at the Museum of Modern Art, voiced similarly catholic sentiments in an article published in 1960 in *Daedalus,* the journal of the American Academy of Arts and Sciences. Despite the erudite forum, the argument is simplistic, much more so than anything Sander ever claimed. "Long before the birth of a word language the caveman communicated by visual images. The invention of photography gave visual communication its most simple, direct, universal language."[24] Steichen went on to tout the success of his Museum of Modern Art exhibition, *The Family of Man,* which by 1960 had been seen by "some seven million people in the twenty-eight countries." He continued, introducing a crude tautological psychologism into his view of photographic discourse: "The audiences not only understand this visual presentation, they also participate in it, and identify themselves with the images, as if in corroboration of the words of a Japanese poet, 'When you look into a mirror, you do not see your reflection, your reflection sees you.'"[25] Steichen, in this moment of fondness for Zen wisdom, understandably neglected to mention that the Japanese recipients of the exhibition insisted on the inclusion of a large photographic mural depicting the victims of the atomic bombings of Hiroshima and Nagasaki, thus resisting the ahistoricity of the photo essay's argument.

The Family of Man, first exhibited in 1955, may well be the epitome of American cold war liberalism, with Steichen playing cultural attaché to Adlai Stevenson, the would-be good cop of U.S. foreign policy, promoting a benign view of an American world order stabilized by the rule of international law. *The Family of Man* universalizes the bourgeois nuclear family, suggesting a globalized, utopian family album, a family romance imposed on every corner of the earth. The family serves as a metaphor also for a system of international discipline and harmony. In the foreign showings of the exhibition, arranged by the United States Information Agency and cosponsoring corporations like Coca-Cola, the discourse was explicitly that of American multinational capital and government — the new global management team — cloaked in the familiar and musty garb of patriarchy. Nelson Rockefeller, who had served as president of the MoMA board of trustees between 1946 and 1953, delivered a preview address that is revealing in terms of its own father fixation.

Rockefeller began his remarks in an appropriately internationalist vein, suggesting that the exhibition created "a sense of kinship with all mankind." He went on to say that "there is a second message to be read from this profession of Edward Steichen's faith. It demonstrates that the essential unity of human experience, attitude and emotion are perfectly communicable through the medium of pictures. The solicitous eye of the Bantu father, resting upon the son who is learning to throw his primitive spear in search of food, is the eye of every father, whether in Montreal, Paris, or in Tokyo."[26] For Rockefeller, social life begins with fathers teaching sons to survive in a Hobbesian world; all authority can be metaphorically equated with this primary relationship.

A close textual reading of *The Family of Man* would indicate that it moves from the celebration of patriarchal authority —which finds its highest embodiment in the United Nations — to the final construction of an imaginary utopia that resembles nothing so much as a protracted state of infantile, preoedipal bliss. The best-selling book version of the exhibition ends with the following sequence. First, there appears an array of portraits of elderly couples, mostly peasants or farmers from Sicily, Canada, China, Holland, and the United States. The glaring exception in regard to class is a Sander portrait of a wealthy German landowner and his wife. Each

Figure A: August Sander, *Untitled* (Peasant Couple from the Leuscheid) 1931. From series
Menschen und Landschaften (People and Landscapes). Photograph courtesy The Museum
of Modern Art, New York.

picture is captioned with the repeated line from Ovid, "We two form a multitude." From these presumably archetypal parent figures we turn the page to find a large photograph of the United Nations General Assembly, accompanied by the opening phrases of the U.N. Charter. The next page offers a woman's lower body, bedecked in flowers and standing in water. The following five pages contain smaller photographs of children at play throughout the world, ending with W. Eugene Smith's famous photograph of his son and daughter walking from darkness into light in a garden. The final photograph in the book is quite literally a depiction of the oceanic state, a picture by Cedric Wright of churning surf.

A case could also be made for viewing *The Family of Man* as a more-or-less unintentional popularization of the then-dominant school of American sociology, Talcott Parsons's structural functionalism. Parsons's writings on the family celebrate the modern nuclear family as the most advanced and efficient of familiar forms, principally because the nuclear family establishes a clear-cut division of male and female roles. The male function, in this view, is primarily "instrumental" and oriented towards achievement in the public sphere. The female function is primarily "expressive" and restricted to the domestic sphere. Although *The Family of Man* exhibits a great deal of nostalgia for the extended family engaged in self-sufficient agrarian production, the overall flow of the exhibition's loosely knit narrative traces a generalized family biography that adheres to the nuclear model.[27]

The familialism of *The Family of Man* functions both metaphorically and in a quite specific, literal fashion as well. For audiences in the advanced capitalist countries, particularly in the United States, the celebration of the familial sphere as the exclusive arena of all desire and pleasure served to legitimate a family-based consumerism. If nothing else, *The Family of Man* was a massive promotion for family photography, as well as a celebration of the power of the mass media to represent the whole world in familiar and intimate forms.[28]

The Family of Man, originating at the Museum of Modern Art but utilizing a mode of architecturally monumentalized photo-essayistic showmanship, occupies a problematic but ideologically convenient middle position between the conventions of high modernism and those of mass culture. The modernist category of the solitary author was preserved, but at the level of editorship. The exhibition simultaneously suggested a family album, a juried show for photo hobbyists, an apotheosis of *Life* magazine, and the magnum opus in Steichen's illustrious career.

A lot more could be said about *The Family of Man,* particularly about its relation to the domestic sexual politics of the cold war and about its exemplary relation to the changing conventions of advertising and mass-circulation picture magazines in the same period. This will have to wait. My main point here is that *The Family of Man,* more than any other single photographic project, was a massive and ostentatious bureaucratic attempt to *universalize* photographic discourse.

Five hundred and three pictures taken by 273 photographers in 68 countries were chosen from 2 million solicited submissions and organized by a single, illustrious editorial authority into a show that was seen by 9 million citizens in 69 countries in 85 separate exhibitions, and into a book that sold at leat 4 million copies by 1978 — or so go the statistics that pervade all accounts of the exhibition. The exhibition claims to fuse universal subject and universal object in a single moment of visual truth and visual pleasure, a single moment of blissful identity. But this dream rings hollow, especially when we come across the following oxymoronic construction in Carl Sandburg's prologue to the book version of the exhibition: Sandburg describes *The Family of Man* as a "multiplication table of living breathing human faces."[29] Suddenly, arithmetic and humanism collide, forced by poetic license into an absurd harmony. Here, yet again, are the twin ghosts that haunt the practice of photography: the voice of a reifying technocratic objectivism and the redemptive voice of a liberal subjectivism. The statistics that seek to legitimate the exhibition, to demonstrate its value, begin to carry a deeper sense: the truth being promoted here is one of enumeration. This is an aestheticized job of global accounting, a careful cold war effort to bring about the ideological alignment of the neocolonial peripheries with the imperial center. American culture of both elite and mass varieties was being promoted as more universal than that of the Soviet Union.

A brief note on the cultural politics of the cold war might be valuable here. Nelson Rockefeller, who welcomed *The Family of Man* with the characteristic exuberance noted above, was the principal architect of MoMA's International Circulating Exhibitions Program, which received a five-year grant from the Rockefeller Brothers' Fund beginning in 1952. Under the directorship of Porter McCray, this program exhibited American vanguard art abroad, and, in the words of Russell Lynes "let it be known especially in Europe that America was not the cultural backwater that the Russians during that tense period called 'the cold war' were trying to demonstrate that it was."[30] Eva Cockcroft has convincingly shown that this nongovernmental sponsorship was closely allied with CIA efforts to promote American high culture abroad while circumventing the McCarthyist probings of right-wing congressmen who, for example, saw Abstract Expressionism as a manifestation of the international communist conspiracy.[31] But since the formal rhetoric of *The Family of Man* was that of photo-journalistic realism, no antagonism of this sort developed; and although a number of the photographers who contributed pictures to the exhibition were or had been affiliated with left parties or causes, Steichen himself, the grand author of this massive photo essay, was above suspicion. Thus *The Family of Man* was directly sponsored by the USIA, and openly embraced by the cosponsoring corporations as a valuable marketing and public relations tool. The exhibition was intended to have an immense *popular* appeal, and was more extensively circulated than any other MoMA production. Even medium-sized cities in the United States, Canada, Europe, Australia, Japan, and the Third World received the show. For example, in India it turned up in Bombay, Arga, New Delhi, Ahmedabad, Calcutta, Madras, and Trivandrum. In South Africa *The Family of Man* traveled to Johannesburg, Capetown, Durban, Pretoria, Windhoek (Southwest Africa), Port Elizabeth, and Uitenboge. In domestic showings in New York State alone, the original MoMA exhibition was followed by appearances in Utica, Corning, Rochester, and Binghamton. Shades of American television, but with higher pretensions.

From my reading of the records of foreign showings, it seems clear that the *The Family of Man* tended to appear in political "hot spots" throughout the Third World. I quote from a United States Information Agency memo concerning the exhibition in Djakarta in 1962: "The exhibition proved to have wide appeal . . . in spite of the fact that . . . the period coincided with a circus sponsored by the Soviet Union, complete with a performing bear. The exhibit was opened with a reception to which members of the most important target groups in Djakarta were invited."[32]

In a more lyrical vein, Steichen recalled the Guatemala City showing in his autobiography, *A Life in Photography:*

> A notable experience was reported in Guatemala. On the final day of the exhibition, a Sunday, several thousand Indians from the hills of Guatemala came on foot or muleback to see it. An American visitor said it was like a religious experience to see

> these barefoot country people who could not read
> or write walk silently through the exhibition
> gravely studying each picture with rapt attention.
>
> Regardless of the place, the response was
> always the same . . . the people in the audience
> looked at the pictures and the people in the pic-
> tures looked back at them. They recognized each
> other.[33]

At the risk of boring some readers with more statistics, allow me to
recall that in 1954, only fourteen months earlier, the United States
directly supported a coup in Guatemala, overthrowing the demo-
cratically elected Government of Jacobo Arbenz, who had received
72 percent of the popular vote in the 1950 elections. American
pilots flew bombing missions during the coup. When Arbenz took
office, 98 percent of the land in Guatemala was owned by 142 people, with corporations counted as individuals. Arbenz nationalized
200,000 acres of unused United Fruit Company land, agreeing to
pay for the land with twenty-five-year bonds, rather than engaging
in outright expropriation. In establishing the terms of payment, the
Guatemalan government accepted the United Fruit valuation of
the land at $600,000, which had been claimed for tax purposes.
Suddenly United Fruit claimed that the disputed land was worth
$16 million, and approached the U.S. State Department for assist-
ance. Secretary of State John Foster Dulles, who was both a United Fruit stockholder and a former legal counsel to the firm, touted
the successful invasion and coup as a "new and glorious chapter in
the already great tradition of the American States."[34] Following the
coup the U.S.-sponsored dicatorship of Colonel Castillo Armas
dismantled agrarian reform and disenfranchised the 70 percent of
the population that could, in Steichen's words, "neither read nor
write." In this context, "visual literacy" takes on a grim meaning.

Finally, my last exhibit concerning this cold war extrava-
ganza: a corporate commentary on the showing of *The Family of
Man* in Johannesburg in 1958 attempted to link the universalism of
the exhibition to the global authority of the commodity: "At the
entrance of the hall the large globe of the world encircled by bottles
of Coca-Cola created a most attractive eye catching display and
identified our product with *Family of Man* sponsorship."[35] And
thus an orbiting soft drink answered the technological challenge of
sputnik. *The Family of Man* worked to make a bottled mixture of
sugar, water, caramel color, and caffeine "humanly interesting" —
to recall Steichen's expressed ambition for his advertising work of

the late 1920s and 1930s. In the political landscape of apartheid, characterized by a brutal racial hierarchy of caloric intake and forced separation of black African families, sugar and familial sentiment were made to commingle in the imagination.

Clearly, both the sexual and international politics of *The Family of Man* are especially interesting today, in light of the headlong return of American politics to the familialism and interventionism of a new cold war, both domestic and international in scope. *The Family of Man* is a virtual guidebook to the collapse of the political into the familial that so characterizes the dominant ideological discourse of the contemporary United States. In a sense, *The Family of Man* provides a blueprint of sorts for more recent political theater; I'm thinking here of the orchestrations of the Vietnam POW "homecoming" and the return of the American hostages from Iran. It would be a mistake, however, not to realize that *The Family of Man* eschewed the bellicosity and racism that accompanies these latter dramas; in this, it represented the limit of an official *liberal* discourse in the cold war era.[36] The peaceful world envisioned by *The Family of Man* is merely a smoothly functioning international market economy, in which economic bonds have been translated into spurious sentimental ties, and in which the overt racism appropriate to earlier forms of colonial enterprise has been supplanted by the "humanization of the other" so central to the discourse of neocolonialism.[37]

Again, what are we to make of the argument that photography constitutes a universal language? Implicit in this claim is the suggestion that photography acts as a miraculous universal solvent upon the linguistic barriers between peoples. Visual culture, having been pushed to an unprecedented level of technical refinement, loses specificity, cultural difference is cancelled, and a "common language" prevails on a global scale. Paradoxically, a medium that is seen as subtly responsive to the minutest details of time and place delivers these details through an unacknowledged, naturalized, epistemological grid. As the myth of a universal photographic language would have it, photography is more natural than natural language, touching on a common, underlying system of desire and understanding closely tied to the senses. Photography would seem to be a way of *knowing* the world directly — this is the scientistic aspect of our faith in the powers of the photographic image. But photography would also seem to be a way of *feeling* the world directly, with a kind of prelinguistic, affective openness of the visual sense — this is the aestheticist aspect of our faith in the medium. As a symbolic practice, then, photography constitutes not a universal language but a paradoxical yoking of a primitivist, Rousseauian dream, the dream of romantic naturalism, with an unbounded faith in a technological imperative. The worldliness of photography is the outcome, not of any immanent universality of meaning, but of a project of global domination. The language of the imperial centers is imposed, both forcefully and seductively, upon the peripheries.

III. Universal Equivalent

Photography was dreamed of and slowly invented under the shadow of a fading European aristocracy; it became practical and profitable in the period of the continental European revolutions of 1848, the period in which class struggle first took the clear form of an explosive political confrontation between bourgeoisie and urban proletariat waged against the conflict-ridden backdrop of everyday industrial production. Photography proliferated, becoming reproducible and accessible in the modern sense, during the late nineteenth-century period of transition from competitive capitalism to the financially and industrially consolidated monopoly form of capitalist organization. By the turn of the century, then, photography stood ready to play a central role in the development of a culture centered on the mass marketing of mass-produced commodities.

Perhaps more than any other single technical invention of the mid nineteenth century, photography came to focus the confidence and fears of an ascendant industrial bourgeoisie. This essay is an attempt to understand the contradictory role played by photography within the culture dominated by that class. As we have seen briefly and will see again, this role combined a coldly rational scientism with a sentimental and often antirational pursuit of the beautiful.

But my argument here seeks to avoid simple deterministic conclusions: to suggest that the practice of photography is entirely and inseparably bound by capitalist social relations would be reductive and undialectical in the extreme. As a social practice photography is no more a "reflection" of capitalist society than a particular photograph is a "reflection" of its referential object. Conversely, photography is not a neutral semiotic technique, transparently open to both "reactionary" and "progressive" uses. The issue is much more complicated than either extreme would have us believe. Although I want to argue here that photography is fundamentally related in its normative way of depicting the world to an epistemology and an aesthetics that are intrinsic to a system of commodity exchange, as I've suggested before, photography also needs to be understood as a simultaneous *threat* and *promise* in its relation to the prevailing cultural ambitions of a triumphant but wary western bourgeoisie of the mid nineteenth century. The historical context was one of crisis and paradox; to forget this is to risk achieving an overly harmonized understanding of the contradictory material and symbolic forces at work in the development of bourgeois culture.

With this warning in mind, I'd like to turn to an extraordinary text written by the American physician, essayist, and poet, Oliver Wendell Holmes, published in 1859 in the *Atlantic Monthly.* Holmes is in many senses an exemplary, even if unique, figure in nineteenth-century New England culture. Furthermore, he embodies the oscillating movement between scientism and aestheticism that so pervades the discourse of photography. Holmes was both a practical man of science — an advocate of positivism — and a genteel man of letters — the archetypal Boston Brahmin, Autocrat, Poet, and Professor of the Breakfast Table. He was a founding member of the American Medical Association and, in company with Emerson, Lowell, and Longfellow, a founder of the *Atlantic Monthly.* Characteristically, Holmes's writing veers between surgical metaphors and allusions to the classics. Perhaps there was no American writer who was better prepared, both rhetorically and ideologically, to envelop photography in the web of Culture.

Holmes's essay "The Stereoscope and the Stereograph" was one of many optimistic early attempts to both philosophize and prognosticate about photography. Significantly, English and American physicians seem to have been prominent in voicing unqualified enthusiasm for the powers of the camera. Holmes, however, goes to hyperbolic extremes. Citing Democritus, he suggests that photography establishes a means of capturing the visual effluvia that are continuously "shed from the surface of solids."[38] Arguing, as was common at the time, that photographs are products of the sun's artistry, he coins the phrase "mirror with a memory,"[39] thereby implying that the camera is a wholly passive, reflective, technical apparatus. In this view nature reproduces itself. Thus, while Holmes casually prefaces his discussion of photography with a mention of the railroad, the telegraph, and chloroform, it would seem that photography constitutes a uniquely privileged technical invention in its refusal or inability to dominate or transform the realm of nature. Photography would seem to offer an inherently preservationist approach to nature. So far, there is nothing in Holmes's argument that is not relatively common to what is by now the thoroughly institutionalized discourse of photographic naturalism.

But the essay takes a rather bizarre turn as Holmes ventures to speculate about the future of photography in a conclusion that seems rather prototypical of science fiction, even if entirely dead-pan in its apocalyptic humor: *"Form is henceforth divorced from matter.* In fact, matter as a visible object is of no great use any longer, except as the mould on which form is shaped. Give us a few negatives of a thing worth seeing, taken from different points of view, and that is all we want of it. Pull it down or burn it up, if you please."[40] [Holmes's italics] Perhaps it is important to interject that Holmes is discussing the stereograph apparatus, the most effective of nineteenth-century illusionistic machineries in its ability to reconstruct binocular vision and thus offer a potent sensation of three-dimensional depth. (Holmes invented a hand-held stereo viewer and was an avid collector of stereo views.)

Also, like the diorama and the lantern-slide show, the stereoscope delivered a total visual experience: immersed within the field of the illusion, eyes virtually riveted to the sockets of the machine, the viewer lost all sense of the pasteboard or glass material substrate of the image. Despite the slight discomfort caused by the weight of the machine, the experience was one of disembodied vision, vision lacking the illusion shattering boundary of a frame. Thus the stereo process was particularly liable to give rise to a belief in dematerialized form.

Would it be absurd for me to suggest that Holmes is describing something analogous to the capitalist exchange process, whereby exchange values are detached from, and exist independently of, the use values of commodities? The dominant metaphor in Holmes's discussion is that of bourgeois political economy; just as use value is eclipsed by exchange value, so the photographic sign comes to eclipse its referent. For Holmes, quite explicitly, the photograph is akin to money. The parallel with political economy becomes even more apparent as Holmes continues: "Matter in large masses must always be fixed and dear: form is cheap and transportable. We have got hold of the fruit of creation now, and need not trouble ourselves with the core. Every conceivable object of Nature and Art will soon scale off its surface for us."[41]

But we are not simply talking about a global political economy of signs, we are also invited to imagine an epistemological treasure trove, an encyclopedia organized according to a global hierarchy of knowledge and power. Diderot's ghost animates Holmes's Yankee enthusiasm: "The time will come when a man who wishes to see any object, natural or artificial, will go to the Imperial, National, or City Stereographic Library and call for its skin or form, as he would for a book at any common library."[42] How prophetic and typical that an American, writing in an aggressively expanding republic, should invoke the fictitious authority of empire in his vision of the future. Finally, Holmes gets down to brass tacks: "Already a workman has been traveling about the country with stereographic views of furniture, showing his employer's patterns in this way, and taking orders for them. This is a mere hint of what is coming before long."[43] (In fact, by 1850, traveling clock salesmen are known to have carried boxes of daguerreotypes illustrating their line of products.) Holmes's vision of an expanded system of photographic advertising leads to a direct appeal for an expanded economy of images: "And as a means of facilitating the formation of public and private stereographic collections, there must be arranged a comprehensive system of exchanges, so that there might grow up something like a universal currency of these banknotes, on promises to pay in solid substance, which the sun has engraved for the great Bank of Nature."[44] Note that Holmes, true to the logic of commodity fetishism, finds the origin of this moneylike aspect of the photograph, not in human labor, but in a direct "miraculous" agency of Nature. Recall Marx's crucial definition of the commodity fetish, first published in 1867, in the first volume of *Capital:*

> The definite social relation between men themselves . . . assumes here, for them, the fantastic form of a relation between things. In order, therefore, to find an analogy we must take flight into the misty realm of religion. There the products of the human brain appear as autonomous figures endowed with a life of their own, which enter into relations both with each other and with the human race. So it is in the world of commodities with the products of men's hands. I call this the fetishism which attaches itself to the products of labour as soon as they are produced as commodities, and is therefore inseparable from the production of commodities.[45]

For Holmes, photographs stand as the "universal equivalent," capable of denoting the quantitative exchangeability of all sights. Just as money is the universal gauge of exchange value, uniting all the world goods in a single system of transactions, so photographs are imagined to reduce all sights to relations of formal equivalence. Here, I think, lies one major aspect of the origins of the pervasive formalism that haunts the visual arts of the bourgeois epoch. Formalism collects all the world's images in a single aesthetic emporium, tearing them from all contingencies of origin, meaning, and use. Holmes is dreaming of this transcendental aesthetic closure, while also entertaining a pragmatic faith in the photograph as a transparent gauge of the real. Like money, the photograph is both a fetishized end in itself and a calibrated signifier of a value that resides elsewhere, both autonomous and bound to its referential function:

> To render comparison of similar objects, or of any that we may wish to see side by side, easy, there should be a stereographic *metre* or fixed standard of focal length for the camera lens . . . . In this way the eye can make the most rapid and exact comparisons. If the "great elm" and Cowthorpe Oak, the State-House and Saint Peter's were taken on the same scale, and looked at with the same magnifying power, we should compare them without the possibility of being misled by those partialities which might make us tend to overrate the indigenous vegetable and the dome of our native Michel Angelo.[46]

In what may be a typically American fashion, Holmes seems to be confusing quantity with quality, even in modestly suggesting the inferiorities of the American natural and architectural landscape. More generally, Holmes shares the pervasive faith in the mathematical truth of the camera.

Oliver Wendell Holmes, like most other promoters of photography, manages to establish a false discursive unity, shifting schizophrenically from instrumentalism to aestheticism, from Yankee pragmatism and empiricism to a rather sloppy romanticism, thus recalling that other related incongruity, Ralph Waldo Emerson's linkage of the "natural fact" and the "spiritual fact."[47] The ideological custodians of photography are forced periodically to switch hats, to move from positivist to metaphysician with the turn of a phrase. It is the metaphysician who respiritualizes the rationalized project of photographic representation. Thus Holmes in a later essay on photography, speaks of carte-de-visite portraits as "the

sentimental 'greenbacks' of civilization."[48] All of this is evidence of
a society in which economic relations appear, as Marx put it, "as
material relations between persons and social relations between
things."[49] Holmes ends his earlier essay with an appropriately ideal-
ist inversion of the Promethean myth: "a new epoch in the history
of human progress dates from the time when He . . . took a pencil
of fire from the hand of the 'angel standing in the sun' and placed it
in the hands of a mortal."[50] So much for bourgeois humanism:
Prometheus is no longer an arrogant rebel but a grateful recipient
of divine favors. And so technical progress is reconciled with theology. Photography, as it was thus conceived in mid nineteenth-
century America, was the vocation of pious accountants.

IV. Conclusion

A final anecdote to end this essay, much too long already.
Crossing this cavernous main floor of New York's Grand Central
Station recently, I looked up to see the latest installment in a thirty-
odd year series of monumental, back-illuminated dye-transfer
transparencies; a picture, taken low to the wet earth of rural Ireland, a lush vegetable apparition of landscape and cottage was
suspended above this gloomy urban terminal for human traffic.
With this image — seemingly bigger and more illusionistic, even in
its stillness, than Cinerama — everything that is absent it made
present. Above: stillness, home, hearth, the soil, the remote old
country for many travelers, an affordable or unaffordable vacation
spot for others, a seductive sight for eyes that must strain hurriedly
in the gloom to read timetables. Below: the city, a site for the
purposeful flow of bodies. Accompanying this giant photograph, a
caption read, as nearly as I can remember: "PHOTOGRAPHY:
THE UNIVERSAL LANGUAGE/EASTMAN KODAK
1880-1980."

And what of the universality of this name, Kodak, unknown to any language until coined in 1888 by George Eastman,
inventor of roll film, pioneer in horizontal and vertical corporate
integration, in the global mass-marketing of consumer goods?
Eastman offered this etymological explanation in 1924 in *American
Photography:* "Philologically, therefore, the word 'kodak' is as
meaningless as a child's first 'goo.' Terse, abrupt to the point of
rudeness, literally bitten off by firm unyielding consonants at both
ends, it snaps like a camera shutter in your face. What more could
one ask?"[51] And so we are introduced to a "language" that is

Figure B: Installation detail from the exhibition *Family of Man,* organized by Edward Steichen at the Museum of Modern Art, New York, 1955. Exhibition design by Paul Rudolph. Photograph by Ezra Stoller, courtesy The Museum of Modern Art, New York.

primitive, infantile, aggressive — the imaginary discourse of the machine. The crucial question remains to be asked: can photography be anything else?

Notes

[1]An earlier, shorter version of this essay was published in the *Australian Photography Conference Papers,* Melbourne, 1980. I'm grateful to the editors of the *Working Papers on Photography,* Euan McGillvray and Matthew Nickson, for the opportunity to present the preliminary version there.

[2]In 1790, Kant separated knowledge and pleasure in a way that fully anticipated the bastard status of photography: "If art which is adequate to the *cognition* of a possible object performs the actions requisite therefore merely in order to make it actual, it is *mechanical* art; but if it has as its immediate design the feeling of pleasure, it is called *aesthetical* art." Immanuel Kant, *Critique of Judgement,* trans. J. H. Bernard, New York, 1951, p. 148.

A number of texts seem relevant to the question of photographer as mere "appendage to the machine." Of specific importance is Bernard Edelman's *Ownership of the Image: Elements for a Marxist Theory of Law,* London, 1979. Less directly related, but valuable are Harry Braverman's *Labor and Monopoly Capital,* New York, 1974, Alfred Sohn-Rethel's *Intellectual and Manual Labor,* London, 1978, and an essay by Raymond Williams, "The Romantic Artist," in *Culture and Society,* New York, 1958, pp. 30-48.

[3]I am grateful to Sally Stein for discussions about the relation between scientific management and the development of a mechanized visual culture in the early twentieth century, and especially for showing me an unpublished essay written in 1980 on this issue, "The Graphic Ordering of Desire: Modernization of *The Ladies' Home Journal,* 1914-1939." Her criticisms and support were very important. Also, Bruce Kaiper, deserves thanks for a lucid essay, "The Human Object and Its Capitalist Image," *Left Curve,* no. 5, 1976, pp. 40-60, and for a number of conversations on this subject.

[4]For an earlier discussion of the relation between symbolist and realist photography see my "On the Invention of Photographic Meaning," *Artforum,* XIII, no. 5, 1975, pp. 36-45.

[5]A useful introduction to some of the cultural implications of an international capitalist economy can be found in Samir Amin's "In Praise of Socialism," in *Imperialism and Unequal Development,* New York, 1977, pp. 73-85. In this connection, a recent and perhaps sardonic remark by Harold Rosenberg comes to mind: "Today, all modes of visual excitation, from Benin idols to East Indian chintz, are both contemporaneous and American." (Harold Rosenberg, "The Problem of Reality," in *American Civilization: A Portrait from the Twentieth Century,* ed. Daniel J. Boorstin, London, 1972, p. 305).

[6]See Richard Rudisill, *Mirror Image: The Influence of the Daguerreotype on American Society,* Albuquerque, 1971, p. 201.

[7]"The Daguerreolite," *The Daily Chronicle* (Cincinnati), 17 January 1840, 2, quoted in Rudisill, *Mirror Image,* p. 54.

[8]See Helmut and Alison Gernsheim, *L. J. M. Daguerre: The History of the Diorama and the Daguerreotype,* New York, 1968, pp. 88, 99.

⁹François Arago, "Report," in Josef Maria Eder, *History of Photography,* trans. Edward Epstean, New York, 1945, p. 235. The earliest English translation of this address appears in L. J. M. Daguerre, *A Historial and Descriptive Account of the Daguerreotype and the Diorama,* London, 1839.

¹⁰Arago, "Report," pp. 234-35.

¹¹Edward Said, *Orientalism,* New York, 1978.

¹²August Sander, "Photography as a Universal Language," trans. Anne Halley, *Massachusetts Review,* XIX, no. 4, 1978, pp. 674-75.

¹³*Ibid.,* p. 675.

¹⁴*Ibid.,* p. 679.

¹⁵Alfred Döblin, "About Faces, Portraits, and Their Reality: Introduction to August Sander, *Antlitz der Zeit"* (1929), in *Germany: The New Photography, 1927-33,* ed. David Mellor, London, 1978, p. 58.

¹⁶August Comte, *Cours de philosophie positive* (1830-42) in *August Comte and Positivism: The Essential Writings,* ed. Gertrud Lenzer, New York, 1975. Lenzer's introduction is especially valuable.

¹⁷Johann Caspar Lavater, *Essays on Physiognomy,* trans. Henry Hunter, London, 1792, I, preface, n. p. This is the first English translation of *Physiognomische Fragmente, zur Beförderung der Menschenkenntniss und Menschenliebe,* Leipzig and Winterhur, 1775-78.

¹⁸I am preparing an essay that deals with the relation between physiognomy and instrumental realism in much greater detail. Much of this work revolves around a study of the two principal schools of late nineteenth-century European criminology, the Positivist School of the Italian forensic psychiatrist Cesare Lombroso and the Statistical School of the French police official Alphonse Bertillon. Lombroso advanced the profoundly racist and long-lived notion of an atavistic criminal *type,* while Bertillon, applying the social statistics developed by the Belgian statistician Adolphe Quételet in the 1820s and 1830s, sought to identify absolutely the criminal "individuality." Bertillon's method of police identification, which linked a series of anthropometric measurements to a photographic *portrait parlé,* or "speaking likeness," was the first "scientific" system of police intelligence. Perhaps the most striking example of the quantification inherent in these searches for the absolute, objective truth of the incarcerated body is found, not in criminological literature, but in the related field of medical psychiatry.

I would like to cite one example to emphasize the nature of this thinking. Hugh Welch Diamond, a minor English psychiatrist and founding member of the genteel Photographic Society, attempted to use photographic portraits of patients in the Surrey Country Women's Asylum for empirical research, therapy, and surveillance of the inmate population. Diamond read a paper on his work to the Royal Society in 1856. "The photographer, on the other hand, needs in many cases no aid from any language of his own, but prefers rather to listen, with the pictures before him, to the silent but telling language of nature . . . the picture speaks for itself with the most marked pression and indicates the *exact* point which has been reached in the *scale* of unhappiness between the first sensation and its utmost height. [Italics mine. Hugh W. Diamond, "On the Application of Photography to the Physiognomic and Mental Phenomena of Insanity" in *The Face of Madness: Hugh W. Diamond and the Origin of Psychiatric Photography,* ed. Sander L. Gilman, Secaucus, N.J., 1977, p. 19.]

I have found the work of Michel Foucault particularly valuable in considering these issues, especially his *Discipline and Punish: The Birth of the Prison,* New York, 1977. My interest in this area began in conversations with Martha Rosler; her video "opera" *Vital Statistics of A Citizen, Simply Obtained* (1976) is an exemplary study of the power of measurement science over the body, with a feminist inflection that is absent in the work of Foucault.

[19]Lavater, *Essays on Physiognomy,* p. 13.

[20]Anne Halley, "August Sander." *Massachusetts Review,* XIX, no. 4, 1978, pp. 663-73. See also Robert Kramer, "Historical Commentary," in *August Sander: Photographs of an Epoch,* Philadelphia, 1980, pp. 11-38, for a discussion of Sander's relation to physiognomic traditions.

[21]Fascist ideology is overtly metaphysical in character, depending in large measure on cults of racial and national superiority and on the ostentatious display of charismatic authority. Nevertheless, the actual functioning of the fascist corporate state demands the sub rosa exercise of a bureaucratic rationalism that is profoundly rooted in positivist notions of the commanding role of science and of technical elites. Nazi ideologues felt the need, in fact, to legitimate the führer cult scientifically. One text in particular is relevant to our discussion of Sander and physiognomy. Alfred Richter in his *Unser Führer im Lichte der Rassenfrage und Charakterologie,* Leipzig, 1933, sought to demonstrate the racial ideality and innate political genius of Adolf Hitler and the host of top party officials by means of handsomely lit formal portraits that were accompanied by flattering physiognomical analyses. This research-project-cum-souvenir-album provides unintended evidence that the seemingly charismatic authority of the fascist leader has the quality of an apparition, an Oz-like aspect that requires amplification through the media and legitimation through an appeal to the larger, abstract authority of Science. In this light, Hitler shines as the embodiment of a racial principle. In its assault on parliamentary pluralism, fascist government portrays itself not only as a means of national salvation but as the organic *expression* of a nonrational, biologically driven will to domination.

[22]Sander, "Photography as a Universal Language," p. 678.

[23]Walter Benjamin in "A Short History of Photography," [1931], trans. Stanley Mitchell, *Screen,* XIII, Spring 1972, p. 24, quotes a very explicit and often-cited statement by Brecht in this regard: "For, says Brecht, the situation is 'complicated by the fact that less than at any time does a simple *reproduction* of *reality* tell us anything about reality. A photograph of the Krupp works or GEC yields almost nothing about these institutions. Reality proper has slipped into the functional. The reification of human relationships, the factory, let's say, no longer reveals these relationships. Therefore something has actually to be *constructed*, something artificial, something set up.'"

One could argue that even the *assemblage* of portraits pursued by Sander merely reproduces the logic of assigned individual places, and thus of reification.

[24]Edward Steichen, "On Photography," reprinted in Nathan Lyons, ed., *Photographers on Photography,* Englewood Cliffs, N.J., 1966, p. 107.

[25]*Ibid.*

[26]Nelson Rockefeller, "Preview Address: 'The Family of Man,'" *U.S. Camera 1956,* ed. Tom Maloney, New York, 1955, p. 18. I'm grateful to Alex Sweetman for calling my attention to this article.

[27]See Talcott Parsons et al., *Family, Socialization, and Interaction Progress,* New York, 1955, and the critique provided in Mark Poster, *Critical Theory of the Family,* New York, 1978, pp. 78-84. Barbara Ehrenreich and Deirdre English, *For Her Own Good: 150 Years of Experts' Advice to Women,* New York, 1978, are excellent on the issue of familial ideology in the postwar period.

[28]Russell Lynes presents evidence that Steichen's appointment to the position of director of the MoMA department of photography in 1947 involved an unsuccessful plan to bring direct funding from photographic corporations into the museum. Although unsurprising today, in an era of direct corporate funding, this was a novel move in the late 1940s. Russell Lynes, *Good Old Modern,* New York, 1973, pp. 259-60.

[29]Carl Sandburg, "Prologue," *The Family of Man,* New York, 1955.

[30]Lynes, *Good Old Modern,* p. 233.

[31]Eva Cockcroft, "Abstract Expressionism, Weapon of the Cold War," *Artforum,* XII, no. 10, 1974, pp. 39-41. See also Max Kozloff, "American Painting During the Cold War," *Artforum,* XI, no. 9, 1973, pp. 43-54; William Hauptman, "The Suppression of Art in the McCarthy Decade," *Artforum,* XII, no. 2, 1973, pp. 48-52. Of general interest is Christopher Lasch's "The Cultural Cold War: A Short History of the Congress for Cultural Freedom," in *Towards a New Past: Dissenting Essays in American History,* ed. Barton Bernstein, New York, 1969, pp. 322-59. It is interesting, if not terribly relevant to my present argument, to note that Harry Lunn, currently (in 1981) regarded as the biggest photographic dealer in the U.S., was a principal agent in the CIA's infiltration of the National Student Association in the 1950s and 1960s, according to Sol Stern, "NSA and the CIA, A Short Account of International Student Politics and the Cold War," *Ramparts,* V, no. 9, March 1967, p. 33.

[32]United States Information Agency memo, subject "Djakarta showing of *Family of Man,"* February 1962. A copy of this memo is in the files of the International Council Office of MoMA.

[33]Edward Steichen, *A Life in Photography,* New York, 1962, n. p.

[34]Department of State White Paper, *Intervention of International Communism in Guatemala.* 1954, p. 33, quoted in David Horowitz, *Free World Colossus,* New York, 1965, p. 160. My summary of events in Guatemala is taken largely from Felix Green, *The Enemy,* New York, 1971, pp. 196-98. with some references to Horowitz, pp. 160-81.

[35]*Coca-Cola Overseas,* December 1958, p. 15.

[36]Writing in *Commentary* in 1955, the conservative critic, Hilton Kramer, attacked *The Family of Man* for displaying liberal naïveté in an era of harsh political realities, claiming that the exhibition was "a reassertion in visual terms of all that has been discredited in progressive ideology." Hilton Kramer, "Exhibiting the Family of Man," *Commentary,* XX, no. 5, October 1955.

[37]For further criticism of *The Family of Man* from the political left see Roland Barthes, "The Great Family of Man," in *Mythologies,* trans. Annette Lavers, New York, 1972, pp. 100-02. I also found an unpublished English translation of an essay by Edmundo Desnoes, "The Photographic Image of Underdevelopment" (translator unknown) extremely valuable. This essay appeared in Spanish in *Punto de Vista,* Havana, 1967.

[38]Oliver Wendell Holmes, "The Stereoscope and the Stereograph," *Atlantic Monthly,* III, no. 20, June 1859, p. 738. My attention was directed to this essay by an insightful article by Harvey Green, "'Pasteboard Masks,' the Stereograph in American Culture, 1865-1910," in Edward W. Earle, ed. *Points of View: The Stereograph in America — A Cultural History,* Rochester, N.Y., 1979, p. 109.

[39]Holmes, "Stereoscope," p. 739.

[40]*Ibid.,* p. 747.

[41]*Ibid.,* p. 748.

[42]*Ibid.*

[43]*Ibid.*

[44]*Ibid.*

[45]Karl Marx, *Capital,* trans. Ben Fowkes, New York, 1977, I, p. 165.

[46]Holmes, "Stereoscope," p. 748.

[47]Ralph Waldo Emerson, "Nature," *The Collected Works of Ralph Waldo Emerson,* I, Cambridge, 1971, p. 18.

[48]Oliver Wendell Holmes, "Doings of the Sunbeam," *Atlantic Monthly,* XIII, no. 49, July 1863, p. 8.

[49]Marx, *Capital,* I, p. 166.

[50]Holmes, "Stereoscope," p. 748.

[51]George Eastman, quoted in J. M. Eder, *History of Photography,* trans. E. Epstean, New York, 1945, p. 489.

After Allan Sekula:

Audience:
As a curator, I would like to say that it's very easy to attack the *Family of Man* show . . . Can you explain why it is still a best-selling catalogue twenty years later? Is photography itself an impe-rialistic art form or is the publishing industry, the museum for example, and so on, responsible?

Allan Sekula:
Well, I think there are features of photography that are inherently tied to a logic of domination — and a logic of a kind of conflation of abstraction and representation — that I think have profoundly dominating implications. I think that leads us to a whole set of problems about technological determinism, about the extent to which we can call a form or particular technology inherently tied to certain politics. The dominant tendency, of course, is to see tech-nology as neutral. I don't think that's true. I think specific forms of technology develop out of specific political contexts and demands. And the proliferation of photography can't be disassociated from the development of specific kinds of power. The extent to which a certain kind of realism is institutionalized in socialist countries is also an indication of the extent to which positivism is the dominant theory of knowledge in those countries.

As for *Family of Man*, yes in some ways it is a very easy target and at this point because the dominant discourse in American photography and western European photography and other pho-tographies as well in the developed capitalist countries is one of auteurism — it's an easy show to discredit in those terms. You know, to see it as a kind of arrogant editorial project and many photographers resent that show. At the same time it is — I confess to a kind of crude thinking and wearing heavy boots in terms of talking about this exhibition, but I think that the cultural history of the 50's is both misunderstood and important to understand at this point, in the United States. That's one reason why I wanted to deal with it. I have long felt the inadequacy of some of the critical readings of *Family of Man* that have come from the left. The short essay by Roland Barthes is illuminating in many ways, but I think there is more to be said. There is also an essay by a Cuban critic and novelist Edmondo Desnoyez, published in a book called *Punte de Vista*, which has some interesting arguments about that exhibition.

I think that Steichen is an incredibly important ideological figure or character in the history of photography, because he embodies this false unification of mass culture and high culture. You know, he is someone who has both a career as an avant-gardist, as a man who made so called 'master prints', and as someone who easily negotiated a rather luminous spot for himself in the cultural industry working for Vogue and Condé-Nast publications. And aside from my own sort of desire to attack someone like Steichen which I am perfectly willing to own up to, I think he is an important target because he embodies a certain mythology to the extent that this culture does encode its cultural myths in a personality. We have to deconstruct that personality, that appearance.

Audience:
What then would you propose as an ideologically correct use of the photographic medium? What work or what artist or what photographer?

Allan Sekula:
I am not going to do that. (laughter) I am not saying that to be abusive to the question. There are some models for work which begins to interrogate the dominant forms — I think of the work of Heartfield for example. But at the same time there are incredible limits to Heartfield. And I have found that I have looked more to cinema for models. In some ways the problem is not to make a new kind of photography, but to re-examine how we constitute photography as an object of critical speculation. And then move to the problem of a kind of work which may well be hybridized.

So I could say that I tend to be sympathetic to work which — as a recent exhibition in Germany was titled "Renounces The Single Image" — renounces what I think is the fetish of the single image, and bases itself on principles of montage, either relational sets of images, or images and text or images and gestures. You know, kind of theatrical use of imagery. But I think that's very open and there's a kind of experimentation going on in various places in Great Britain, in Germany and the U.S. But it's all very marginal stuff.

I mean I could name collaborations. I could name projects. But one reason that I resist that is because of a kind of nominalism that people in the visual arts have, where they — particularly in photography, where there is not a heavy theoretical apparatus. People want to know your list of names — you know — you've got some good names — you've got some bad names. What's the good list.

And I would like to sort of resist that to some extent.

Audience:
I feel that we are looking at these photographs from a 1980's viewpoint and that you are commenting on them from a 1950's viewpoint, that they meant something different in the 50's than what they do now.

Allan Sekula:
Well, of course, the meaning shifts historically, and also the project of the historian is very much to write history from the problematics of the present. I mean I wouldn't go on about this if it weren't for certain tendencies in American culture today. — Both intrinsic to the sphere of art and larger than that.

Audience:
May I ask a last question. Do you know how this project, the *Family of Man* started? Do you know who was in charge of it? Do you know all the mechanics of it? Because it seems to me that you are talking about Sandburg and Steichen, who had been very well known as a duo in the United States since 1941, I think, when they organized the show called the *Road to Victory* at the Museum of Modern Art. Did they get a new assignment during the 50's in order to promote the cold war?

Allan Sekula:
I think that in a way Steichen's affiliation with the centres of cultural power in the U.S. was so almost organic, in a sense, that there were just tacit assumptions that certain projects were ennobling. The business of the *Road to Victory* and the various wartime exhibitions as well as the book of the Blue Ghost — I think it is a combination of factors. One is entrepreneurial, a kind of bureaucratic entrepreneurial behaviour, in that Steichen had a collaboration throughout the late 40's with a man named Tom Mahoney who was the editor of a magazine called *The U.S. Camera*, which was a marketing magazine which produced rather handsome portfolios of photographic prints and yearly annuals which Steichen was a judge for. And at that point, of course, Steichen was a star, essentially; he was a celebrity. Like Margaret Bourke-White he was almost a Hollywood persona. And according to Russell Lynes, Tom Mahoney proposed to the Board of Trustees at the Museum

of Modern Art that Steichen be brought into the museum in 1947 with direct corporate backing. And that corporate backing would be monies from the various photographic corporations like Sylvania, Kodak, and so on.

That was the first time that anyone had proposed that there should be a direct connection between a particular form of corporate capitalism and a specific form of high cultural promotion. I mean, you are essentially talking about the Rockefeller history of MOMA, of laundered money. You know, there are oil wells somewhere, and somehow that turns into a Picasso. And there is a mediation that is rather complicated and it has to do with surplus value, a certain amount that the ruling class has to spend on culture. And here we are talking about a direct form of sponsorship which of course is much more familiar to us today, with the increase in both corporate and state intervention in the arts. Well, that ideal was greeted with a certain amount of resistance by members of the MOMA board. In fact, one of the reasons why it was greeted with resistance was because it involved the making subordinate of Beaumont Newhall, who was there as the Curator of Photography, and had built a collection, done very rigorous, good, solid, scholarly work, in terms of establishing photography as an art-historically credible medium. So Steichen came in without the corporate backing and without this big kind of impresario version of a kind of cult of photographic promotion.

He claims in his autobiography that he had had the idea of *Family of Man* in the 40's. I may be slightly wrong about this, but you get the sense that it is sort of like the antidote for the war-like material which is an earlier theme in his biography in terms of his work in the First World War. But Steichen tends to travel in more or less liberal circles in New York, that is, the anti-McCarthyist. Something I don't make clear enough, I think, in this exposition is that there are aspects of the *Family of Man* that are quite clearly waving the flag of liberalism. The text begins with the banned passage from the Molly Bloom soliloquy in *Ulysses* and so on. It was no longer banned in the 50's, but it was a kind of announcement of Steichen's cultural progressivism.

I think that it's clear from Rockefeller's address that there is a sense of the appropriateness of this exhibition for the system of transnational capital. But I don't think that there is any conspiracy. I don't think you are asking that. That's about all that comes to mind, and I'm not sure that it's adequate. There is more to be found out. The USIA part of it is very hard to determine. If you go to the MOMA you try to discover who controlled where it went and when and why and how. They can't tell you anything and they are very careful about that because they realize what that kind of question means and of course the USIA is a now-defunct agency. It has been absorbed into a new agency, and so you have to find these veterans of the State Department and talk to them personally and I am hoping that if I do more work on this that I will actually go find some people who were responsible for foreign exhibition decisions.

Clement Greenberg

To Cope With Decadence

Our Western culture has been in a singular position the past 150 years and maybe more. It's the only high urban culture — civilization — that's still quite alive. I can think of only one precedent in this respect: Sumer, five thousand years ago, which is said to be the first literate culture, and in being the first was the only high urban culture extant for a while.

By a culture that's still quite alive, I mean one that's still developing, one in which change fulfils potentialities. To be sure, a culture or civilization can be developing in certain directions and not in others. But no matter what particular direction or directions are taken as indices, all the non-Western urban cultures seem now long decayed when not, as in most cases, altogether dead and gone. (Japan may look like an exception, but the only aspects under which its culture develops seem the Westernized ones.)

What's not just singular but unique and altogether unprecedented in Western culture's present position is that its reach is earth-wide, that it's become the first global urban culture, one that intrudes everywhere and threatens to dominate everywhere, among tribal as well as urban peoples. This is an utter historical novelty. It's not just because Western power, with its industrial and pre-industrial technology has laid waste, and lays waste, to all other cultures. All other urban cultures had run their courses or (like the Incan and Aztec) were in a very "late" stage before Western force or influence ever intruded upon them. (Yes, the West has over-run pre-urban cultures that may have still been thriving, but non-Western civilizations had been doing that long before, if not on the same scale.) Western "imperialism," for all its energy and aggressiveness from the 16th century on, was at the same time sucked into exotic urban spaces by a kind of vacuum that became one of culture as well as power (except in Japan). There was an excruciating coincidence in the fact that Western Europe had summoned up the energy, the force, and the technical means to intrude upon other urban cultures just when these had everywhere lost, or were on the point of losing, their vitality. And it was part of the coincidence that Western culture itself, *qua* culture, was at the height of its vitality. It hasn't been by force or enterprise alone that the West has invaded all those exotic spaces, which were spaces of mind as well as of place.

To begin with, Western art and ways of art did not march everywhere in step with imperialist power. Nor does it do so today, any more than Western ways of thinking or Western technology does. Western pictorial and sculptural illusionism penetrated, hundreds of years ago, where Europeans had hardly been, and proved as irresistible as Greco-Roman illusionism had two thousand years before in areas that Alexander's or Rome's armies never reached. Yet just as Indian artists converted Hellenistic lifelikeness into something integrally their own, so Far Eastern artists did two thousand years later with Western lifelikeness. Only, by the 19th century Indian and Chinese artistic tradition, and by the mid-19th Japanese too, had become too feeble, too worn, to assimilate anything to good effect any more, whether from other traditions or from lived life.

In this century, and especially since, and despite, the retreat of Western imperialism after the last world war, the influence of Western culture, and of Western art, on other places of urban culture has increased to an extreme. Now it's no longer a question of the irresistibility of illusionism, now it's become the effect pure and simple of continuing vitality of Western art (as of Western science, technology, and even scholarship). That vitality shows itself nowadays in Modernism. Modernist art goes away from illusionism, yet in its Modernist phase Western art has spread itself more "seriously" than it did before. What I could see for myself, visiting Japan and India in the 1960s, was that artists there weren't Westernizing simply as part of a general effort to Westernize or modernize in their countries. In much greater part it was because of the perception of how much better, how much more alive, recent art from the West was than anything being done in traditional ways at home. At the same time Modernist art seemed to offer them a range of directions in which to be themselves as neither Western art before nor their home traditions any longer did.

Now there is such a thing as truly international art, visual art anyhow (including architecture). But it remains Western art, stays charged from and centered in the West. There, alas, the fate of high art over the only world we know is being decided, because there alone high art, high urban art, remains fully alive and fully rooted.

The spread of Western culture doesn't appear to affect its internal situation. Just as the course of Greco-Roman culture wasn't, seemingly, affected by its spreading beyond its homeland or, on the other hand, even by the incursions of barbarian outsiders. Western culture, with its art, seems to keep on evolving according to its own inner logic, its entelechy, uninfluenced at bottom by events at large. I'm not going to argue about how that autonomy maintains itself (of course it's not absolute). Nor would I assert it, necessarily, as a hard and fast fact, but it has been, and is, a very useful working hypothesis; it's hard to make sense of the history of culture or of art without entertaining the notion of autonomy.

And yes, I've been talking in Spenglerian terms. Cultures and civilizations do run their "biological courses." The evidence says that, and the evidence forces me to accept Spengler's scheme in largest part. (This doesn't mean that I don't find the climate of his mind repellent. And he can be silly. Even I have caught him out in an error of fact. Nevertheless, certain of his insights are large, and they hold up.)

A feeling of "lateness" was already in the air in the West by the middle of the 19th century. My reading hasn't been wide enough to tell me how explicit it was made, but it was there implicitly among certain "esthetes," especially in France; there as a mood maybe more than anything else. Today a feeling of "lateness" abounds in many different ways, showing itself confusedly. Not that journalists and critics think that Western culture is in the late stage that Spengler said it had entered with the 19th century. When they talk of "post-Modern," "post-Modernist," and "post-industrial" they mean only that something has finished and something new is taking its place. They expect new beginnings. Their talk is superficial — as if there were anything in sight that was replacing industrialism, and as though Modernism in the arts were just one episode among others. But what this talk symptomatizes is not superficial. The sense of "lateness" goes deeper than the "post" vogue.

If Western lateness, which means Western decline, is an actual fact, then our culture is headed — in Spengler's scheme — toward the same fate that overtook all previous, all other high cultures. It will become lifeless in the same way. But this will mean, as it now looks, far more than it did in those previous cases. Because then there'll be no more living high urban culture anywhere, the Western being, as I've pointed out, the only such culture still alive right now. (Spengler saw Russia as coming to the rescue as it were: that is the Russian as the next new high urban culture. But the prospect is too remote to concern anybody, including Russians themselves, for the time being.)

It's as though the first full-fledged Modernists in France, back in the 1850's (Baudelaire, Flaubert, Gautier, Manet, et al.), set out deliberately to upset Spengler's scheme of decadence and decline beforehand. Modernism in the arts emerged in answer to what was felt as a radical lowering of standards — esthetic standards — and it remains that answer. Modernism, or the avant-garde if you please, is one more new and unique historical phenomenon, another way in which the West has produced or witnessed an historical novelty. (I seem to detect tentatives towards something like an avant-garde in the remoter past of Chinese and Japanese pictorial art, but all of them aborted.)

In the upshot it looks as though it remains to Modernism alone to resist decline and maintain the vitality of the Western arts, and by doing that to maintain the vitality of high art in general, of high art anywhere — given that high art lives now only on Western terms. The vitality of art means the upholding of esthetic standards. (When I say art I mean all the arts, including literature.) Esthetic standards happen in this time to be far more precarious than those of science or scholarship or technology (in time past they weren't; it was the opposite). Western science and technology don't seem to be threatened yet by decline. Spengler was as wrong in seeing this sixty-five years ago as in seeing in Modernist art nothing but signs of decadence. Nay, he was even wronger: nominally Modernist, would-be Modernist — or post-Modernist — art is shot through with evidence of impotence, but this still doesn't compromise authentic, genuine Modernism, which can, and continues to, define itself only by superior quality. By the same token it's true Modernism alone that still copes with "lateness" and decline.

After Clement Greenberg:

Audience:
I see you talk basically as a defense, basically of capitalism and western imperialism trying to separate culture from the fact of the imperialist — the economic situation itself. What I would like specifically to ask you about — you mention two instances in France, in 1848 and 1870, where historical situations never really affected the course of art itself. I was wondering if the crucial fact here is that in both those situations the class that was in power, the middle class, maintained power; and I don't see how there is going to be a drastic change in art when the class that controls the means of production of art itself maintains that control.

Clement Greenberg:
Urban art has always been elitist art — I hate that word elitist. But as Marx was maybe the first to point out, I don't think he was actually the first — high urban art was always produced for an upper class that enjoyed dignified leisure. Now, it remains to this day that our best art is still produced for an elite. And the best art ever made, I think, is high-urban art in large part, and urban art — high urban art — has always been produced for an upper, ruling, exploiting — exploitative class if you want — that's a sad fact. To register that fact, to constate it as the French would say, does not mean to approve of it. Now . . . French art — the best French art continued, as before in a sense, to all these political crises — all these social crises — sure let's say the upper class in France was not really shaken by these crises. I'll put it in your terms. I'll accept them for the moment. Now do you disagree?

Audience:
I don't disagree. But Tim Clark has shown in his study of Courbet after 1848, history had a lot of influence on the way Courbet formed his art. Maybe you don't consider that to be high art. Maybe I am not clear on the definitions.

Clement Greenberg:
Courbet is high art, indeed he is, good Lord. If he isn't, then, who is? But what kind of influences did the events — the political events — have on Courbet's art after '48? It's true, he may have changed his subject, but his way of painting didn't change. I am a formalist, I look at the pictures first. I look at the pictures first and how they

look, and what they have to tell comes next. Which is not to say that literature has no place in pictorial art. Indeed it has. There has been great pictorial literature, but in this present case — in the case of Courbet — his painting again suffers I feel only towards the end of his life and maybe his Swiss exile had something to do with that, I think. He began to fall off before then. Fundamentally his art was not affected by current events *I maintain.*

Goya the same. Goya's case is the same. There is a controversy going on now among critics as to how important it is to — how relevant Picasso's personal life is to his art. Now, I happen to side with those who don't think it is all that relevant though it is damn interesting. And looking at art of the past. Art by people whose lives are largely unknown to us. In looking at exotic art — the Hindu sculpture — or Chinese painting — Japanese painting — where we know so little, really, of the historical context in which these works of art were created, and far, far less about the creators themselves, at least in India. It seems to me not to matter. And this is a matter of my experience. I have to point to my experience. It is all I have to go by, and at the risk of paying myself a compliment, in Japan — I spent two months in Japan and most of the time I —when I looked at art — it was at the older art and I met some Japanese art historians, and curators and so forth, and I found that my uninfluenced responses to Japanese art were not so far away from theirs. And I was not surprised by that. No, I wasn't. You know — I should have been, other people were, and . . . Once you immerse yourself in exotic art you begin to get to feel at home in it and the same thing happened in India where I likewise spent two months. I looked mostly at the old art, and found that what art the Indians or the British before them had chosen to put into the museums, and what — especially temple sculpture — they had chosen to leave exposed to the elements, so forth — the difference showed a lot of taste, that they did house the best art sculpture, and now you can say of course that I was influenced by the fact I saw things in the museum as I wouldn't have been when I saw sculpture in an open field, as in Khajurao — the Jain Temple things which were quite good. I feel pretty sure that I wasn't influenced by that.

Now the point is, my acquaintance with Indian history is very small, and so is my acquaintance with Japanese history; and in any case many of the works I saw in both places were not datable within more than fifty or a hundred year reach — you had to say circa. Because nothing, almost nothing, had a precise year assigned to it except Japanese painting of the 15th century, and that I felt once again history matters and all that, but when you are face to face with art you are — well as Schopenhauer said maybe transcending history, and maybe transcending your own person, too — your own personality, connecting art and literature with history is valid, and should be done: but in the showdown, aesthetic experience, that's it for me.

(clapping)

What an enlightened audience, I must say.

Audience:
You have spent a long time this morning denying that imperialism has anything to do with the dominance of western art and western culture.

Clement Greenberg:
No, don't say anything — doesn't have all that much to do —

Audience:
Okay — little — it has had little to do with the dominance of western art and western culture.

Clement Greenberg:
Western art particularly yes.

Audience:
And instead you've explained that dominance through reference to the aesthetic vitality of western art. You haven't once defined what you mean by aesthetic vitality. And it appears as if you are hiding behind those two words in order to explain away the dominance of western art.

Clement Greenberg:
Aesthetic vitality and what other words? What's the other word?

Audience:
Aesthetic vitality of high art.

Clement Greenberg:
Western art shows its vitality still by producing works in all forms, all the genres, of superior aesthetic quality. That's a tautological

answer I know. But you see elementary lessons in aesthetics — as Emmanuel Kant, once again I have to say this — you can't prove an aesthetic judgment. You can't demonstrate it. I can't prove that Raphael is better than Norman Rockwell, the way I can prove that two plus two equals four to anyone who is sane, but if I choose to think that Rockwell is better than Raphael, you can't show me otherwise.

Audience:
Well, perhaps we can't ask for proof, but we can ask for analysis.

Clement Greenberg:
Analysis is descriptive in the showdown. Analysis doesn't convey in the end anything that's an aesthetic judgment. I can analyze a Rockwell at as great a length as I can a Raphael any day. Don't misunderstand me, Miss — there are certain axioms about aesthetic experience that have to be repeated over and over again. There must be a cultural reason for it because it's not true in Japan and I have never been any further into China than Kowloon, but I have a feeling it wasn't true in China either. I'd known that aesthetic experience is intuitive and, as intuitive experience, it cannot be taken apart by discourse.

(clapping)

T. J. Clark

More on the Differences Between Comrade Greenberg and Ourselves

In the issue of *Partisan Review* for Fall 1939 appeared an article by Clement Greenberg entitled 'Avant-Garde and Kitsch.' It was followed four issues later, in July-August 1940, by another wide-ranging essay on modern art called 'Towards a Newer Laocoon'. I think one is entitled to treat these two articles as staking out the ground for Greenberg's later practice as a critic and setting down the main lines of a theory and history of culture since 1850 —since, shall we say, Gustave Courbet and Charles Baudelaire. Greenberg reprinted 'Avant-Garde and Kitsch', making no attempt to tone down its mordant hostility to capitalism, as the opening item of his collection of critical essays, *Art and Culture*, in 1961. 'Towards a Newer Laocoon' was not reprinted, perhaps because the author felt that its arguments were made more effectively in some of his later, more particular pieces — the essays on 'Collage' or 'Cézanne', for example, or the brief paragraphs on 'Abstract, Representational and So Forth'. I am not personally sure that the author was right to omit the piece: it is noble, lucid and extraordinarily balanced, it seems to me, in its defense of abstract art and avant-garde culture; and certainly its arguments are taken up directly, sometimes almost verbatim, in the more famous theoretical study of 1965 with the bolder title 'Modernist Painting.'[1]

The essays of 1939 and 1940, I am saying, display already Greenberg's main preoccupations as a critic. They argue for those preoccupations and commitments, and the arguments adduced, as the author himself admits at the end of 'Towards a Newer Laocoon', are largely historical. "I find", so Greenberg writes there, "that I have offered no other explanation for the present superiority of abstract art than its historical justification. So what I have written has turned out to be an historical apology for abstract art."

The author's profferred half-surprise at having thus "turned out" to be composing an apology in the historical manner should not of course be taken literally. For it was historical consciousness, Greenberg had argued in 'Avant-Garde and Kitsch', which was the key to the avant-garde's achievement — its ability, that is, to salvage something from the collapse of the bourgeois cultural order. To put you in mind of the sentences — they are crucial ones to the essay as a whole —: "a part of Western bourgeois society", Greenberg writes, "has produced something unheard of heretofore: avant-garde culture. A superior consciousness of history — more precisely, the appearance of a new kind of criticism of society, an historical criticism — made this possible. [. . .] It was not accident, therefore, that the birth of the avant-garde coincided chronologically — and geographically, too — with the first bold development of scientific revolutionary thought in Europe." By which last he means, need I say it, preeminently the thought of Marx; to whom the reader is grimly directed at the end of the essay, after a miserable and just description of Fascism's skill at providing "art for the people", with the words: "Here, as in every other question today, it becomes necessary to quote Marx word for word. Today we no longer look towards socialism for a new culture — as inevitably as one will appear, once we do have socialism. Today we look to socialism *simply* for the preservation of whatever living culture we have right now."

It is not intended as some sort of revelation on my part that Greenberg's cultural theory was originally Marxist in its stresses, and indeed in its attitude to what constituted explanation in such matters. I point out the Marxist and historical mode of proceeding as emphatically as I do partly because it may make my own procedure, later in this paper, seem a little less arbitrary. For I shall fall to arguing in the end with these essays' Marxism and their history, and I want it understood that I think that to do so *is* to take issue with their strengths, and their main drift.

But I have to admit there are difficulties here. The essays in question are quite brief. They are, I think, extremely well written: it was not for nothing that *Partisan Review* described Clement Greenberg, when he first contributed to the journal early in 1939, as "a young writer who works in the New York customs house" — fine, redolent avant-garde pedigree, that! The language of these articles is forceful and easy, always straightforward, blessedly free from Marxist conundrums. Yet the price paid for such lucidity, here as so often, is a degree of inexplicitness — a certain amount of

elegant skirting round the difficult issues, where one might otherwise be obliged to call out the ponderous armory of Marx's concepts, and somewhat spoil the flow of the prose from one firm
statement to another. The Marxism, in other words, is quite largely
implicit; it is stated on occasion, with brittle and pugnacious final-
ity, *as* the essays' frame of reference, but it remains to the reader to
determine just how it works in the history and theory presented —
what that history and theory depend on, in the way of Marxist
assumptions about class and capital or even base and superstruc-
ture. That is what I intend to do in this paper: to interpret and
extrapolate from the texts, even at the risk of making their Marxism declare itself more stridently than the "young writer" seems to
have wished. And I should admit straight away that there are
several points in what follows where I am genuinely uncertain as to
whether I am diverging from Greenberg's argument, or explaining
it more fully. This does not worry me overmuch, as long as we are
alerted to the special danger in this case, dealing with such transparent yet guarded prose; and as long as we can agree that the
project in general — pressing home a Marxist reading of texts
which situate themselves within the Marxist tradition — is a reasonable one.[2]

I should therefore add a word or two to conjure up the
connotations of 'Marxism' for a writer in 1939 in *Partisan Review.* I
do not need to labour the point, I hope, that there *was* a considerable and various Marxist culture in New York at this time; it was
not robust, not profound, but not frivolous or flimsy either, in the
way of England in the same years; and it is worth spelling out how
well the pages of *Partisan Review* in 1939 and 1940 mirrored its
distinction and variety, and its sense of impending doom. The
number of the journal in which the 'Newer Laocoon' was published
began with an embattled article by Dwight MacDonald entitled
'National Defense: the Case for Socialism', whose two parts were
headed 'Death of a World' and 'What Must We Do To be Saved?'
The article was a preliminary to the 'Ten Propositions on the War'
which MacDonald and Greenberg were jointly to sign a year later,
in which they argued — still in the bleak days of 1941 — for
revolutionary abstention from a war between capitalist nation-
states. A bleak time, then, in which Marxist convictions were often
found hard to sustain. But still a time characterized by a certain
energy and openness of Marxist thought, even in its moment of
doubt. MacDonald had just finished a series of articles — an excellent series, written from an anti-Stalinist point of view — on Soviet

cinema and its public. (It is one main point of reference in the
closing sections of 'Avant-Garde and Kitsch'.) Edmund Wilson in
Fall 1938 could be seen pouring scorn on the Marxist Dialectic, in
the same issue as André Breton and Diego Rivera's manifesto,
'Towards a Free Revolutionary Art'. Philip Rahv pieced out 'The
Twilight of the Thirties' or 'What is Living and What is Dead' in
Marxism. Victor Serge's *Ville Conquise* was published, partly, in
translation. Meyer Schapiro took issue with *To the Finland Station,*
Bertram Wolfe reviewed Souvarine's great book on Stalin.

And so on. The point is simply that this *was* a Marxist
culture — a hectic and shallow-rooted one, in many ways, but one
which deserved the name. Its appetite for European culture — for
French art and poetry in particular — is striking and discriminate,
especially compared with later New York French enthusiasms. This
was the time when Lionel Abel was translating Lautréamont, and
Delmore Schwartz *A Season in Hell.* The pages of *Partisan Review*
had Wallace Stevens alongside Trotsky, Paul Eluard next to Allen
Tate, 'East Coker' — I am scrupulous here — following 'Marx and
Lenin as Scapegoats.' No doubt the glamour of all this is misleading; but at least we can say, all reservations made, that a comparable roster of names and titles from any later period would look
desultory by contrast, and rightly so.

Greenberg's first contribution to the magazine, in early
1939, was a review of Bertold Brecht's *A Penny for the Poor,* the
novel taken from the *Threepenny Opera.* In it he discussed, sternly
but with sympathy, the "nerve-wracking" formal monotony which
derived, so he thought, from Brecht's effort to write a parable — a
consistent fiction — of life under capitalism. In the same issue as
'Avant-Garde and Kitsch' there appeared an account of an inter-
view which Greenberg had had, the previous year, with Ignazio
Silone. The interviewer's questions told the tale of his commitments
without possibility of mistake: "What, in the light of their relations
to political parties," he asked, "do you think should be the role of
revolutionary writers in the present situation?"; and then, "When
you speak of liberty, do you mean *socialist* liberty?", and then,
"Have you read Trotsky's pamphlet, *Their Morals and Ours?* What
do you think of it?"

I am aware of the absurdity of paying more heed to Greenberg's questions than to Silone's grand replies; but you see the
point of all this, for anyone trying in the end to read between the
lines of 'A Newer Laocoon'. And I hope that when, in a little while,
I use the phrase "Eliotic Trotskyism" to describe Green-

berg's stance, it will seem less forced a coinage. Perhaps one should even add Brecht to Eliot and Trotsky here, since it seems that the example of Brecht was specially vivid for Greenberg in the years round 1940, representing as he did a difficult, powerful counter-example to all the critic wished to see as the main line of avant-garde activity — standing for active engagement in ideological struggle, not detachment from it, and suggesting that such struggle was not necessarily incompatible with work on the *medium* of theatre, making that medium explicit and opaque in the best avant-garde manner. (It is a pity that Greenberg, as far as I know, wrote only about Brecht's novels and poetry.[3] Doubtless he would have had critical things to say also about Brecht's epic theatre, but the nature of his criticism — and especially his discussion of the tension between formal concentration and political purpose here — might well have told us a great deal about the grounds of his ultimate settling for "purity" as the only feasible artistic ideal.)

All this has been by way of historical preliminary: as usual with such things it has gone on too long, but I hope it has been fair, and I believe it is necessary to what follows. If we are to read the essays of 1939 and 1940, this, I think, is the history we need to bear in mind.

Let me begin my reading proper, then, by stating in summary form what I take to be the arguments of 'Avant-Garde and Kitsch' and 'Newer Laocoon'. They are, as I have said already, historical explanations of the course of avant-garde art since the mid-19th century. They are seized with the strangeness of the avant-garde moment — that moment in which "a part of Western bourgeois culture . . . produced something unheard of heretofore." Seized with its strangeness, and not specially optimistic as to its chances of survival in the face of an ongoing breakdown of bourgeois civilization. For that *is* the context in which an avant-garde culture comes to be: it is a peculiar, indeed unique, reaction to a far-from-unprecedented cultural situation — to put it bluntly, the decadence of a society, the familiar weariness and confusion of a culture in its death-throes. The text is explicit on this: Western society in the 19th century reached that fatal phase in which, like Alexandrian Greece or late Mandarin China, it became "less and less able . . . to justify the inevitability of its particular forms" and thus to keep alive "the accepted notions upon which artists and writers must depend in large part for communication with their audiences." Such a situation is usually fatal to seriousness in art. At the end of a culture, when all the verities of religion, authority, tradition and style — all the ideological cement of society, in other words — are either disputed or doubted, or believed in for convenience's sake and not held to *entail* anything much — at such a moment "the writer or artist is no longer able to estimate the response of his audience to the symbols and references with which he works." In the past that had meant an art which therefore left the really important issues to one side, and contented itself with "virtuosity in the small details of form, all larger questions being [mechanically, listlessly] decided by the precedent of the old masters."

Clearly, says Greenberg, there has been a "decay of our present society" — the words are his — which corresponds in many ways to all these gloomy precedents. What is new is the course of art in this situation. No doubt bourgeois culture is in crisis, more and more unable since Marx "to justify the inevitability of its particular forms"; but it has spawned, half in opposition to itself, half at its service, a peculiar and durable artistic tradition — the one we call modernist, and which Greenberg then called, using its own label, avant-garde. "It was to be the task of the avant-garde", I am quoting now from the 'Newer Laocoon', "to perform in opposition to bourgeois society the function of finding new and adequate cultural forms for the expression of that same society, without at the same time succumbing to its ideological divisions and its refusal to permit the arts to be their own justification." There are several stresses here, worth distinguishing.

First, the avant-garde is "part of Western bourgeois society", and yet in some important way estranged from it: needing, as Greenberg phrases it, the revolutionary gloss put on the very "concept of the 'bourgeois' in order to define what they were *not*", but at the same time performing the function of finding forms "for the expression" of bourgeois society, and tied to it "by an umbilical cord of gold." Here is the crucial passage: ". . . it is to the [ruling class] that the avant-garde belongs. No culture can develop without a social base, without a stable source of income. [We might immediately protest at this point at what seems to be the text's outlandish economism: "social base" is one thing, "source of income" another; the sentence seems to elide them. But let it pass for the moment.] . . . in the case of the avant-garde this [social base] was provided by an elite among the ruling class of that society from which it assumed itself to be cut off, but to which it has always remained attached by an umbilical cord of gold." That is the first stress: the contradictory belonging — together-in-opposition of the avant-garde and its bourgeoisie; and the sense —the pressing and anxious sense — of that connection-in-difference being attenuated, being on the point of severance. For "culture is being abandoned by those to whom it actually belongs — our ruling class": the avant-garde, in its specialization and estrangement, *had always been* a sign of that abandonment, and now it seemed as if the breach was close to final.

Second, the avant-garde is a way to protect art from "ideological divisions." "Ideological confusion and violence" are the enemy of artistic force and concentration: art seeks a space of its own apart from them, apart from the endless uncertainty of meanings in capitalist society. It is plain how this connects with my previous wondering about Greenberg on Brecht, and I shall not press the point here, except to say that there is a special and refutable move being made in the argument: to compare the conditions in which, in late capitalism, the meanings of the ruling class are actively disputed, with those in which, in Hellenistic Egypt, say, established meanings stultified and became subject to scepticism —this is to compare the utterly unlike. It is to put side by side a time of economic and cultural dissolution — an epoch of weariness and unconcern — and one of articulated and fierce class struggle. Capital may be uncertain of its values, but it is not weary; the bourgeoisie may have no beliefs worth the name, but they will not admit as much: they are hypocrites, not sceptics. And the avant-garde, I shall argue, has regularly and rightly seen an *advantage* for art in the particular conditions of "ideological confusion and violence" under capital; it has wished to take part in the general, untidy work of negation, and has seen no necessary contradiction (rather the contrary) between doing so and coming to terms once again with its "medium".

But I shall return to this later. It is enough for now to point to the second stress, and to the third: the idea that one chief purpose of the avant-garde was to oppose bourgeois society's "refusal to permit the arts to be their own justification." This is the stress which leads on to the more familiar — and trenchant — arguments of the essays in question, which I shall indicate even more briefly: the description of the *ersatz* art produced for mass consumption by the ruling classes of late capitalism as part of their vile stage-management of democracy, their pretending — it becomes perfunctory of late — "that the masses actually rule"; and the subtle account of the main strands in the avant-garde's history, and the way they have all conspired to narrow and raise art "to the expression of an absolute." The pursuit has been purity, whatever the detours and self-deceptions. "The arts lie safe now, each within its 'legitimate' boundaries, and free trade has been replaced by autarchy. Purity in art consists in the acceptance . . . of the limitation of the medium . . . . The arts, then, have been hunted back [the wording is odd and pondered] to their mediums, and there they have been isolated, concentrated and defined." The logic is ineluctable, it "holds the artists in a vise", and time and again it overrides the most impure and ill-advised intentions: "a good many of the artists," this is the 'Newer Laocoon' again, "— if not the majority — who contributed to the development of modern painting came to it with the desire to exploit the break with imitative realism for a more powerful expressiveness, but so inexorable was the logic of the development that in the end their work constituted but another step towards abstract art, and a further sterilization of the expressive factors. This has been true, whether the artist was Van Gogh, Picasso or Klee. All roads lead to the same place."

This is enough of summary. I do not want now, whatever the temptation, to pitch in with arguments about specific cases — is that *true* of Van Gogh; and what is the balance in collage between medium and illusion; and so on and so forth? The argument of course provokes such exclamations, as arguments should do. But I want to restrict myself, if I can, to describing the argument's general logic, inexorable or not, and choosing my examples as arguments with that overall gist.

Let me go back to the start of 'Avant-Garde and Kitsch'. It seems to be an unstated assumption of that article — and an entirely reasonable one, I believe — that there once was a time, before the avant-garde, when the bourgeoisie, like any normal ruling class, possessed a culture and an art which was directly and recognizably its own. And indeed we know what is meant by the claim: we know what it means, whatever the provisoes and equivocations, to call Chardin and Hogarth bourgeois painters, or Richardson and Defoe novelists of the middle class. We can move forward a century and still be confident in calling Balzac and Stendhal likewise, or Constable and Géricault. Of course there are degrees of difference and dissociation always: Balzac's politics, Géricault's alienation, Chardin's royal clientele: but the bourgeoisie, we can say, in some strong sense *possessed* this art: the art enacted, clarified and criticized the class's experience, its appearance and values; it responded to its demands and assumptions. There was a distinctive bourgeois culture; this art is part of our evidence for just such an assertion.

But it is clear also that from the later 19th century on the distinctiveness and coherence of that bourgeois identity began to fade. "Fade" is too weak and passive a word, I think. I should say that the bourgeoisie was obliged to dismantle its focused identity, as part of the price it paid for maintaining social control. As part of its struggle for power over other classes, subordinate and voiceless as they were in the social order, but not placated, it was forced to dissolve its claim to culture — and in particular forced to revoke the claim, which is palpable in Géricault or Stendhal, say, to take up and dominate and preserve the absolutes of aristocracy, the values of the class it displaced. "It is Athene whom we want," Greenberg blurts out in a footnote once, "formal culture with its infinity of aspects, its luxuriance, its large comprehension."[4] Add to those qualities intransigeance, intensity and risk in the life of the emotions, fierce regard for honour and desire for accurate self-consciousness, disdain for the commonplace, rage for order, insistence that the world cohere: these are, are they not, the qualities we tend to associate with art itself, at its highest moments in the Western tradition, but they are specifically feudal ruling-class superlatives; they are the ones the bourgeoisie believed they had inherited; and the ones they chose to abandon because they became, in the class struggles after 1870, a cultural liability.

Hence what Greenberg calls *kitsch. Kitsch* is the sign of bourgeoisie contriving to lose its identity, forfeiting the inconvenient absolutes of *Le Rouge et le Noir* or the *Oath of the Horatii*. It is an art and a culture of instant assimilation, of abject reconciliation to the everyday, of avoidance of difficulty, pretence to indifference, equality before the image of capital.

Modernism is born in reaction to this state of affairs. And you will see, I hope, the peculiar difficulty here. There had once been, let me say it again, a bourgeois identity and a classic 19th-century bourgeois culture. But as the bourgeoisie built itself the forms of mass society, and thereby entrenched its power, it devised a massified pseudo-art and pseudo-culture, and destroyed its *own* cultural forms — they had been, remember, a long time maturing, in the centuries of patient accommodation to and difference from aristocratic or absolutist rule. Now Greenberg says, I think rightly, that some kind of connection exists between this bourgeoisie and the art of the avant-garde. The avant-garde is engaged in finding forms for the expression of bourgeois society that is the phrase again from the 'Newer Laocoon'. But what could this mean, ex-

actly, in the age of bourgeois decomposition so eloquently described in 'Avant-Garde and Kitsch'? It seems that modernism is
being proposed as bourgeois art in the absence of a bourgeoisie, or,
more accurately, as aristocratic art in the age when the bourgeoisie
abandons its claims to aristocracy. And how will art keep aristocracy alive? By keeping *itself* alive, as the remaining vessel of the
aristocratic account of experience and its modes; by preserving its
own means, its media; by proclaiming those means and media *as* its
values, as meanings in themselves.

This is, I think, the crux of the argument. It seems to me
that Greenberg is aware of the paradox involved in his avant-garde
preserving *bourgeoisie*, in its highest and severest forms, for a bourgeoisie which, in the sense so proposed, no longer existed. He
points to the paradox but he believes the solution to it has proved
to be, in practice, the density and resistance of artistic values *per se.*
They are the repository, as it were, of affect and intelligence that
once inhered in a complex form of life, but do so no longer; they
are the concrete form of intensity and self-consciousness, the only one
left, and therefore the form to be preserved at all costs, and somehow kept apart from the surrounding desolation.

It is a serious and grim picture of culture under capitalism,
and the measure of its bitterness and perplexity seems to me still
justified. Eliotic Trotskyism, I called it previously; the cadencies
shifting line by line from *Socialism or Barbarism* to *Shakespeare
and the Stoicism of Seneca.* (And was Greenberg a reader of *Scrutiny,* I wonder? It was widely read in New York at this time, I
believe.[5]) From his Eliotic stronghold he perceives, and surely with
reason, that much of the great art of the previous century, including
some which had declared itself avant-garde and anti-bourgeois,
had depended on the patronage and mental appetites of a certain
fraction of the middle class. It had in some sense *belonged* to a
bourgeois intelligentsia — to a fraction of the class which was
self-consciously "progressive" in its tastes and attitudes, and often
allied not just to the cause of artistic experiment but of social and
political reform. And it is surely also true that in late capitalism this
independent, critical and progessive intelligentsia was put to death
by its own class. For late capitalism — by which I mean the order
emerging from the Great Depression — is a period of cultural
uniformity: a levelling-down, a squeezing-out of previous bourgeois elites, a narrowing of distance between class and class, *and*
between fractions of the same class. In this case, the distance largely
disappears between bourgeois intelligentsia and unintelligentsia: by

our own time one might say it is normally impossible to distinguish one from the other.

(And lest this be taken as merely flippant, let me add that the kind of distance I have in mind — and distance here does not mean detachment, but precisely an active, uncomfortable difference from the class one belongs to — is that between Walter Lippmann's *salon,* say, and the American middle class of its day; or that between the Gambetta circle and the general ambience of *Ordre Moral.* This last is specially to the purpose, since its consequences for culture were so vivid: one has only to remember the achievement of Antonin Proust in his brief tenure of the *Direction des Beaux-Arts,* or Clemenceau's patronage of and friendship for Claude Monet.)

This description of culture is suitably grim, as I say, and finds its proper echoes in Eliot, Trotsky, Leavis and Brecht. And yet — and here at last I modulate into criticism — there seem to me things badly wrong with its final view of art and artistic value. In the rest of this paper I shall offer three, or perhaps four, kinds of criticism of the view; and it would perhaps be useful if I indicated straight away what they are. I shall firstly point to the difficulties involved in the whole notion of art itself becoming an independent source of value. I shall then disagree with one of the central elements in Greenberg's account of that value: his reading of "medium" in avant-garde art. Thirdly, I shall try to recast his sketch of modernism's formal logic in order to include aspects of avant-garde practice which he overlooks or belittles, but which I believe are bound up with those he sees as paramount. What I shall point to here — not to make a mystery of it — are *practices of negation* in modernist art which seem to me the very form of the practices of purity (the recognitions and enactments of medium) which Greenberg extols. Lastly, I shall suggest some ways in which the previous three criticisms are connected; in particular, I shall discuss the relation between those practices of negation and the business of bourgeois artists making do without a bourgeoisie.

I shall be brief, and the criticisms may seem schematic. But my hope is that because they are anyway simple objections, to points in an argument where it appears palpably weak, they will, schematic or not, seem quite reasonable.

The first disagreement could be introduced by asking the following (Wittgensteinian) question: What would it be *like,* exactly, for art to possess its own values? Not just to have, in other words, a set of distinctive effects and procedures, but to have them somehow be, or provide, the standards by which the effects and procedures are held to be of worth? I may as well say at once that there seem, on the face of it, some insuperable logical difficulties here; and they may well stand in the way of ever providing a coherent reply to the Wittgensteinian question. But I much prefer to give — or to sketch — a kind of *historical* answer to the question, in which the point of asking it in the first place might be made more clear.

Let us concede that Greenberg may be roughly right when he says in 'Avant-Garde and Kitsch' that "a fairly constant distinction" has been made by "the cultivated of mankind over the ages" "between those values only to be found in art and the values which can be found elsewhere." But let us ask how that distinction was actually made — made and maintained, as an active opposition — in practice, in the first heyday of the art called avant-garde. For the sake of vividness we might choose the case of the young speculator Dupuy, whom Camille Pissarro described in 1890 as "mon meilleur amateur", and who killed himself the same year, to Pissarro's chagrin, because he believed he was faced with bankruptcy. One's picture of such a patron is necessarily speculative in its turn, but what I want to suggest is not anything very debatable. It seems clear from the evidence that Dupuy was someone capable of savouring the *separateness* of art, its irreducible difficulties and appeal. That was what presumably won him Pissarro's respect, and led him to buy the most problematic art of his day. (This at a time, remember, when Pissarro's regular patrons, and dealers, had quietly sloped off in search of something less odd.) But I would suggest that he also saw — and in some sense insisted on — a kind of consonance between the experience and value that art had to offer and those that belonged to his everyday life. The consonance did not need to be direct, and indeed could not be. Dupuy was not in the market for animated pictures of the Stock Exchange — the kind he could have got from Jean Béraud — or even for scenes *à la Degas* in which he might have been offered back, dramatically, the shifts and upsets of life in the big city. He seems to have purchased landscapes instead, and had a taste for those painted in the neo-Impressionist manner — painted, that is, in a way which tried to be tight, discreet and uniform, done with a disabused orderliness, seemingly scientific, certainly analytic. And all of these qualities, we might guess, he savoured and required as the signs of art's detachment.

Yet surely we must also say that his openness to such qualities, his ability to understand them, was founded in a sense he had of some play between those qualities occurring in art and the same occurring in life — occurring in his life, not on the face of it a happy one, but one at the cutting edge of capitalism still. And when we remember what capitalism *was* in 1890, we are surely better able to understand why Dupuy invested in Georges Seurat. For this was a capital still confident in its powers, if shaken; and not merely confident, but scrupulous; still in active dialogue with science, still producing distinctive rhetorics and modes of appraising experience; still conscious of its own values — the tests of rationality, the power born of observation and control — ; still, if you wish, believing in the commodity as a [perplexing] form of freedom.

You see my point, I hope. I believe it was the interplay of these values and the values of art which made the distinction between them an active and possible one — made it a distinction at all, as opposed to a rigid and absolute disjunction. In the case of Dupuy, there was difference-yet-consonance between the values which made for the bourgeois's sense of himself in practical life, and those he required from avant-garde painting. The facts of art and the facts of capital were in active tension. They were still negotiating with each other; they could still at moments, in particular cases like Dupuy's, contrive to put each other's categories in doubt.

This, it seems to me, is what is meant by "a fairly constant distinction [being] made between those values only to be found in art and the values which can be found elsewhere." It is a negotiated distinction, with the critic of Diderot's or Baudelaire's or Fénéon's type the active agent of the settlement. For critics like these, and in the art they typically address, it is true that the values a painting offers are discovered, time and again and with vehemence, as different and irreducible. And we understand the point of Fénéon's insistence; but we are the more impressed by it precisely because the values are found to be different as part of a real cultural dialectic; by which I mean that they are visibly under pressure, in the text, from the demands and valuations made by the ruling class in the business of ruling — the meanings it makes and disseminates, the kinds of order it proposes as its own. It is this pressure — and the way it is enacted in the patronage relation, or in the artist's imagining of his or her public — which keeps the values of art from becoming a merely academic canon.

I hope it is clear how this account of artistic standards — and particularly of the ways in which art's separateness as a social practice is secured — would call into question Greenberg's hope that art could become a provider of value in its own right. Yet I think I can call that belief in question more effectively simply by looking at one or other of the facts of art which Greenberg takes to have become a value, in some sense: let me look, for simplicity's sake, at the notorious fact of "flatness". Now it is certainly true that the literal flatness of the picture surface was recovered at regular intervals as a striking fact by painters after Courbet. But I think that the question we should ask in this case is *why* that simple, empirical presence went on being interesting for art? How could a fact of effect or procedure stand in for value in this way? What was it that made it vivid?

The answer is not far to seek. I think we can say that the fact of flatness was vivid and tractable — as it was in the art of Cézanne, for example, or that of Matisse — because it was made to stand for something: some particular and resistant set of qualities, taking their place in an articulated account of experience. The richness of the avant-garde, as a set of contexts for art in the years between 1860 and 1918, say, might thus be re-described in terms of its ability to give flatness such complex and compatible values —values which necessarily derived from elsewhere than art. It could stand, that flatness, as an analogue of the "popular" — something therefore conceived as plain, workmanlike and emphatic. Or it could signify "modernity," with flatness meant to conjure up the mere two dimensions of posters, labels, fashion prints and photographs. Equally, unbrokenness of surface could be seen — by Cézanne, for example — as standing for the truth of *seeing,* the actual form of our knowledge of things. And that very claim was repeatedly felt, by artist and audience, to be some kind of aggression on the latter: flatness appeared as a barrier to the ordinary bourgeois's wish to enter a picture and dream, to have it to be a space apart from life, in which the mind would be free to make its own connections.

My point is simply that flatness in its heyday *was* these various meanings and valuations; they were its substance, so to speak, they were what it was seen *as.* Their particularity was what made it vivid — made it a matter to be painted over again. Flatness was therefore in play — as an irreducible, technical "fact" of painting — with all of these totalizations, all of these attempts to make it a metaphor. Of course in a sense it resisted the metaphors, and the painters we most admire insisted also on it as an awkward, empirical quiddity; but the "also" is the key word here: there was no fact without the metaphor, no medium without it being the vehicle of a complex act of meaning.

This leads me directly to my third criticism of Greenberg's account. It could be broached most forcefully, I think, by asking the question: how does the medium most often *appear* in modernist art? If we accept (as we ought to, I feel) that avant-garde painting, poetry and music are characterized by an insistence on medium, then what kind of insistence has it been, usually? My answer would be — it is hardly an original one — that the medium has appeared most characteristically as the site of negation and estrangement.

The very way that modernist art has insisted on its medium has been by negating that medium's ordinary consistency — by pulling it apart, emptying it, producing gaps and silences, making it stand as the opposite of sense or continuity, having matter be the synonym of resistance (and why, after all, should matter be "resistant"? It is a modernist piety with a fairly dim ontology appended). Modernism would have its medium be *absence* of some sort — absence of finish or coherence, indeterminacy, a ground which is called on to swallow up distinctions.

These are avant-garde strategies; and I am not for a moment suggesting that Greenberg does not recognize their part in the art he admires. Yet he is notoriously uneasy with them, and prepared to declare them extrinsic to the real business of art in our time —the business of each art "determin[ing], through the operations peculiar to itself, the effects peculiar and exclusive to itself." (The phrase is quoted from the essay of 1965 on 'Modernist Painting.') It is Greenberg's disdain for the rhetoric of negation which underlay, one supposes, the ruefulness of his description of Pollock as, after all, a "Gothic" whose art harked back to Faulkner and Melville in its "violence, exasperation and stridency."[6] It is certainly the same disdain which determines his verdict on Dada, which is only important, he feels, as a complaisant topic for journalism about the modern crisis (or the shock of the new). And one does know what he means by the charge; one does feel the fire of his sarcasm, in 1947, when he writes — he is in the middle of dealing well with Pollock's unlikely achievement —: "In the face of current events, painting feels, apparently, that it must be epic poetry, it must be theatre, it must be an atomic bomb, it must be the rights of Man. But the greatest painter of our time, Matisse, preeminently demonstrated the sincerity and penetration that go with the kind of greatness particular to 20th century painting by saying that he wanted his art to be an armchair for the tired business man."[7]

It is splendid, it is salutary, it is congenial. Yet surely in the end it will not quite do as description. Surely it is part of modernism's problem — even Matisse's — that the tired business man be so weary and vacant, and so little interested in art as his armchair. It is this situation — this lack of an adequate ruling class to address — which goes largely to explain modernism's negative cast.

I think that finally my differences with Greenberg centre on this one. I do not believe that the practices of negation which Greenberg seeks to declare mere *noise* on the modernist message can be thus demoted. They are simply inseparable from the work of self-definition which he takes to be central: inseparable in the case of Pollock, for certain, or Miro, or Picasso, or for that matter Matisse. Modernism is certainly that art which insists on its medium, and says that meaning can henceforth only be found in *practice*. But the practice in question is extraordinary and desperate: it presents itself as a work of interminable and absolute decomposition, a work which is always pushing "medium" to its limits — to its ending — to the point where it breaks or evaporates or turns back into mere unworked material. That is the form in which medium is retrieved or reinvented: the fact of Art, in modernism, *is* the fact of negation.

I believe that this description imposes itself: that it is the only one which can include Mallarmé alongside Rimbaud, Schoenberg alongside Webern, or (dare I say it?) Duchamp beside the Monet of the *Nymphéas.* And surely that dance of negation has to do with the social facts I have spent most of my time rehearsing — the decline of ruling-class elites, the absence of a "social base" for artistic production, the paradox involved in making bourgeois art in the absence of a bourg. oisie. Negation is the sign inside art of this wider decomposition: it is an attempt to *capture* the lack of consistent and repeatable meanings in the culture — to capture the lack and make it over into form.

I should make the extent of this, my last disagreement with Greenberg, clear. The extent is small but definite. It is not of course that Greenberg fails to recognize the rootlessness and isolation of the avant-garde; his writing is full of the recognition, and he knows as well as anyone the miseries inherent in such a loss of place. But he does believe — the vehemence of the belief is what is most impressive in his writing — that art can substitute *itself* for the values capitalism has made valueless. A refusal to share that belief — and that is finally what I am urging — would have its basis in the following three observations: First, to repeat, that negation is inscribed in the very practice of modernism, as the form in which art appears to itself as a value. Second, that that negativity does not appear as a practice which *guarantees* meaning or opens out a space for free play and fantasy — in the manner of the joke, for example or even of irony — but rather, negation appears as an absolute and all-encompassing fact, something which once begun is cumulative and uncontrollable; a fact which swallows meaning altogether. The road leads back and back to the black square, the hardly differentiated field of sound, the infinitely flimsy skein of spectral colour, speech stuttering and petering out into etceteras or excuses. ("I am obliged to believe that these are statements having to do with a world . . . But you, the reader, need not . . . And I and You, Oh well . . . The poem offers a way out of itself, hereabouts . . . But do not take it, wholly . . ." And so on.) On the other side of negation is always emptiness: that is a message which modernism never tires of repeating, and a territory into which it regularly strays. We have an art in which ambiguity becomes infinite, which is on the verge of proposing — and does propose — an other which is comfortably ineffable, a vacuity, a vagueness, a mere mysticism of sight.

There is a way — and this again is something which happens *within* modernism, or at its limits — in which that empty negation is in turn negated. And that brings me back finally to the most basic of Greenberg's assumptions: it brings me back to the essays on Brecht. For there is an art — a modernist art — which has challenged the notion that art stands only to suffer from the fact that now all meanings are disputable. There is an art — Brecht's is only the most doctrinaire example — which says that we live not simply in a period of cultural decline, when meanings have become muddy and stale, but rather in a period when one set of meanings — those of the cultivated classes — is fitfully contested by those who stand to gain from their collapse. There is a difference, in other words, between Alexandrianism and class struggle. The 20th century has elements of both situations about it, and that is why Greenberg's description, based on the Alexandrian analogy, applies as well as it does. But the end of the bourgeoisie is not, or will not be, like the end of Ptolemy's patriciate. And the end of its art will be likewise unprecedented. It will involve, and has involved, the kinds of inward-turning that Greenberg has described so compellingly. But it will also involve — and has involved, as part of the practice of modernism — a search for another place in the social order. Art wants to address someone, it wants something precise and extended to do; it wants *resistance,* it needs criteria; it will take risks in order to find them, including the risk of its own dissolution.[8] Greenberg is surely entitled to judge that risk too great, and even more to be impatient with the pretence of risk so dear to one fringe of modernist art and its patrons — all that stuff about blurring the boundaries between art and life, and the patter about art being "revolutionary". Entitled he is, but not in my opinion right. The risk is large and the chatter odious; but the alternative, I believe, is on the whole worse. It is what we have, as the present form of modernism: an art whose object is nothing but itself, and which never tires of discovering that that self is pure as only pure negativity can be, and which offers its audience that nothing, tirelessly and, I concede, adequately made over into form. A verdict on such an art is not a matter of taste — for who could fail to admire, very often, its refinement and ingenuity — but involves a judgement, still, of cultural possibility. Thus, while it seems to me right to expect little from the life and art of late capitalism, I still draw back from believing that the best one can hope for from art, even *in extremis,* is its own singular and perfect disembodiment.

Notes

[1]*Art and Literature,* Spring 1965, p.193-201.

[2]This carelessness distinguishes the present paper from two recent studies of Greenberg's early writings, S. Guilbaut's 'The New Adventures of the Avant-Garde in America', *October,* Winter 1980, and F. Orton and G. Pollock's '*Avant-Gardes* and Partisans Reviewed,' *Art History,* September 1981. I am indebted to both these essays, and am sure that their strictures on the superficiality — not to say the opportunism — of Greenberg's Marxism are largely right. (Certainly Mr. Greenberg would not now disagree with them.) But I am nonetheless interested in the challenge offered to most Marxist, and non-Marxist, accounts of modern history by what I take to be a justified, though extreme, pessimism as to the nature of established culture since 1870. That pessimism is characteristic, I suppose, of what Marxists call an ultraleftist point of view. I believe, as I say, that a version of some such view is correct, and would therefore wish to treat Greenberg's theory *as if* it were a decently elaborated Marxism of an ultraleftist kind; one which issues in certain mistaken views (which I criticize) but which need not so issue, and which might still provide, cleansed of those errors, a good vantage for a history of our culture.

[3]The essay on the poetry, from 1941, is reprinted in *Art and Culture.*

[4]In 'Avant-Grade and Kitsch'.

[5]Mr. Greenberg informs me the answer here is Yes, and points out that he even once had an exchange with Leavis, in *Commentary,* on Kafka — one which, he says, "I did not come out of too well."

[6]In 'The Present Prospects of American Painting and Sculpture', *Horizon,* Oct. 1947, p.20-30.

[7]In 'Art', *Nation,* 8 March 1947, p.284.

[8]This is not to smuggle in a demand for Realism again by the back door; or at least, not one posed in the traditional manner. The weakness or absence in modern art does not derive, I think, from a lack of grounding in "seeing" (for example) or a set of Realist protocols to go with that; but rather from its lack of grounding in some (any) specific practice of representation, which would be linked in turn to other social practices — embedded in them, constrained by them. The question is not, therefore, whether modern art should be figurative or abstract, rooted in empirical commitments or not so rooted, but whether art is now provided with sufficient constraints of any kind — notions of appropriateness, tests of vividness, demands which bring with them measures of importance or priority. Without constraints, representation of any articulacy and salience cannot take place. (One might ask if the constraints which modernism declares to be its own, and sufficient — those of the medium, or of private emotion and inner truth — are binding, or indeed coherent; or, to be harsh, if the areas of practice which it points to as the *sites* of such constraint — medium, emotion, even 'language' (sacred cow) — are existents at all, in the way that is claimed for them.)

After T. J. Clark:

Audience:
I think that you are raising a question which I am very pleased to
see being raised. I think that possibly you might have been as
intrigued as I was to hear Mr. Greenburg announce his interest in
Spengler now. And I was thinking how curious it would be — or
how curious it really is that somebody who emerges from a peculiar
moment in the development of — I guess I would have to agree —a
Marxist interpretation of modern culture in the late 30's — today
finds himself unable to do otherwise than quote Spengler and
Schopenhauer.

The irony that I see in that has to do with something that appears in the beginning of Greenburg's work. Which is that — and I
think you pointed this out — that somehow in that period of the
late thirties — or the American Marxism of the late 30's — there
was a hint of Spengler even at that moment. And that in some
cases, in some sense Greenberg's career, to those who have
watched it carefully for a long time, maybe more than any other,
perhaps because of its purity, represents the continuing working out
from a kind of hidden place of that Spenglerism which is latent in
the early period. In that sense also there is an ironic sense in which
purity in the Greenbergian sense represents a kind of melancholic
withdrawal. The melancholic element, or the pessimistic element in
the late thirties Marxism you label Eliotic Trotskyism, and you
seem to identify the presence of this pessimism (or at least it's not
clear how to identify the presence of this pessimism) in that Marxist
milieu or possibly the disoriented Marxist milieu with the presence
of Trotsky.

And I think that opens a question which certainly moves forward in time, but definitely also opens questions that go back to the
period possibly that Buchloh was talking about yesterday, arising
from the first Russian revolution. That question appears to be
open. I am thankful for the opening, but I am not positive exactly
what you want to say about that.

T. J. Clark:
Well thank you for the questions which are very thoughtful. The
first thing to say is that this is a sort of curiously uneasy situation in
that I am going to have to, in some sense, speak for someone who
is here, but — and anyway he can dispute it, so I am sure he
disputes most of it — but there is one thing I wish to stress which is

that I believe there are perfectly reasonable grounds on which one could retreat from the kinds of commitments and descriptions like the Marxist commitments and descriptions that I have rehearsed. I have not retreated from them — right — I find them more vivid and more usable on the whole than the assumptions that Greenberg now operates with. But we must remember what those grounds are: that for instance, the history of the so-called socialist world and the working class movement in our time, the history of Stalinism and of the Chinese Revolution, for many Marxists produced serious grounds on which cultural hope in that direction became impossible or jejune and that one was forced to reconcile oneself with the few remaining progressive elements within American capitalist culture. I don't on the whole agree, you see, with that analysis, but it is not an unreasonable one, given the extremity of the Stalinist phenomenon.

Secondly, I suppose that really connects with what I mean by Eliotic Trotskyism and the degree of pessimism. I mean Trotsky is there simply — he is a complex example — but what I meant by that was that he is there as the spokesman for the degree of risk involved in the whole project of civilization in the 1920's and 30's. I mean it's the Trotskyism of that sense that the choice is socialism or barbarism. That fascism, to which I would also add American capital and Stalinism, represents such a monstrous form of capitalist social order — state capitalist or private capitalist social order, that we are face to face with the possibility of the end of cultural organization — the end of cultural values as we know it.

So — and I think that is a perfectly right and proper pessimism or right and proper degree of extremism in the posing of the cultural question. It is not of course peculiar to Trotsky — the Frankfurt school thinkers of the same time have a very similar sense of what the cultural question — what the question of civilization involves. It is now very fashionable to attack them as, you know, the petty bourgeois nihilist pessimists, but I think that on the whole that attack comes from a kind of revived Stalinism which I hold despicable in its sense of what Stalinism and Fascism really represent.

Clement Greenberg:
May I correct you. . .

T. J. Clark:
Yes, surely yes.

Clement Greenberg:
I didn't reprint the "New Laocoon" because it was misunderstood,
as I told you, to mean that I saw purity as a value myself. I was
describing something. And that subsequently in another piece I
wrote ("Modernist Painting") I was describing something, not sub-
scribing to it. Nor did I ever imply that the values of art are
aesthetic values which were to be substituted for other values. I
believe that the aesthetic values, ultimate though they may be, are
not the supreme values. There are higher values than aesthetic
values and I think I have made that explicit only when prompted
by misunderstandings like yours. Thank you.

T. J. Clark:
Okay. Can I just ask you — well, I mean I reply in the form of a
question inevitably. If — I don't quite see how one is to read —read
your account of art and it's course as other than a proposal that,
first of all, that the question of culture and its survival proposes
itself as an urgent one in our time. Secondly, that art is the one
main possible carrier of cultural value — and thirdly that we have
somehow to accept a situation in which there is no longer a dialectic between other values and artistic values. A tension — a difference, but a tension. And that somehow or other descriptively, as
you said, you described the course of avant-garde art as a securing
of the specialness and purity, the irreducible presence of its medium
as its value. Now, if that is not substitutionism I don't know what
is, really.

Clement Greenberg:
Aesthetic experience may overlap with other kinds, but it does take
place in a realm of its own.

T. J. Clark:
Yes, I agree.

Clement Greenberg:
And to — its barbarism as Thomas Mann once said, "To take
aesthetic values and introduce them into questions of morality,"
say, and he is critical of Nietzsche for that reason. Now I have never
felt that morality should in any sense be affected by the aesthetic
factor. That's an absolute separation. How you can make it any
more emphatic than by saying it is absolute, I don't know. It simply
is a fact that I don't see art as having *ever*, in a real sense, affected

the course of human affairs.

T. J. Clark:
No, but that is not the argument between us. The argument is, what are the conditions in which a set of vivid and irreducible artistic processes and values remain vivid, remain usable, remain securable as a separate realm, as a realm with a richness and intensity. Now I was suggesting that the separateness of artistic value in its richness as a realm of value to which artists and their patrons subscribe is dependent on a rather complex cultural dialetic, and that your account of late capitalism is an account of that dialectic ceasing, and in that sense it's a substitutionism in that there is nothing left for art but its own values. They are no longer in active interplay with other values which they refuse to be subsumed under, or fused with, but with which they interact.

Clement Greenberg:
Alright. You are raising questions here that — again I am going to sound supercilious — betray that fact that you haven't read enough aesthetics. See, aesthetic values are ultimate. I know I sound awfully supercilious.

T. J. Clark:
That's alright. I don't mind.

Clement Greenberg:
But aesthetic value is an ultimate value, you see. Art may serve other ends than itself, but insofar as the aesthetic constitutes value it's an end in itself. I think the greatest philosopher my country ever produced, Peirce, saw that — to the point where he said ultimate values in general, let's say, someone dear to you is really cherished aesthetically — in the aesthetic mode. Now . . .

T. J. Clark:
Could I reply to you on my aesthetic readings. I mean . . .

Clement Greenberg:
Art and society interact, therefore the values interact. That's true, but in any given instance — historical instance — yes in actual fact the values do interact — religion and art the most conspicuous case — and yet . . .

T. J. Clark:
They are different.

Clement Greenberg:
. . . in the end, in the end, it doesn't deprive us from the pleasure of
a Titian — deriving pleasure of a Titian without being in the least
Christian. And Rembrandt, or Piero. And that's what happens
—it's not — yes we can think, oh they're inexplicably involved with
one another.

T. J. Clark:
Yes — what we are to reply to you here — what we are arguing
about is not the autonomy of a realm of artistic practice and artistic
evaluation. It is — we are arguing about the grounds on which that
autonomy is secured. Now — and — we are also arguing on our
reading of Kant. I don't agree with your reading of the *Critique of
Judgment* — which I have actually sort of, you know, flipped
through. And you know — it is one thing to argue for an irreducibility of a realm of judgment or aesthetic value. It is another thing
to argue that that irreducibility stands in an absolute disembodied
otherness from other realms of judgment and value. And that is not
what Kant . . .

Clement Greenberg:
That's not implied . . .

T. J. Clark:
But look . . .

Clement Greenberg:
I am not taking my point of departure from Kant here. I am taking
. . .

T. J. Clark:
It's the best.

Clement Greenberg:
. . . let's say — what's been written — alright Croce too, even
though I think Kant is superior. I consult my own experience and
my experience of other people's experience reports how religious
art finally got secularized not — I mean in the present — but
retroactively, and you will have to conclude then that aesthetic

value is self-justifying, ultimate. I keep harping on that because — alright — the conditions under which the Persian miniature was produced and appreciated have a hell of a lot to do with it all. But in the end we have this kind of alembication let's say. The whole question of the aesthetic here is taken too much for granted. We appreciate aesthetically — experience aesthetically ever so many things that arc not art — that are not art — and you have to go easy then.

T. J. Clark:
Well look, alright. Let me just — I will sort of up the pace slightly — because the difference between us is a serious one and you know the fact that you could raise applause earlier on — you know — by that statement . . .

Clement Greenberg:
Only from the artists in the gallery . . . (laughter and clapping) I'm sorry — that was demagoguery.

T. J. Clark:
Exactly. But I — it may or may not be true. Probably a few curators and dealers applauded, too . . . That's the problem right. That you unfortunately have become — I really do say this with respect — and I hope the paper demonstrates the respect — you have become a spokesman for a kind of devastating artistic self-satisfaction and laziness . . . (laughter and clapping) . . . I am not saying that that applies to all the artists you approve of. I am saying that because your vision — the crisis — the extremity of the situation of art in our time is presented now in such a stripped-down form that it gives license to those who say there is no problem, it's the aesthetic realm, let's get on with the job, don't talk, painter paint — all the clichés, and this is a danger.

Clement Greenberg:
I don't mind you saying that. That doesn't bother me. And let me say I appreciate your talk very much and felt highly complimented by it.

Nicole Dubreuil-Blondin

Feminism and Modernism: Paradoxes

The woman-paradigm has been ignored by all the major approaches to modernism, notably by structural linguistics which can be said to have provided contemporary critical thought with its most privileged models:[1]

> . . . even though early writers noted the difference in male and female linguistic usage, all linguists —or nearly all — act as if the question had never arisen: Saussure's notion of *langue,* and Chomsky's model of competence both seem to exclude the recognition of any such variance.

American formalism, dominating art-criticism in the post-war decades, was equally unmoved by the rise of a feminine problematic. Defining modernism as an auto-critical enterprise leading to the definition of specificity of each art-form, formalism translated the history of art since Manet into Wölffinnian terms of formal evolutionary cycles of refinement; thus it impeded the possibility of a typically feminine contribution. In its dialectical history, in fact, formalism naturalizes the producer of art and deals only with the connections between works. One of the few women to be seriously dealt with is Helen Frankenthaler. Michael Fried analyses her work as a stage in a design problem inaugurated by Pollock's drips and completed in Morris Louis' work.[2] In an attempt to map all the significant productions of the plastic arts' constant self-renewal, formalism pursues an aesthetic of the masterpiece, linking the great masters of the present with the great masters of the past. The facts have shown clearly that for reasons other than entirely aesthetic ones woman and the category of the "great master" have never gone together well.[3]

Yet even though formalist criticism is not too concerned with the artists, its vocabulary and its rhetoric none the less fashion "personalities" to measure up to the works. An analysis of the terms used in Greenberg's criticism to talk about Pollock and his work shows a constant recourse to manifest male power. There the artist, full of energy, is defined by his forcefulness, his frustration, his innate violence — a rugged and brutal character reminiscent of the myth of the all-conquering American hero. The work itself is situated in the same terms: monumental, brave, intense, extravagant, and powerful.[4] So the difficulties Pollock's wife Lee Krasner had in affirming herself, and Greenberg's harsh judgement of her, should be no surprise.[5]

> I never went for her paintings. She immolated her-
> self to Pollock. Lee should have had more faith in
> herself and more independence.

The criticism itself is ultimately inscribed within a particular sexual politics. When the formalist critic does not show his blatant misogyny — as is often the case with Greenberg — he employs an objective discourse in which only his educated eye is apparent. Rosalind Krauss recalls Philip Leider's astonishment about her age.[6] The tone of formalist criticism made her seem older than she really was. And, without a signature, even the sex of the author could be mistaken. The cold authoritarianism and the judgemental imperialism, detached from the text, made the criticism seem not only "old" but "male".

From the heart of the formalist fortress, then, it seems unthinkable to approach the problematic of feminine art. But recent transformations in the avant-garde are nonetheless provoking reflections on the place of the feminine dimension in art. For example, in America we have witnessed a theoretical and actual affirmation of women artists over the last fifteen years, sustained by an ever larger group of critics and art-historians. We can even see at the heart of the avant-garde a type of consecration relatively unheard of for women. Some women, like Eva Hesse, find themselves in the pantheon of the creators of contemporary art paradigms because of their specifically feminine practice, marked by the experience of a sexed body. Others, like Judy Chicago, are resolutely feminist, totally devoted (on formal, iconographic, material and socio-political levels) to the expression of "femininitude". Such a radical position would once have earned no more than a *succès de scandale*. But it was an almost academic reception given by the spectators who lined up in close ranks for a long wait, their heads buried in huge catalogues, to see the tables for the *Dinner Party* at the San Francisco Museum.

Women avant-garde: we can sense today the formation of a new and forceful alliance whose complexity has not yet been thoroughly examined and which at first sight seems to have found a paradoxical formulation. Must the woman-paradigm be considered as the model rupture, the total "other", the definitive subversion that will finally reconcile aesthetics and politics? Does its forceful arrival on the contemporary art-scene mark an assault on an enemy territory that must be conquered and rebuilt on better foundations? Or is not the avant-garde itself undergoing profound changes in its post-modernist phase,[7] its new configurations corresponding exactly to the problematics of women's art? Will that art be simply another chapter — albeit a chapter particularly rich in plastic propositions — of the dominant art that is now creating history?[8]

The question of women's relations to contemporary art was implicitly allowed at a conference in Montreal in September 1979. Although the position of women had been solicited (with Lucy Lippard as its representative), it had no real official voice and was not discussed as such. Yet it made itself felt beneath each critique, each explanation of the classic notions of American formalism. Formalism was attacked for its rationalist imperialism and authoritarianism, and found itself trampled beneath appeals to the emotions and to the imaginary. Its classic formal analysis was threatened by the infiltration of new, more autobiographical substance; art was beginning to entertain more open and more ambiguous structures.

The dogma of the specificity of medium and of the flatness of surface was to be replaced by a real critical function that would attempt the insertion of art into the social (trying to avoid the traps of a party line, however). At the source of this interrogation of formalism we find the fractured condition of contemporary art-practice: fractured, in the sense that its multiple aspects by far exceed the traditional categories while none of these aspects is dominant (the formalism of the fifties and sixties related above all to painting); these are fragmented and individual propositions, appearing to escape any form of categorization or grouping. Ultimately, in the background of an artistic map peppered with islands, we find a change in the relation between artistic and political power: this marks the end of the unilateral and preponderant influence of the United States over the western world.

Within this new geography there seems to be room for the feminine problematic. Lucy Lippard, the missing link in the Montreal conference and the most widely known championer of women's art, can serve here as an Ariadne, providing the thread for an exploration of the labyrinthine relations between feminine art-practice and the complicated field of postmodernity. Lippard seems a figure cut to exactly the size of the present situation. From an historico-formalist position in the sixties, she found herself ardently defending minimal art because of its resistance to the strict ortho-doxy of formalism. She then became involved with political debate and feminist militancy, trying to put into question once more the meaning of art and critical procedures; her astounding lucidity and her capacity for self-analysis allowed her to understand fully the position of her own discourse at its every stage.

The introduction to her book *From the Center* (now consi-dered a classic on the relation of women and art) speaks of a double rupture at the heart of feminist critical consciousness: a rupture with formalist criticism as a dominant discourse, expressed in the following terms:[9]

> I recognized now the seeds of feminism in my re-volt against Clement Greenberg's patronization of artists, against the imposition of the taste of one class on everybody, against the notion that if you don't like so-and-so's work for the 'right' reasons, you can't like it at all, as well as against the 'mas-terpiece' syndrome, the 'three great artists' syn-drome and so forth.

A rupture, too, on the level of an art-practice that seems to be the perfect antithesis of 'male' production and that establishes new criteria. Still in the introduction to *From the Center,* Lippard makes much of her perplexity about the almost total inversion of perspective on the question of the character and conditions of creativity in the two sexes. She had believed that the serious artist worked in big studios with all the professional advantages; she found women artists working in the corner of a man's studio, in the kitchen or in their own rooms. American art, whatever its ambi-tion, seemed to demand large scale; women preferred more modest dimensions — either by necessity or by choice. The importance of men's art was measured by what formal advances it made on previous art; women, more hesitant and more vulnerable, were more open to the sharing of their experiences and were sustained more by personal confidence. Thus in Lippard's book the criticism and practice of women's art is straight away presented as a retreat from the ideology of formalism.

With the help of the autobiographical remarks that under-pin *From the Center* we can interpret Lippard's voluntary critical marginalization as the corollorary of a particular social marginali-zation of the artistic field. Several formalist critics of Lippard's generation hold university degrees wielding both learned academic discourse and theoretical argumentation equally proficiently. From their positions in universities or in the major museums they enjoy an institutional prestige which affirms their position of authority. Lippard presents herself and her career as an "anti-academic rebel-lion" and chooses art rather than English Literature because she refused to be dictated to in terms of what she should think; she abandons her college studies to go to Paris and wander around the galleries; she tries social work, dedicating herself to teaching Eng-lish and geography to Aztec children; she is refused work in galler-ies because she does not answer to the "pretty" worker stereotype; she it taken on as an art-history researcher and begins her training solely in order to be paid more per hour for her work; she remains even now a freelance, despite her work for several prestigious jour-nals such as *Arts, Artforum,* and *Art International;* she is in close touch with artists, often those who are not in the mainstream of American art. These days, she frequents feminists and feminist circles that have little artistic recognition. She used to be friendly with the group of minimalists ostracized by Post Painterly Abstrac-tion formalism (the Bowery Boys, as opposed to the Black Moun-tain Boys, and including Robert and Sylvia Mangold, Frank Viner, Dan Graham, Ray Donarski, Eva Hesse, Tom Doyle, Sol Le Witt and Robert Ryman — all little known when Lippard was defending them).

Since my own reflections are concerned to discover, through the critical theory and the actual work of artists cham-pioned by Lippard, the inter-relations between women's art and the art of the avant-garde, the critical engagement with the first princi-ples of formalism must be examined more closely. An early collec-tion of articles, aptly titled *Changing,* [10] gives an account of the period with the Bowery Boys in the latter half of the sixties. This series of essays is devoted largely to minimal art and its gradual progression toward conceptual art. The collection tries to define a practice that escapes the modernist orthodoxy. First of all, it is interesting to see that the collection deals with African Art, Dada, Surrealism, and Pop Art as well — procedures that can be included in Gene Swenson's "other tradition". That term designates an art that transgresses mere formal problems and embraces content (subliminally, if not overtly), starting with a suggestive iconography and opening out onto a general reflection on vision, and considering art's relation to the social. Reticent about the luminaries of Post Painterly Abstraction (she thinks that Stella reaches a point of crisis with his *Protractor* series and she accuses Jules Olitski of feebleness and of superficial beauty), Lippard prefers Ad Reinhardt whose rejective purism implies a moral engagement with the world.

And yet it is in her analysis of minimalism and conceptual art that Lippard notates the main deviations from formalist norms — deviations that will be more marked in certain categories of feminist art. Because it abandons strict medium specificity and points toward the demise of painting, and because it assumes an experience that departs from form in order to take into account the environment, minimal art is presented as the first blow to be struck against the ideology of modernism. That is why it is condemned for its theatricality by Michael Fried.[11] Formalism relied upon a few structural *a prioris* that acted as indices of "modernism" — affirmation of the support surface, all-over or deductive composition guaranteeing the picture's self-referential and auto-critical dimension. Lippard, on the other hand, is interested in any sort of deviation that threatens the regularity of structure or that opens up paths other than the consideration of medium specificity. She notes, for example, the arrival of an eccentric type of abstraction that is founded upon the irregular forms carried by untreated materials and that will have a considerable impact on post-minimal art: Robert Morris' felts, Bruce Nauman's strips of latex. An organic or erotic metaphor is continually at play here because of the suggestive nature of the contours and palpable qualities of these materials. Radically opposed to geometric form, this tendency also suggests the use of mixed solutions that combine the regular and the irregular within the same structure. Eva Hesse excels at this kind of juxtaposition of contraries, introducing into her work a certain discontinuity, strange and unexpected effects that are alien to art of the formalist persuasion. Another method of disrupting the regularity or rationality of structure consists in introducing a distortion between the conceptual aspect of a system and its perception. This is what is arrived at in the deliberately perverse perspectives of Ron Davis that always deny depth in the design, undercutting it by the sheer brilliance of colour. The pastels that hover on the surface of a Larry Poons mask an infrastructure of mathematical regularity. The concrete experience of a Sol LeWitt construction produces effects (classical beauty, presence) unforeseen in his system's intellectual construction. Everywhere there are profoundly ambiguous relationships: the meaning of the work is never immediate but must be won through uncertainty. A final aspect of this perversion of structure consists in the repetition of a single form to the point of absurdity; the obsessive development of a system. Carl Andre and Hanne Darboven excell in this sort of compulsive activity that turns into a fixation.

As well as deconstructing the kinds of structure favoured by formalism the art that Lippard defends in *Changing* can offer a broadening of aesthetic experiences. The notion of experience is, of course, crucial to the Greenbergian concept of modernism because it is in an unique and novel encounter with each work that a judgement of relevance and competence can be made. There is something audacious and defiant about formalist judgement but it remains excessively reliant upon the notion of medium specificity and is too much concerned with comparisons to the great art of the past. The experience of postformalism is more usually informed by a non-artistic "content". Pop Art, indeed, mimics the perception of the modern world just as much as it mimics the perception of modernist painting. Since Michael Fried's development of the idea of optical space, formalist experience has appealed primarily to the eye. The postformalist art that Lippard defines calls upon the imagination, re-awakens the unconscious and has commerce with the whole human body: the sense of touch, for example, is continually appealed to through soft forms and materials. Reference to nature, prohibited after Newman's decision to move the horizontal through the axis of the vertical line, makes its return in many different ways: through organic metaphors, or more subtly through the shift of attention from form to process, through the investigation of energy transformations, or through the use of nature as both support and material. Those primitive connotations, so dear to Action Painting, resurface. Lawrence Weiner's Land Art takes on the figure of a ritual. Minimal constructions seem to be wrapped in the mysterium, evoking memories of ancient ziggurats and pyramids (Tony Smith's sculptures deal with this mysterious covering, echoing Mayan Pyramids constructed over pre-classical temples). By rejecting all forms of pictorial illusion (even optical) and by insisting on the quiddity of the art-work, minimalism recalls attention to the real space of the art-object's installation and finally opens out onto a political dimension. *Changing* discusses the collosal proportions of some minimal structures (those of Smith and Bladen) but is equally concerned with the public nature of open-air sculpture and with the question of spectator participation.

Lippard conceives of this period of formalism's disintegration as one of an impossible synthesis of irrecncilable elements. Modernist theory was fond of dialectic of opposites provided that those opposites could be transcended by formal solutions to the problems posed. In Greenberg's view, Post Painterly Abstraction is a progression from Painterly Abstraction because it reconciles colour to the opening of field. On the other hand, he cannot approve of Jasper Johns' brilliant oscillations between paintings and objects.[12] It is with a similar series of tensions that Lippard ends her analyses in *Changing* — art as art is there confronted by an art that turns toward life, abstraction is confronted by figuration, classical construction by romantic emotion, the conceptualizing approach by a more intuitive attitude. At this point Lippard still declines to disrupt contradiction in favour of a definitively anti-formalist option. She rejects, for example, reference that is too direct or too specific. She enjoys the work of James Rosenquist because it does not display openly the very personal connotations of the subject matter. The work does not really tell a story — it is more like a sort of visual boomerang. She reacts in the same way to exhalations of emotion, associated with the occasional vagueness and confusion in fifties expressionism. The art of today, claims Lippard, purports to be specific and factual above all. It remains serious, moral and difficult (all qualities that are quite in accordance with a formalist ethic, tainted with puritanism). It implies a fear of the pleasure principle and rests upon a base of self-abnegation. It is amusing to consider that the art condemned in *Changing* for its facile nature sometimes exhibits the very same qualities as are conventionally attributed to the feminine world. Thus Lippard reproaches the decorative prettiness of certain abstract practices such as Olitski's. The use of art as a political tool is also excluded, as is activism in the field of art. Lippard is wary of arguments, labels, demonstrations and group solidarity. Art should ultimately be of the avant-garde, or not at all. There are some artists who have retreated into the "private" practice of abstraction or figuration and whose only desire is to perform good work in the haven of the difficult choices to be made in high intensity art. Lippard is not interested in them at all. A demanding art transmits its demands to criticism. There is no reason for the rarified atmosphere of aesthetic pleasure to be darkened by emotions and daily obsessions, by past, present or future, or in a word by "human experience." And what about "feminine experience"?

As we saw above from the introduction to *From the Center,* that experience is presented for Lippard as almost the inverse of the usual experience of avant-garde art. Small spaces, small works, small aesthetic certainties, compensated by a great propensity for communicating about the problems of creativity: *that* is what is found in woman's space. This feeling of displacement in relation to the norms echoes the revelatory character assumed, according to Lippard, by the discovery of art's repressed feminine dimension. It was during a vacation abroad in a little fishing village in which she isolated herself with her five year old son in order to write fiction (an activity that she had long wanted to develop as her "real" career) that Lippard realized that her writing sprang not so much from herself as from her artist friends — the men especially. Wanting to write for herself, she went on to assume her own femininity and thus to rejoin the community of women. Ironically, it was fiction that made her aware of things she had for too long ignored or refused to deal with. But this was not the first break for Lippard. Years of political activism had already removed her from the purely aesthetic domain and had obliged her to approach anew the function of art.

Reading the articles in *From the Center* that sum up five years of engagement with feminist questions, we might still be surprised to see the continuity between that book and *Changing.* Women's art, interrogated as a structure that carries meaning, is close in many respects to the postformalist art analyzed in the earlier collection. For example, it is significant that feminine art (art produced by women) is not clearly distinguished from feminist art (art that tries to explore carefully and with commitment all aspects of women's experience as it is dictated by nature or culture). Lippard's book presents stars from both camps, side, by side, like Eva Hesse and Mary Miss on the one hand, and Judy Chicago and Faith Ringold on the other. Few completely unknown names crop up in the course of her monographs, whose production is suitably tied to all the great options of postmodernist art. Minimalism proper is a dead letter but conceptual art survives. Added to that are Body Art, performance, Land Art, the creation of environments and a few figurative paintings . . . . There are few examples that arise out of recent paradigms either through definitive artisanal decisions (the use of traditional female materials is always transcended by the political dimension — Faith Ringold — or by posing of a formal problem — Brenda Miller) or through the adoption of outmoded "styles" revived within a feminist procedure (except for a few rather problematic realist images, no return to pre-war movements can be perceived).

The question of format constitutes a good example of the intersection between postmodernist art and women's art as they are analysed by Lippard. Having announced that women were deciding, often by necessity, to work within smaller dimensions Lippard actually cites very few modestly sized objects in this book. Alongside a small work by Hannah Wilke (13″ × 13″ × 1½″) and a few of Louise Bourgeois' touchables, we see Jo Baer's huge paintings (22″ × 96″ × 4″) and Reeva Potoff's imposing polyurethane sculpture (3′4″ × 12′ × 15′1″).[13] The problem of dimension — as in many formalist postmodernist practices — is no longer explicitly posed in terms of object format. It is transposed to landscape scale (and yet Lippard does not analyse why so many women excell in Land Art), or is evaluated as an extension of systems and networks (in the case of artists who work with mass-media and with audiovisuals, among others).

Trying to map out a significant women's structure within aesthetic experience Lippard reaches a series of propositions that recall the plastic and theoretical options of *Changing. From the Center* is in fact concerned with procedures that mark a detour from modernist form. The women's structure is described there as an apparent absence of order (feeble design, ennervation, flexible treatment and soft touch), or even as a *trapped* order, messy and fragmented (the grid, the modernist structure *par excellence,* suffers repeated assaults). Eva Hesse's 1968 *Fiberglass* uses "containers" 20″ high, all sufficiently similar to suggest a system; but the profiles of each unit vary continuously and they are distributed in a way that appears to be random. As in certain postformalist practices, order can be seen elsewhere taken to extremes by the obsessive repetition of elements and the proliferation of detail. The closed rows of crayoned lines arranged by Agnes Martin on her canvases have nothing to do with logical exposition or classical clarity *(Untitled 7,* 1974). They are always at the edge of invisibility. Lippard is concerned also with other recurrent structural aspects of women's art and suggests that what we find there is a surplus of meaning, a feminine investment of worldy experience. Rounded forms, or forms with a central kernel (circle, domes, spheres, cylinders, pouches) abound, she says, in women's production along with layered superimpositions, folds, veils, all producing an effect of sedimentation or envelopment. A constant play of interior and exterior arises from these structural preferences. In Lippard's book all sorts of examples overlap, from Cynthia Carlson's almost surreal graphics *(Untitled,* a 1970 painting, neatly suggests a vaginal opening), to the more devolved experiences of Land Art like the well sunk by Mary Miss in the Connecticut countryside *(Sunken Pool,* 1974). Besides appropriating certain privileged configurations, women often use a palette and materials that are traditionally given as feminine: pastels, especially pinks, appear all over. Women return to natural materials, soft, tactile and sensual, handled with techniques that are almost domestic (rolling, folding, weaving, sewing, embroidering). And yet these choices cannot be said to be exclusive to women. Centered images, circular or not, were already distinguishing marks of Post Painterly Abstraction and even of Pop Art (Jasper Johns' targets, or Kenneth Noland's). Transforming these images into flowers or breasts does little to solve the problem (we will come back to this later). The same reaction comes too with the palette and materials. Lippard seems to disapprove of Olitski's almost feminine, seductive appeal achieved in the range of hues and tones he chooses. With the proliferation of resins and acrylics in the sixties the painterly palette had lent itself to a whole range of connotations, such as those of the urban commercial environment, scorned by "great" formalist art as much as feminine connotations are. The use of soft and tactile materials was already apparent in the art of Oldenburg who used them with an "appropriate technique" — sewing, which Oldenburg entrusted to his wife Pat!

Beyond these strictly formal considerations, we can say that the return of the autobiographical subject and the opening up of the art-field onto political considerations are both part of the new dimension explored by women's art and by postmodernist art in general. Women are recounting an original experience at both biological and social levels. The ritual transposition of domestic work and the exploration of intimate spaces both form a large part of the feminine proposition, manifested in objects (Marjorie Strider's brooms that work in conjunction with an "organic" drain — *Brooms,* 1972), or in procedures (Mierle Laderman Uncles, in a performance, cleans the floor of the Wadsworth Atheneum Museum — *Washing, Maintenance: Maintenance Art Activity III,* 22 July, 1973). Archetypal connotations (the return to mother-earth) are apparent in certain constructions, in Land Art and in performances (Alice Aycock digging into gallery floors — *Simple Network of Underground Wells and Tunnels,* 1975). Indeed, in all the branches of recent art that take the body as object, as support or as communicating vehicle, the contribution of women seems especially dynamic and stimulating for the work of men. In video and performance art women may use a relation to the imperial but problematic body that has presided over their individual and collective histories. Taking the stage, playing roles, standing in front of the mirror: woman has always had a privileged relationship to these situations. (Eleanor Antin exploits the phenomenon by having herself photographed as a star ballerina — *The Artist as Prima Ballerina,* 1973). Lippard emphasizes that this ground never needed to be prepared by men. The exploration of the body and analysis of one's relations to self and others also have their more extreme side, always threatening to spill over from the avant-garde. They are not always distinguishable from pure and simple neuroses. In France this art sometimes sinks to the level of lewd exhibitionism: "beautiful" bodies are always popular. Adrian Piper's U.S. performances, however, are threatening — although at certain moments she cannot distinguish between art and merely bizarre behaviour.

Lippard's readings lead to the conclusion that there are many links between women's art and postmodernist art. The current interest of (and interest in) women's artistic productions is not the only consequence of a new relation of forces in the art world in the social. An "inside" complicity favors a more open critical approach that allows the rise of women's art.

It could be objected here that to explore the relationship between women's art and postmodernist art via Lucy Lippard is to falsify the debate at its source. This criticism is faithful to both of these two areas, and this has more than once thrown it into startling contradiction. So we can suggest that the mobility and the pluralism seen in women's art and the art described in *Changing* are more a product of the tentativeness and heterogeneity of Lippard's approach than of the art itself (many people in fact regard both minimal and conceptual art as prolongations of the authoritarian rationalism of modernism). We could also say that Lippard is continuing to "change" and that the analysis of her two published collections largely blocks other more radical critical engagement. Nonetheless it would seem that her examination of this transitional moment retains its pertinence in relation to what the conjunction of women's art and postmodernist practices brings to light. It provides evidence of the difficulty of finding a "place" for the exercise of women's art, and questions the foundation of the delimitation of a feminine specificity at a moment when the quest for *any* specificity — medium specificity in particular — is being put into question.

It is, besides, the systematic exploration and the unconditional defence of a feminine territorialism[14] that seems to sanction the real change for Lippard and, this time, makes her relationship with postmodernism more than problematic. If the specific analyses of *From the Center* are witness to women's production as the undermining of dominant, phallocratic modernism, the very act of regrouping from *another* "center" and the militancy that underlies such a gesture give pause for thought. Critical reaction in fact risks being turned into authority.

It is revealing to find a similar ambiguity in some of the artists that Lippard defends. Judy Chicago is especially relevant here because she is the most complete paradigm of engaged feminism and because she proposes its emblem — the centered form. An examination of her major work, the *Dinner Party,* shows that by mimicking postmodernist strategies she takes control of the field of art in the name of social struggle, and she thus turns art away from its internally reflexive dimension.

Judy Chicago's iconography needs first to be questioned. On the structural level the centered image already belonged to the critical register of modernist painting, whether in the ready-made form of Jasper Johns' targets or as the result of the minimalist reorganisation of the paint surface such as we find in the work of Frank Stella or Kenneth Noland. In the heyday of formalism it bespoke an epistemology of pictorial function: it checked European-style composition whose assymetries and carefully balanced tensions remain filled with narrative content, recalling something beyond the painting itself; it returned attention to the painting surface as the place where meaning is inscribed through the work of colour. What, then, can be said about the surplus of content that Judy Chicago's procedures bring? Is it the art of a postmodernist to transform the centered image into a flower, a butterfly, the vulva, or to endow the vacuity of a now ruined structure (its critical interaction with the history of the medium having been exhausted) with a symbol of the eternal feminine?

This symbolisation appears more like a regression, however much the polysemic richness of the reference might make it appear otherwise. Meaning is imposed from the outside (according to the author's own intentions) and points toward the recognition of an absolute outside to the work: imaged femininity. Instead of investigating within the work itself the function of signification — perhaps by the inscription of a biologically or socially marked subject — Chicago's symbolic centered form prevents any internal critical move. It invests a structure formally consecrated by modernism, the profit of whose prestige it reaps. The centered image thus becomes an icon, a banner (a support that Chicago uses with predilection at the entrance of the *Dinner Party),* rallying a convocation of feminist forces. Art is mobilised for social action.

And yet the *Dinner Party* exceeds the problem of the centered image. On the conceptual level as well as the political the project is ambitious; on a wider level it poses the question of the recuperation of postmodernity. Does it not take history as its object (the history of women's contribution to culture and humanity) while aligning itself with those facets of postmodernist art that proceed by constant reference to the past? Does it not attack the specificity of medium by attaching to the debate about the compartmentalising of genres, a debate about their hierarchy (the *Dinner Party* itself making an almost exclusive appeal to artisanal practices)? Does it not imply a critical return to the notion of the author and the conditions of the work's production?

The answer to these questions is, not really. The reason for this must be imputed to the same strategies of appropriation that allow Judy Chicago to use the centered figure as a vehicle for the feminist message. This symbolic installation, the *Dinner Party,* makes use of the museum (instead of the painting surface) in order to play with its prestige to Chicago's own advantage and in order to consecrate the relation of women to the development of the world. Consecration of the "master artist" (mistress artist?), first of all, since it is the name of Judy Chicago herself that remains attached to the title and that serves as a guarantee. The consecration of the artisan — and we no longer know whether to appreciate it for technical execution (the hours of patient work solidified into the confection) or for the aura conferred upon it by the preciousness of the materials used, or for the solemn nature of the event. The *Dinner Party* finally marks the return to the museum full of beautiful and well-made works, the like of which have not been seen for some time. The consecration, in the end, of a history of women that takes off from myth and proposes a long list of "positive" models drawn from a list of famous names.

Last Supper, or Holy Grail, with female participants, this installation takes on the character of the definitive ritual: the ritual of a fictional meal to which the spectator is mentally invited, a processionary ritual which leads the gathered crowd around slowly from the bannered ante-chamber to the main dining room. So this is the site of ritual whose ceremony the spectator completes; the *Dinner Party* evokes spaces that are charged with energy, like caverns, grottos, temples, megalithic fields where women artists can go to be refreshed and to reactivate the myth of the mother-goddess. These pilgrimages to the source are what Gloria Orenstein was speaking of at the conference on the representation of the great goddess in women's art (Montreal, February 1981). The emotion aroused by her piece (emotion that Lippard sees as an index to the value of a work as art) has more to do with this common attachment to the ritual act than with the artistic experience proper. This sort of ritual never goes against itself by providing a critique in the field of art itself, nor does it denounce, for example, the way the museum neutralizes and ritualizes any potential critique of the art. The *Dinner Party's* goals are enlistment and mobilisation. It affirms more than it questions.

The above remarks might lead us to a re-evaluation of *From the Center*. The text allows it to be understood that in time the different tendencies of women's art will reveal their common roots and will define a specific ethos. Only the underdeveloped state of the present circumstance prevents us from seeing this clearly at the moment. On the contrary, it seems to me that this book uses these apparent likenesses to cover over the fault lines between those women artists who pursue their critique of modernism through the immanence of their work, and the militants whose practice is governed by a sort of transcendence — the "cause's" transcendence, the eternal feminine. It is interesting to note that this political or mystical skid occurs elsewhere than in Lippard's book; it often takes its justification from iconography. It is because of their "representing" various figures of the mother-goddess (from the Shaman to the germinating seed) that certain artists were grouped together at Orenstein's conference. Stylized illustrations went side by side with performance without having any effect on the rhetorical commentary.

Counter all this, how much more interesting it is to see procedures that graft experiences, sociologically or biologically marked as feminine, onto a more profound questioning of the function of meaning production in art. A case in point is the video-performance by Rita Myers *(Slow Squeeze 1,* 1973, 10 minutes) described by the artist herself in *Changing:*[15]

> The camera is trained on myself, lying on my back with my arms extended over my head. My body extends across the width of the monitor, feet and fingertips just within its lateral boundaries. The monitor is used as a feedback device. The camera

begins a very slow zoom in, which is at first unde-
tectable. As this zoom begins to shrink the field of
the monitor, I am forced to relinquish the space
occupied by my body in its initial position. My
goal is to remain within the boundaries of the monitor as its field progressively diminishes. In the end,
the space allowed me is extremely compressed, and
my body is curled in on itself, as tight as possible.

This is, without doubt, the transcription of a "typically"
feminine experience. The absence of vital space, the feeling of com-
pression and the incapacity to act are shown as woman's lot in
society. It is still possible to read the work in terms of agressivity
and rape — terms to which the phallic nature of the lens is (mor-
phologically and functionally) not foreign. We can discern here
archetypal connotations of a return to the mother's breast in the
body's process of folding itself up and trying to maintain itself in
the visual field (the action functions here as the opposite of the
birth ritual exalted in some feminisms).

This work avoids the traps of illustration and expression by
holding firmly to a sort of epistemology of vision. In fact it deals
with the function of frame, the delimitation of semantic field and
the control that a reading trajectory can impose in any such delim-
ited field. As is often the case with video, other media are invoked
— theatre, cinema, and even painting — and their privileged construction of meaning is played upon by putting them in the frame,
by catching them in vision. By refusing to be diverted or cut off by
the objective approach, Rita Myers puts forward an art that de-
nounces such controls. This is a regression that allows itself a
critical dimension and seems to be more in accord with a postmodernist realization than with any regressive return to figuration or to
the symbol as witness to the cause of women.

A modest example, this video none the less demonstrates
the necessity of commentary, of some articulation of the action
combined with its iconography and narrativity in the process of
perception, and the necessity of making the proper critical function
of the work emerge in the context of art's recent past. Greenberg's
modernism was sensitive to a particular and immanent criticism,
but held a much too restrictive view of the work's content. For its
part, the social history of art too often neglects the self-referential
dimension in its haste to attach the work to the socio-economic
infra-structure of the time. If women's art (like the best of post-
modernist art) undermines the certainty of these two positions —

formalist and Marxist — that will indubitably constitute its major contribution to "human culture".

(translation by Paul Smith)

Notes

*The first part of this text is a slightly modified version of an article called "De quel centre? La situation paradoxale de l'art des femmes," *Bulletin de la Galerie Jolliet,* no. 5, March 1981.

[1]Anne-Marie Houdebine, "Les femmes et la langue," *Tel Quel,* 74, Winter 1977.

[2]*Morris Louis,* New York, Abrams p.11.

[3]An excellent article on this question is Linda Nochlin's "Why have there been no great women artists?" in *Art and Sexual Politics,* eds. T. B. Hess and E. C. Baker, New York, 1973, p.1-39.

[4]Nicole Dubreuil-Blondin, "Number One," in *Jackson Pollock: Questions,* Musée d'Art Contemporain, Montréal, 1979, p.64.

[5]Quoted by Cindy Nemser, "Lee Krasner's Paintings, 1946-1949", *Artforum,* Dec. 1973, p.64.

[6]Rosalind Krauss, "A View of Modernism," *Artforum 11: 1,* Sept. 1972, p.48.

[7]The term postmodernist is used here in preference to postmodern so as to mark its provenance in the American context which is the ground of the present article in respect to both the body of art and the theory dealt with.

[8]Even if postmodernism is regarded by some theoreticians as marking the end of history, or at least of an evolutionary concept of the history of modernity in art, and even if institutions and markets are in some way confused by the complexity of contemporary artistic productions, we must still recognize that recent trends in art nonetheless are consecrated by the media and institutions (even video and performance have their exegetes just as Post Painterly Abstraction did in its time; art works will perhaps pass into the history of art without a plastic "aura" but with a theoretical aura that has been constructed around them).

[9]*From the Center: Feminist Essays on Women's Art,* New York, Dutton 1976, p.3. Further references to this book will not be given since it is the main object of my analysis. The same for *Changing* (see note 10).

[10]*Changing: Essays in Art Criticism,* New York, Dutton 1971.

[11]"Art and Objecthood", in *Minimal Art: A Critical Anthology,* ed. G. Battcock, New York, Dutton 1968, p.116-147.

[12]"After Abstract Expressionism", in *New York Painting and Sculpture: 1940-1970,* ed. H. Geldzahler, New York, Dutton 1969, p.360-365.

[13]As Lucy Lippard is in a position to know, men too are nowadays quite fond of small format.

[14]I am grateful to René Payant for drawing my attention to a text which connects the pursuit of territory to a fascist ideology, Guy Scarpetta's *Eloge du cosmopolitisme,* Paris, Grasset 1981.

[15]*Op. cit.,* p.54.

After Nicole Dubreuil-Blondin

Allan Sekula:
I am a little curious about your reading of Lucy Lippard — the points in her career as a critic. It seems to me that in looking at Lucy's more recent work, that she has made a certain break with what may be a kind of orthodoxy, or kind of institutionalized feminism that I think has emerged in American visual art precisely around projects like the *Dinner Party*. And I think some of the indications of that in Lucy's work are her turn to doing somewhat more journalistic criticism and more general cultural criticism.

I am thinking about her article on retrochic in the *Village Voice* with the kind of return of mannerist, fascist and racist mannerisms in American culture and punk culture and in some of the culture of fashion.

Also, I think Lucy has begun to very explicitly work toward a socialist feminist position which is of course a minority position within U.S. feminism, but one which is gaining strength and developing a real discourse, among feminists. I've seen it, for example, in the Women's Building in Los Angeles, where there has been in my time in Los Angeles a certain real legitimate distrust. A quite understandable distrust on the part of women artists in Los Angeles of the culture of the left and absolutely no communication with that culture. And if I could characterize the Women's Building I think it had tended to have a strong notion of feminism which involved concepts of matriarchy and so on. And in around 1978 there began to be certain movements between people involved in, for example, the socialist community school in Los Angeles who — male socialists began to understand the importance of the feminist critique and feminist artists who began to understand the need to deal with political economy and we saw projects, for example like the work of Suzanne Lacy and Leslie Leibowitz dealing with a didactic strategy — a theatrical strategy for dealing with rape. And I think Lucy increasingly deals with those kinds of issues.

Her support recently has been of projects like the Times Square show which is a weird amalgam of marginal art projects like Fashion Moda in the South Bronx — projects like the social art documentation project. So that in a sense I think she has moved somewhat.

Nicole Dubreuil-Blondin
Yes. Well I did say that she has been changing since. Changing.

That's true. And I did take these two books just because I wanted to enquire at this moment when there was this sort of joining. I just wanted to enquire about the structural relationship. Of course, my point of view was probably basically structural. I knew about her more political activities, but I just decided to analyse this part and maybe you are right to bring them in.

Thomas Crow

Modernism and Mass Culture in the Visual Arts

I

What are we to make of the continuing involvement between modernist art and the materials of low or mass culture?
From its beginnings, the artistic avant-garde has discovered, renewed, or re-invented itself by identifying with marginal, 'non-
artistic' forms of expressivity and display — forms improvised by
other social groups out of the degraded materials of capitalist manufacture. Manet's "Olympia" offered a bewildered middle-class
public the flattened pictorial economy of the cheap sign or carnival
backdrop, the pose and allegories of contemporary pornography
superimposed over those of Titian's "Venus of Urbino". For both
Manet and Baudelaire, can we separate their invention of powerful
models of modernist practice from the seductive and nauseating
image the modern city seemed to be constructing for itself? Similarly, can we imagine the Impressionist invention of painting as a
field of both particularized and diffuse sensual play separately from
the new spaces of commercial pleasure the painters seem rarely to
have left — spaces whose packaged diversions were themselves
contrived in an analogous pattern? The identification with the social practices of mass diversion — whether uncritically reproduced,
caricatured, or transformed into abstract Arcadias —remains a
durable constant in early modernism. The actual debris of that
world makes its appearance in Cubist and Dada collage as part of a
more aggressive renewal of the deconstructive course of the avant-
garde. Even the most austere and hermetic twentieth-century ab-
stractionist, Piet Mondrian, in his final "Boogie-Woogie" series,
anchored the results of decades of formal research in a delighted
discovery of American traffic, neon, and commercialized black
music. In recent history, this dialectic has repeated itself most vividly in the paintings, assemblages, and happenings of the artists

who arrived on the heels of the New York School: Johns, Rauschenberg, Oldenburg, and Warhol.

How fundamental is this repeated pattern to the history of
modernism? At the outset, the terms in which the question is posed
ought to be clarified. So far, I have been using the words avant-
garde and modernism in a roughly equivalent way: modernism
designating the characteristic practice which goes on within the
social and ideological formation we call the avant-garde. But there
remains a tension or lack of fit between the two terms which might
have a bearing on the meaning of this observed connection between
modernism and appropriated low culture. Modernism as a word
carries connotations of an autonomous, inward, self-referential and
self-critical artistic practice; our usual use of the term avant-garde is
on the other hand much more inclusive, encompassing extra-
artistic styles and tactics of provocation, group closure, and social
survival. We might choose to see the record of avant-garde appropriation of devalued or marginal materials as part of the latter,
extrinsic and expedient in relation to the former. Yes, time and
again low-cultural forms are called on to displace and estrange the
deadening givens of accepted practice, and some residuum of these
forms is visible in many works of modernist art. But might not such
gestures be seen as only means to an end, weapons in a necessary,
aggressive clearing of space, which are discarded when their work is
done? This has been the prevailing argument on those occasions
when modernism's practitioners and apologists have addressed the
problem. This is the case even in those instances where the inclusion of refractory material drawn from low culture was most conspicuous and provocative. In the early history of modernist painting, these would be Manet's images of the 1860's and Seurat's
depiction in the 1880's of the cut-rate commercial diversions of
Paris. And in each instance we have an important piece of writing
by an avant-garde artist which addresses the confrontation between
high and low culture, but assigns the popular component to a
securely secondary position.

In the case of Manet, the argument comes from Mallarmé
in 1876.[1] It is true, he states, that the painter began with Parisian
low-life: ". . . something long hidden, but suddenly revealed. Cap-
tivating and repulsive at the same time, eccentric, and new, such
types as were needed in our ambient lives." But Mallarmé, in the
most powerful reading of Manet's art produced in the nineteenth
century (or since), regarded these subjects as merely tactical and
temporary. He was looking back at the work of the sixties with

relief that the absinthe drinkers, dissolute picnics, and upstart whores had faded from view. What was left was a cool, self-regarding formal precision, dispassionate technique as the principal site of meaning, behind which the social referent retreats; the art of painting overtakes its tactical arm and restores to itself the high-cultural autonomy it had momentarily abandoned. The avant-garde schism had, after all, been prompted in the first place by the surrender of the academy to the philistine demands of the modern marketplace — the call for finish, platitude, and trivial anecdote. The purpose of modernism was to save painting, not sacrifice it to the debased requirements of yet another market, this time one of common amusement and cheap spectacle. For Mallarmé, Manet's aim "was not to make a momentary escapade or sensation, but . . . to impress upon his work a natural and general law." In the process, the rebarbative qualities of the early pictures — generated in an aggressive confrontation with perverse and alien imagery — are harmonized and resolved. The essay concludes with the voice of an imaginary Impressionist painter who flatly states the modernist credo:

> I content myself with reflecting on the clear and durable mirror of painting . . . when rudely thrown, at the close of an epoch of dreams, in the front of reality, I have taken from it only that which properly belongs to my art, an original and exact perception which distinguishes for itself the things it perceives with the steadfast gaze of a vision restored to its simplest perfection.

Despite the distance which separates their politics, a parallel argument to Mallarmé's was made by *"un camarade impressionniste"* in 1891 in the pages of the anarchist journal *La Révolte.*[2] Entitled "Impressionists and Revolutionaries", his text is a political justification of the art of Seurat and his colleagues to Jean Grave's readership — and the anonymous "impressionist comrade" has been identified as painter Paul Signac. Like Mallarmé's 1876 essay, it is another account by an avant-garde insider that addresses the relationship between iconography drawn from degraded urban experience and a subsequent art of resolute formal autonomy. And similarly, it marks the former as expedient and temporary, the latter as essential and permanent. The Neo-Impressionists, he states, had at first tried to draw attention to the class struggle through the visual discovery of industrial work as spectacle and, "above all", through portraying the kinds of proletarian pleasure that are only industrial work in another guise: in Seurat's "La Parade" for example, the joyless and sinister come-on for Ferdinand Corvi's down-at-heels circus; or the Pavlovian smile of the stolid music-hall patron who anchors the mechanical upward thrust of "Le Chahut".[3] Signac puts it this way:

> . . . with their synthetic representation of the pleasures of decadence: dancing places, music halls, circuses, like those provided by the painter Seurat, who had such a vivid feeling for the degradation of our epoch of transition, they bear witness to the great social trial taking place between workers and Capital.

But this tactic was to be no more permanent than the impulse which in 1890 sent Charles Henry, armed with Signac's posters and charts, off to instruct the furniture workers of the Faubourg Saint-Antoine (the venerable revolutionary district) in Neo-Impressionist color theory.[4] The continuing oppositional character of *Néo* painting does not derive, Signac is quick to say, from those earlier keen dissections of the world of organized diversion, but from an aesthetic developed in their making, one which now can be applied to any subject whatever. The liberated sensibility of the avant-gardist will stand as an implicit exemplar of revolutionary possibility, and the artist will most effectively perform this function by concentration on the self-contained demands of his medium. (This stands as one of the earliest statements of this now well-worn formula of leftist aesthetics.) Signac refuses any demand that his group continue

> a precise socialist direction in works of art, because this direction is encountered much more strongly among the pure aesthetes, revolutionaries by temperament, who, striking away from the beaten paths, paint what they see, as they feel it, and very often, unconsciously supply a solid axe-blow to the creaking social edifice.

Four years later, he would sum up the progress of Neo-Impressionism in a single sentence:[5] "We are emerging from the hard and useful period of analysis, where all our studies resembled one another, and entering that of varied and personal creation." By this time, Signac and company had left behind the subjects and people of the industrial *banlieue* for the Côte d'Azur.

For both of these writers, the relationship between painting and the ordinary diversions of urban life moves from wary identity to determined difference. At the beginning, "rudely thrown, at the close of an epoch of dreams, in the front of reality," as Mallarmé puts it, low culture provides by default the artist's only apparent grasp on modernity. Even this notoriously hermetic and withdrawn poet, like the anarchist-socialist Signac, holds that the advanced artist is necessarily allied with the lower classes in their struggle for political recognition: "The multitude demands to see with its own eyes . . . the transition from the old imaginative artist and dreamer to the energetic modern worker is found in Impressionism." But it goes without saying, for both, that emancipated vision will not come from imitating the degraded habits induced in the multitude by its currently favored amusements. Mass political emancipation will occasion a "parallel" search in the arts — now, thanks to politics, shed of an oppressive, authoritarian tradition — for ideal origins and purified practice.

This idea has been so recurrent an organizing belief in the history of the avant-garde that we could raise it to the status of a group ideology. As such, it will determine the way popular sources are understood by the artists who use them. When we turn to the self-conscious theories of modernism developed subsequently, we find that ideology ratified and made explicit. In an essay which stands as one of Clement Greenberg's more complete statements of formal method, "Collage" of 1959[5], he puts the 'intruder objects' of cubist collage firmly in their place. He belittles the view of some early commentators, like Apollinaire and Kahnweiler, that the technique represented a renewed vision outward, its disruptions sparking attention to a "new world of beauty" dormant in the littered commercial landscape of wall posters, shop windows, and business signs.[6] Greenberg, in contrast, stresses the lack of any such claims coming from Picasso or Braque, continuing, "The writers who have tried to explain their intentions for them speak, with a unanimity that is suspect in itself, of the need for renewed contact with 'reality' (but) even if these materials were more 'real', the question would still be begged, for 'reality' would still explain next to nothing about the actual *appearance* of cubist collage."[7] The word reality here stands for any independent significance the bits of newspaper or woodgrain might retain once inserted into the cubist pictorial matrix. One reads through the entire essay without once finding this even admitted as an interpretive possibility. Collage is entirely subsumed in a self-sufficient dialogue between the flat plane and sculptural effect; the artist's worry over the problem of representation in general precludes representation in the particular.

Thus, as the theory of modernism takes on independent life, these dislodged bits of commercial culture become, even more drastically, means to an end.

II

The testimony of modernism itself then would appear thoroughly to obviate the low culture problem — or indicate that its solution must be pursued in another critical discourse entirely. Certainly to the many partisans of a post-modernist present, who dismiss Greenberg's model as an arbitrary and arid teleology, it would seem foolish to look to the theory of modernism for any help on this issue. Avant-garde borrowing from below necessarily involves questions of heterogeneous cultural practice, of transgressing limits and boundaries. The post-modernists, who profess to value heterogeneity and transgression, find modernist self-understanding utterly closed to anything but purity and truth to media.[8]

The critique of Greenbergian modernism is now well advanced, and its defenders are scarce. But I am pursuing this point in the belief that Greenberg — and the moment of theoretical practice to which he contributed — does have something to tell us, despite this apparent closure against the sphere of low culture. Greenberg's criticism, in fact, offers an explanation for that very act of closure as carried out by Mallarmé, Signac, and all the rest; he brackets the idealism of Mallarmé's mirror of painting and Signac's liberated consciousness in a social and historical frame. Greenberg's critics have almost exclusively focused on the prescriptive outcome of his analysis, and there is some justice in this, in that since 1950 or so Greenberg himself has been rather myopically enamored with those prescriptions. But the later Greenberg has obscured the earlier, his eventual modernist triumphalism pushing aside the initial logic of his criticism and the particular urgency which prompted it.

In 1939, what worried him was not the picture plane; his seminal essay "Avant-Garde and Kitsch"[9] begins with a flat rejection of the limited frame of formal aesthetics: "It appears to me it is necessary to examine more closely and with more originality than hitherto the relationship between aesthetic experience as met by the specific — not the generalized — individual, and the social and historical contexts in which that experience takes place." This is a mildly stated but deeply meant preamble; what occupies his attention is nothing less than a material and social crisis which threatens the traditional forms of nineteenth-century culture with extinction. This crisis has resulted from the economic pressure of an industry devoted to the simulation of art in the form of reproducible cultural commodities, that is to say, the industry of mass culture. In search of raw material, mass culture strips traditional art of its marketable qualities, and leaves as the only remaining path to authenticity a ceaseless alertness against the stereotyped and preprocessed. The name of this path is modernism, which with every success is itself vulnerable to the same kind of appropriation. Ultimately, the surviving autonomous art object becomes a fragile and fugitive thing, withdrawn in the face of the culture industry to the refuge of its material support. By refusing any other demand but the most self-contained technical ones, it closes itself to the reproduction and rationalization that would process its useable bits and destroy its inner logic. From this resistance is derived modernism's inwardness, self-reflexivity, 'truth to media'.

Greenberg makes this plain in "Towards a Newer Loacoon" of 1940,[10] the essay in which he drew out the largely unstated aesthetic implications of "Avant-Garde and Kitsch". "The arts, then," he states, "have been hunted back to their mediums, and there they have been isolated, concentrated and defined . . . . To restore the identity of an art, the opacity of the medium must be emphasized." As stated, this conclusion is provisional and even reluctant, its tone far removed from the complacency of his later criticism. As we have seen, he would come to ratify in an untroubled way the absolute priority of a high modernism over its occasional popular materials. But in his original work, which provided the premises for his subsequent critical practice, that priority is reversed. 'Quality', it is true, remains exclusively with modernist remnants of traditional high culture, but mass culture has determined the form high culture must assume. Mass culture is prior and determining; modernism is its effect.

The point I am making is that the formative theoretical moment in the history of modernism in the visual arts was inseparably an effort to come to terms with cultural production as a whole under late capitalism. Because of this — and only because of this — it was able temporarily to surpass the idealism of the ideologies generated within the avant-garde, an idealism to which it soon tacitly succumbed. Recovering this nearly lost moment of theoretical consciousness can begin to give us a purchase on the low-culture problem, one which the avant-garde itself cannot provide. Interdependence between high and low is at the heart of the theory.

In Greenberg's analysis, mass culture is never left behind in modernist practice, but persists as a constant pressure on the artist, which severely restricts creative 'freedom'. But the pressure is, of course, all in one direction — all repulsion, no attraction; the continued return to vernacular materials on the part of the avant-garde thus remains unexplained.

Greenberg could not admit any positive interdependence between the two spheres because of the rigid distinction he makes between popular culture and the modern phenomenon of kitsch. The former is for him inseparable from some integrated community comparable to the kind that sustained traditional high art; the latter is peculiarly modern, a product of rural migration to the cites and the immigrants' eager abandonment of the folk culture they brought with them. Expanded literacy, the demarcation of assigned leisure outside the hours of work, the promise of heightened diversion and pleasure within that leisure time, set up pressure for a simulated culture adapted to the needs of this new clientele. Kitsch exists to fill a vacuum; the urban worker, whether in factory or office, compensates for the surrender of his personal autonomy to the discipline of the workplace in the intense development of the time left over; lost control over one's life is rediscovered in the symbolic and affective experiences now defined as specific to leisure. But because the ultimate logic of this re-creation (the hyphen restores the root meaning of the term) is the rationalized efficiency of the system as a whole, these needs are met by the same means as material ones: by culture in the form of reproducible commodities.

For those whose cultural horizons are limited to kitsch, subjectivity it thus mirrored and trapped in the lifeless logic of mass production; imagining, thinking, feeling are all done by the machine long before the individual consumer encounters its products: the tabloids, pop tunes, pulp novels, melodramas of stage and film. For this reason, the artist — in any genuine sense of the term —can expect no audience outside those cultivated fractions of the dominant class who maintain in their patronage a pre-modern independence of taste. Greenberg can state categorically,[11]

> The masses have always remained more or less
> indifferent to culture in the process of development
> .... No culture can develop without a social basis,
> without a source of stable income. And in the case
> of the avant-garde, this was provided by an elite
> among the ruling class of that society from which it
> assumed itself to be cut off, but to which it has

always remained attached by an umbilical cord of gold.

In light of this analysis, it is not surprising that he should posit the relationship between modernism and mass culture as one of relentless refusal. The problem remains, however, that the elite audience for modernism endorses, in every respect but its art, the social order responsible for the crisis of culture. The implicit contention of modernist theory — and the name of T. W. Adorno for modern music can be joined to that of Greenberg for the visual arts — was that the contradiction between an oppositional art and a public with appetite for no other kind of opposition could be bracketed off, if not transcended, in the rigor of austere, autonomous practice.

III

There was and is great explanatory and moral power in this position. But there are, it hardly need be said, problems with it. The critics of modernism have tirelessly pointed out that none of its formal innovations have escaped being sleekly incorporated into, first, a new academicism, and subsequently, chic items of upscale consumption and glamorous facades for state and corporate power. By the mid-1960's, painting and sculpture had reached a point of terminal reticence barely distinguishable from expensive vacuity. This sort of critique is by now easy to make, and has settled into glib orthodoxy. It has at times taken the bizarre form of holding the theory somehow responsible for the fate that befell modernist art. I have tried to show that the fashion for anti-modernism has obscured a complex and useful historical account imbedded in Greenberg's early writings. And if we are to surpass Greenberg's conclusion that authentic art must forego interchange with the rest of the culture, we need to question his analysis on a point his critics have largely conceded: the issue of audiences for advanced art.

If we make Manet the beginning of modernism, it would be hard not to admit the general accuracy of Greenberg's dismissal of any but an elite audience. The impulse which moved Signac momentarily to make an audience of those Parisian furniture workers stands out by its extreme rarity in the history of the avant-garde. The fleetingness of those efforts in Berlin, Cologne, and Vitebsk after World War I to re-define avant-garde liberation in working-class terms tells the same story. But oppositional art did not begin with Manet and did not before him always opt for detachment.

The two artists together most responsible for defining advanced art in terms of opposition to established convention, making painting a scene of dispute over the meaning of high culture, were David and Courbet; and the art of each, at least in the critical moments of 1785 and 1850, was about a re-definition of publics. The formal qualities which are rightly seen as anticipating fully-fledged modernism — the dramatic defiance of academic compositional rules, technical parsimony, and compressed dissonance of the "Oath of the Horatii" or "Burial at Ornans" — were carried forward in the name of *another* public, excluded outsiders, whose own emergent or residual signifying practices these pictures managed to address. In the process, 'Rome' or 'the countryside' as privileged symbols in a conflict of ideologies were turned over to the outsiders. The antagonistic character of these pictures can thus be read as duplicating real antagonisms within the audience assembled in the Salon. Already perceived oppositions of style and visual language drawn from the world outside painting were drawn into the space of art and put to work in a real dialectic of publics: the appeal of each artist to the excluded group was validated by the demonstrated hostility of the established, high-minded art public; that hostility was redoubled by the positive response of the illegitimate public; and so on in a self-reinforcing way.[12]

But with the installation of oppositional art within a permanent avant-garde, that group itself comes to replace the oppositional public precariously mobilized by David or Courbet; antagonism is abstracted and generalized; and only then does dependence on an elite audience and luxury-trade consumption become a given. One writer of Greenberg's generation, rather than bracketting off this dependence, made it central to his analysis: this was Meyer Schapiro. In his little-known but fundamental essay of 1936, "The Social Bases of Art" and in "The Nature of Abstract Art" published the following year in the *Marxist Quarterly,*[13] he argued in an original and powerful way that the avant-garde has habitually based its model of artistic freedom on the aimlessness of the strolling, middle-class consumer of packaged diversion. The complicity between modernism and the consumer society is, he maintains, clearly to be read in Impressionist painting:[14]

> It is remarkable how many pictures we have in
> early Impressionism of informal and spontaneous
> sociability, of breakfasts, picnics, promenades,
> boating trips, holidays, and vacation travel. These
> urban idylls not only present the objective forms of

bourgeois recreation in the 1860's and 1870's; they also reflect in the very choice of subjects and in the new aesthetic devices the conception of art solely as a field of individual enjoyment, without reference to ideas and motives, and they presuppose the cultivation of these pleasures as the highest field of freedom for an enlightened bourgeois detached from the official beliefs of his class. In enjoying realistic pictures of his surroundings as a spectacle of traffic and changing atmospheres, the cultivated rentier was experiencing in its phenomenal aspect that mobility of the environment, the market and of industry to which he owed his income and his freedom. And in the new Impressionist techniques which broke things up into finely discriminated points of color, as well as in the 'accidental' momentary vision, he found, in a degree hitherto unknown in art, conditions of sensibility closely related to those of the urban promenader and the refined consumer of luxury goods.

Schapiro's contention is that the advanced artist, after 1860 or so, succumbs to the general division of labor as a full-time leisure specialist, an aesthetic technician picturing and prodding the sensual expectations of other, part-time consumers. The preceding passage is from the 1937 essay; in its predeccessor Schapiro offered an extraordinary iconographic summation of modernism in a single paragraph, one in which its progress is logically linked to Impressionism's initial alliance with the emerging forms of mass culture. If only because of the undeserved obscurity of the text, it is worth quoting at length:[15]

Although painters will say again and again that content doesn't matter, they are curiously selective in their subjects. They paint only certain themes and only in a certain aspect .... First, there are natural spectacles, landscapes or city scenes, regarded from the point of view of a relaxed spectator, a vacationist or sportsman, who values the landscape chiefly as a source of agreeable sensations or mood; artificial spectacles and entertainments — the theatre, the circus, the horse-race, the athletic field, the music hall — or even works of painting, sculpture, architecture, or technology, experienced as spectacles or objects of art; ... symbols of the artist's activity, individuals practic-

ing other arts, rehearsing, or in their privacy; in-
struments of art, especially of music, which suggest
an abstract art and improvisation; isolated intimate fields, like a table covered with private in-
struments of idle sensations, drinking glasses, a
pipe, playing cards, books, all objects of manipulation, referring to an exclusive, private world in
which the individual is immobile, but free to enjoy
his own moods and self stimulation. And finally,
there are pictures in which the elements of professional artistic discrimination, present to some degree in all painting — the lines, spots of color,
areas, textures, modelling — are disengaged from
things and juxtaposed as 'pure' aesthetic objects.

Thus elements drawn from the professional
surroundings and activity of the artist; situations in
which we are consumers and spectators; objects
which we confront intimately, but passively or ac-
cidentally — these are the typical subjects of modern painting . . . . The preponderance of objects
drawn from a personal and artistic world does not
mean that pictures are more pure than in the past,
more completely works of art. It means simply that
the personal and aesthetic contexts of secular life
now condition the formal character of art . . . .

With Schapiro, then, we have an account of modernist
painting that makes the engagement with urban leisure central to
its interpretation. In the hands of the avant-garde, the aesthetic
itself is identified with habits of enjoyment and release produced
quite concretely within the existing apparatus of commercial entertainment and tourism — even, and perhaps most of all, when art
appears entirely withdrawn into its own sphere, its own sensibility,
its own medium.

IV

Schapiro would one day become a renowned and powerful
apologist for the avant-garde, but we find his original contribution
to the debate over modernism and mass culture squarely opposed
to Greenberg's conclusions of a few years later: the 1936 essay was
in fact a forthright anti-modernist polemic, an effort to demonstrate that the avant-garde's claims to independence, to disengage-
ment from the values of its patron class were a sham; "in a society

where all men can be free individuals," he concluded, "individuality must lose its exclusiveness and its ruthless and perverse character."[16] The social analysis underlying Schapiro's polemic, however, is almost identical to Greenberg's. Both see the commodification of culture as the negation of the real thing, that is, the rich and coherent symbolic dimension of collective life in earlier times; both see beneath the apparent variety and allure of the modern urban spectacle only the "ruthless and perverse" laws of capital; both posit modernist art as a direct response to that condition, one which will remain in force until a new, socialist society is achieved.[17] Given these basic points of agreement and the fact that both men were operating in the same intellectual/political milieu, how do we explain the extent of their differences?

One determining difference between Greenberg and Schapiro lay, I think, in the specificity of their respective understandings of mass culture: though each is schematic in his account, Greenberg is more schematic. His use of the term kitsch encompasses practically the entire range of consumable culture, from the crassest proletarian entertainments to the genteel academicism of 'serious' art: "What is academic is kitsch, what is kitsch is academic,"[18] is his view in a pithy sentence. Schapiro, on the other hand, is less interested in the congealed, inauthentic character of cultural commodities taken by themselves than he is in behavior: what are the characteristic forms of experience induced by these commodities? In his discussion of Impressionism, this leads to the historically accurate perception that the people with the time and money fully to occupy the new spaces of urban leisure were primarily middle class. The week-end resorts and *grands boulevards* were, at first, places given over to conspicuous display of a brand of individual autonomy specific to that class, the right clothes and accessories, as well as the right poses and attitudes were required. The new department stores, like Boucicaut's *Bon Marché,* grew spectacularly by supplying the necessary material equipment and, by their practices of sales and promotion, effective instruction in the more intangible requirements of this sphere of life. The economic barriers were enough, in the 1860's and 1870's, to ward off the incursion of other classes. Even such typically working-class diversions of our time as soccer and bicycle racing (Manet planned a large canvas on the latter subject in 1870) began in this period as enthusiasms of the affluent.[19]

In Schapiro's eyes, the avant-garde merely followed a de-centering of individual life which overtakes the middle-class as a whole. It is for him entirely appropriate that the formation of Impressionism should coincide with the Second Empire, that is, the period when bourgeois acquiescence to political authoritarianism was followed by the first spectacular flowering of the consumer society. The two phenomena cannot in fact be separated from one another; the self-liquidation after 1848 of the classical form of middle-class political culture prompted a reconstruction of traditional ideals of individual autonomy and effectiveness in spaces outside the official institutions of society, spaces where conspicuous styles of 'freedom' were made available. That shift was bound up with the increasingly sophisticated engineering of mass consumption, the internal conquest of markets, required for continuous economic expansion. The department store, which assumed a position somewhere between encyclopedia and ritual temple of consumption, is the appropriate symbol for the era. And we are just beginning to understand what a powerful mechanism for socialization it was. It served as one of the primary means by which a bourgeois public, often deeply unsettled by the dislocations in its older patterns of life, was won over to the new order being wrought in its name.[20]

As noted above, this is the historical observation which underlies Greenberg's "Avant-Garde and Kitsch", but his account is incomplete in that it sees kitsch, the *nouveautés* in the cultural display windows, as simply meeting the needs of the productive apparatus: there is a void in urban life, the 'empty' time outside work, which can be filled with any ersatz product whatever; the market for kitsch is credited with no resistance to manipulation. What this picture leaves out is the historical origin of that market in the *suppression* of pre-industrial forms of communal life. Greenberg assumes that the "new urban masses" abandoned their traditional cultural equipment readily and without a fight; actually they found what elements of rural ritual and recreation they brought with them actively opposed by urban authorities and moral reformers. It was the case throughout the industrializing West that the rhythms of work and rest imbedded in rural communal life were held incompatible with urban tranquility and the efficient operation of expanding workshops and factories. The distinctive festive and athletic amusements of the countryside were re-defined in the city as vice and violence, and treated accordingly.[21]

Older forms of community were thus under constant pressure and slowly but surely dismantled. They were not, however, erased. Communal impulses were channeled into new forms of labor association, ranging in their aims from pious improvement to radical conspiracy. In France, the growing sense of grievance and political assertiveness of these groups following the February Revolution in 1848 provoked the crisis of the following June — and the abandonment by the republican bourgeoisie of parliamentary accommodation of working-class demands in favor of a naked show of force. And that strategy led in 1851 to an unprotesting surrender of the central institutions of bourgeois political culture — representative government, parties, legal opposition, a free press — all liquidated in the interests of 'order'. Morny and the upstart Bonaparte brought off their coup without serious resistance from the politicians or intelligentsia.

These early essays of Greenberg and Schapiro, which take as their common subject the sacrifice of the best elements in bourgeois culture to economic expediency, are both visibly marked, as I read them, by the best known interpretation of the 1848-51 crisis in France: that of Marx in the *Eighteenth Brumaire of Louis Bonaparte.* There Marx described the way in which the forcible exclusion of oppositional groups from the political process necessitated a kind of cultural suicide on the part of the republican bourgeoisie, the willed destruction of its own optimal institutions, values, and expressive forms:[22]

> While the *parliamentary party of Order,* by its clamor for tranquility, as I have shown, committed itself to quiescence, while it declared the political rule of the bourgeoisie to be incompatible with the safety and existence of the bourgeoisie, by destroying with its own hands in the struggle against other classes in society all the conditions for its own regime, the parliamentary regime, the *extra-parliamentary mass of the bourgeoisie,* on the other hand, by its servility toward the President, by its vilification of parliament, by its brutal treatment of its own press, invited Bonaparte to suppress and annihilate its speaking and writing section, its politicians and its *literati,* its platform and its press, in order that it might be able to pursue its private affairs with full confidence in the protection of a strong and unrestricted government. It declared unequivocally that it longed to get rid of its own political rule in order to get rid of the troubles and dangers of ruling.

When Schapiro speaks of the "enlightened bourgeois detached

from the official beliefs of his class," he directs us back to the actual process by which that detachment occurred. And out of the desolation of early nineteenth-century forms of collective life, which affected all classes of the city, fractions of the dominant class led the way in colonizing the one remaining domain of relative freedom: the spaces of public leisure. There suppressed community is displaced and dispersed into isolated acts of individual consumption; but those acts can in turn coalesce into characteristic group styles. Within leisure, a sense of solidarity can be recaptured, at least temporarily, in which individuality is made to appear imbedded in group life: the community of fans, aficionados, supporters, sportsmen, experts. Lost possibilities of individual effectiveness within the larger social order are represented as a catalogue of leisure-time roles.[23]

Another contributer to this extraordinary theoretical moment of the later 1930's, Walter Benjamin, makes this point plainly in his study of Baudelaire and Second-Empire Paris. Speaking of the class to which the poet belonged, he states,[24]

> The very fact that their share could at best be enjoyment, but never power, made the period which history gave them a space for passing time. Anyone who sets out to while away time seeks enjoyment. It was self-evident, however, that the more this class wanted to have its enjoyment in this society, the more limited this enjoyment would be. The enjoyment promised to be less limited if this class found enjoyment of this society possible. If it wanted to achieve virtuosity in this kind of enjoyment, it could not spurn empathizing with commodities. It had to enjoy this identification with all the pleasure and uneasiness which derived from a presentiment of its destiny as a class. Finally, it had to approach this destiny with a sensitivity that perceives charm even in damaged and decaying goods. Baudelaire, who in a poem to a courtesan called her heart 'bruised like a peach, ripe like her body, for the lore of love,' possessed this sensitivity. To it he owed his enjoyment of this society as one who had already half withdrawn from it.

V

In his drafted introduction to the never-completed Baudelaire project, Benjamin writes,[25] "In point of fact, the theory of *l'art pour l'art* assumes decisive importance around 1852, at a time when the bourgeoisie sought to take its 'cause' from the hands of the writers and poets. In the *Eighteenth Brumaire* Marx recollects this moment . . . ." Modernism, in the conventional sense of the term, begins in the forced marginalization of the artistic vocation. And what Benjamin says of literature applies as well if not better to the visual arts. The avant-garde leaves behind the older concerns of official public art not out of any special rebelliousness on the part of its members, but because their political representatives had jettisoned as dangerous and obstructive the institutions and ideals for which official art was metaphorically to stand. David's public, to cite the obvious contrasting case, had found in his pictures of the 1780's a way imaginatively to align itself with novel and pressing demands of public life; the *Horatii* and the *Brutus* resonated as vivid tracts on individual resolve, collective action, and their price. Oppositional art meant opposition on a broad social front. Until 1848, there was at least a latent potential for a middle-class political vanguard to act on its discontents, and an oppositional public painting maintained itself in reserve. This was literally the case with the most powerful attempt to duplicate David's early tactics, Géricault's "Raft of the Medusa", which failed to find an oppositional public in the politically bleak atmosphere of 1819. But when the Revolution of 1830 roused Delacroix from his obsession with individual victimization and sexual violence, he reached back to the "Raft". "Liberty's" barricade, heaving up in the foreground, is the raft itself turned ninety degrees; the bodies tumble off its leading rather than trailing edge (Delacroix shifts the sprawling, bare-legged corpse more or less intact from the right corner to the left, precisely marking the way he has transposed his model); the straining pyramid of figures now pushes toward the viewer rather than away. In the first days of the year 1848, the republican Michelet employed the "Raft" in his oratory as a rallying metaphor for national resistance. After February, "Liberty" emerged briefly from its captivity in the storerooms.[26]

1851 ended all this. (It certainly obviated Courbet's effort to shift the address of history painting to a new outsider public, a radical opposition based in the working class.) For a bourgeois public, the idea of a combative and singular individuality, impatient with social confinement, remained fundamental to a generally internalized sense of self — as it still does. But that notion of individuality could henceforth be realized only in private acts of self-estrangement, in distancing and blocking out the gray realities

of administration and production in favor of a brighter world of
sport, tourism, and spectacle. This process was redoubled in the
fierce repression which followed the Commune twenty years later;
between 1871 and 1876, the hey-day of Impressionist formal innovation, Paris was under martial law. And in the following decade,
the Third Republic would orchestrate the return to 'normalcy'
(translate as aggressive policies of re-armament, nationalism,
commercial and colonial expansion) around the most massive pro-
vision of spectacular diversion yet conceived: the Eiffel Tower exhibition of 1889. The event was designed and organized from the
start for the purpose of painless management of political consent; it
did so by transforming the official picture of French society and
empire into an object of giddy, touristic consumption. After the
close of the exhibition, the government, riding a fat electoral victory, unabashedly pronounced the operation a success in just these
terms.[27]

    If the subjective experience of freedom becomes a function
of a supplied identity, one detached from the social mechanism and
contemplating it from a distance, then the early modernist painters
— as Schapiro trenchantly observed in 1936 — lived that role to
the hilt. If we accept his initial position, we might well end our
discussion right here, dismissing, as one kind of Leftist art history
still does, all avant-garde claims to a critical and independent
stance as so much false consciousness. In Schapiro's essay of the
following year, however, there occurs a significant shift in his position. The basic argument remains in place, but we find him using
without irony terms like "implicit criticism" and "freedom" to
describe modernist painting. Of early modernism, he states,[28]

> The very existence of Impressionism which trans-
> formed nature into a private, unformalized field of
> sensitive vision, shifting with the spectator, made
> painting an ideal domain of freedom; it attracted
> many who were tied unhappily to middle-class jobs
> and moral standards, now increasingly problem-
> atic and stultifying with the advance of monopoly
> capitalism.... In its discovery of a constantly chang-
> ing phenomenal outdoor would of which the
> shapes depended on the momentary position of the
> casual or mobile spectator, there was an implicit
> criticism of symbolic and domestic formalities, or
> at least a norm opposed to these.

What has been added here is recognition of some degree of active,
resistant consciousness within the avant-garde. And this extends to

his valuation of middle-class leisure as well. He speaks of an Impressionist "discovery" of an implicitly critical, even moral, point of view. This critical art is not secured through withdrawal into self-sufficiency, but is found in existing social practices outside the sphere of art.

Schapiro creates a deliberate ambiguity in the second essay in that it offers a qualified apology for modernism without renouncing his prior dismissal of all modernist apologetics. How do we interpret that ambiguity? To start, we could note the immediate political and biographical reasons of his shift, which the research of Serge Guilbaut has amply demonstrated.[29] It is, among other things, a step toward his anodyne celebrations of abstract painting in the 1950's.[30] But for the moment, I want to hold these texts apart from their immediate determinations and functions within the political and artistic battles of New York in the 1930's, in the belief that, together, they still provide the most productive access to the modernism/mass culture problem in the visual arts. "The Nature of Abstract Art" is an inconclusive, 'open' text, and it is just this quality, its unresolved oscillation between negative and affirmative positions, that makes it valuable.

The fundamental change in Schapiro's thinking is that he no longer identifies the avant-garde with the outlook of a homogeneous 'dominant' class. Yes, Impressionism belongs to and figures a world of privilege, but there is disaffection and erosion of consensus within that world. The society of consumption as a means of engineering political consent and socially integrative codes was no simple or uncontested solution to the 'problem of culture' under high capitalism. As it displaced resistant impulses, it also gave them a refuge in a relatively unregulated social space where contrary social definitions could survive, and occasionally flourish. Much of this was and is, obviously, permitted disorder. Managed consensus depends on a compensating balance between submission and negotiated resistance within leisure — Marcuse's "repressive de-sublimation". But once that zone of permitted 'freedom' exists, it can be seized by groups which articulate for themselves a counter-consensual identity, an implicit message of rupture and discontinuity. From the official point of view, these groups are defined as deviant or delinquent; we can call them, following contemporary sociological usage, resistant subcultures.[31]

If we wanted briefly to characterize the early avant-garde as a social formation, we could do no better than simply to apply this sociologists' description of these subcultures in general.[32] Their purpose is to

> win space . . . . They cluster around particular
> locations. They develop specific rhythms of inter-
> change, structured relations between members:
> younger to older, experienced to novice, stylish to
> square. They explore 'focal concerns' central to the
> inner life of the group: things always 'done' or
> 'never done', a set of social rituals which underpin
> their collective identity and define them as a
> 'group' instead of a mere collection of individuals.
> They adopt and adapt material objects — goods
> and possessions — and reorganize them into dis-
> tinctive 'styles' which express the collectivity of
> their being-as-a-group. These concerns, activities,
> relationships, materials become embodied in ritu-
> als of relationship and occasion and movement.
> Sometimes, the world is marked out, linguistically,
> by names or an *argot* which classifies the social
> world exterior to them in terms meaningful only
> within their group perspective, and maintains its
> boundaries. This also helps them to develop, ahead
> of immediate activities, a perspective on the imme-
> diate future — plans, projects, things to do to fill
> out time, exploits . . . . They too are concrete,
> identifiable social formations constructed as a collec-
> tive response to the material and situated expe-
> rience of their class.

To make the meaning of that last sentence more precise, the resistant subcultural response is a means by which certain members of a
class 'handle' and attempt to resolve difficult and contradictory
experience common to their class but felt more acutely by the
subcultural recruits. In our own time, youth, black, brown, or gay
identity are the common determining factors; the uneasy and incomplete integration of such groups into the institutions of work,
training, politics, and social welfare necessitates distinctive defensive maneuvers in style, language, and behavior. In the later nineteenth century, an artistic vocation, in the sense established by the
examples of David, Goya, Géricault, Delacroix, Courbet, had become so problematic as to require similar defense. The invention of
the avant-garde constitutes a small, face-to-face group of artists
and supporters as their significant oppositional public, one which is
socially grounded within structured leisure. The distinctive point of
view and iconographic markers of the subculture are drawn from a
repertoire of objects, locations, and behaviors supplied by other

colonists of the same social spaces; avant-garde opposition is drawn out of inarticulate and unresolved dissatisfactions which those spaces, though designed to contain them, also put on display.

VI

At this point, we need to draw distinctions more clearly between kinds of subcultural response. There are those which are no more than the temporary outlet of the ordinary citizen; there are those which are *merely* defensive, in that the group style they embody, though it may be central to the social life of its members, registers only as a harmless, perhaps colourful, enthusiasm. But the stylistic and behavioral maneuvers of certain subcultures will transgress settled social boundaries. From the outside, these will be read as extreme, opaque, inexplicably evasive and for that reason hostile. The dependable negative reaction from figures in authority and the semi-official guardians of propriety and morality will then further sharpen the negative identity of the subculture, help cement group solidarity, and often stimulate new adherents and imitators. Defense passes over into symbolic resistance.

The required boundary transgression can occur in several ways. Where different classes and class fractions meet in leisure-time settings, there is the possibility that objects, styles, and practices with an established significance for one class identity can be appropriated and re-positioned by another group to generate new, dissonant meanings. This shifting of signifiers can occur in both directions on the social scale (or scales). Another means to counter-consensual group statement is to isolate one element out of the normal pattern of leisure consumption, and then exaggerate and intensify its use until it comes to signify the opposite of its intended meaning.

It is easy to think of examples of such semiotic tactics in present-day subcultures; our model of subversive consumption is derived from the analysis of these deviant groups.[33] But we can see, just as easily I think, the same tactics at work in the early avant-garde. The mixing of class signifiers was central to the formation of the avant-garde sensibility. Courbet's prescient excursion into suburban pleasure for sale, the "Young Ladies on the Banks of the Seine" of 1856, showed two drowsing prostitutes in the intimate finery of their betters, piled on past all 'correct' usage of fashionable underclothing.[34] In the next decade, Manet would exploit similar kinds of dissonance. It showed up in his own body; his friend and biographer Proust speaks of his habitual imitation of the speech patterns and peculiar gait of a Parisian street urchin.[35] The subject of both the "Déjeuner" and the "Olympia" is the pursuit of commercial pleasure at a comparably early stage when it necessarily involved negotiation with older, illicit subcultures at the frontier between legality and criminality.[36]

Establishing itself where Courbet and Manet had led, 'classic' Impressionism, the sensually flooded depictions of weekend leisure produced by Monet, Renoir, and Sisley in the 1870's, opted for the second tactic. The life they portray was being lived entirely within the confines of real-estate development and entrepreneurial capitalism; these are images of provided pleasures. But they are images which, by the very exclusivity of their concentration on ease and uncoerced activity, alter the balance between the regulated and unregulated compartments of experience. They take leisure out of its place; instead of appearing as a controlled, compensatory feature of the modern social mechanism, securely framed by other institutions, it stands out in unrelieved difference from the unfreedom which surrounds it.

It is in this sense that Schapiro can plausibly speak of Impressionism's "implicit criticism of symbolic and domestic formalities, or at least a norm opposed to these." But what Schapiro does not address is how this criticism was specifically articulated as criticism: a difference is not an opposition unless it is consistently read as such. This brings us necessarily back to the question of modernism in its conventional aesthetic sense of autonomous, self-critical form — back to Greenberg, we might say. The 'focal concern' of the avant-garde subculture is, obviously, painting conceived in the most ambitious terms available. It was in its particular opposition to the settled discourse of high art that the central avant-garde group style, i.e. modernism, gained its cogency and its point. They were able to take their nearly total identification with the uses of leisure and make that move count in another arena, a major one where official beliefs in cultural stability were particularly vulnerable. The *grands boulevards* and Argenteuil may have provided the solution, but the problem had been established elsewhere: in the evacuation of artistic tradition by academic eclecticism, pastiche, the manipulative reaching for canned effects, all the played-out maneuvers of Salon kitsch. Almost every conventional order, technique, and motif which had made painting possible in the past, had, by this point, been fatally appropriated and compromised by academicism. And this presented immediate practical

1. Edouard Manet, *Before the Mirror,* 1876. Tannhauser Collection, The Solomon R. Guggenheim Museum, New York, N.Y.

2. Georges Seurat, *La Parade* (Invitation to the Side Show), 1887-1888. Collection The Metropolitan Museum of Art, New York, N.Y.

3. Pablo Picasso, *Still Life with Chair Caning,* 1912. Collection Musée Picasso, Paris.

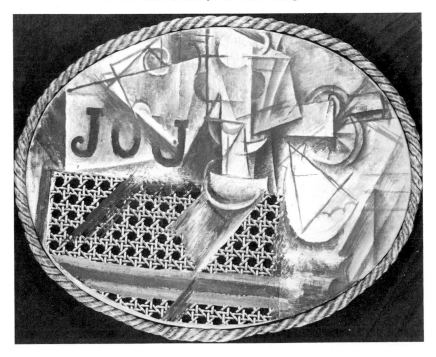

4. Claude Monet, *Regattas at Argenteuil,* n.d. Collection Musées Nationaux du Louvre, Paris.

5. Juan Gris, *The Teacups,* 1914. Collection Kunstsammlung Nordrhein-Westphalen, Duesseldorf.

6. Henri Toulouse-Lautrec, *Affiche pour Jean Avril,* 1891.

7. Henri Matisse, *Luxe Calme et Volupté,* 1904. Private Collection, Paris.

difficulties for the simple making of pictures: how do you compose, that is, construct a pictorial order with evident coherence and closure, without resorting to any prefabricated solutions? The unavailability of those solutions inevitably placed the greatest emphasis — and burden — on those elements of picture-making which seemed unmediated and irreducible: the single vivid gesture of the hand by which a single visual sensation is registered. As tonal relationships belonged to the rhetoric of the schools — rote procedures of drawing, modelling, and chiaroscuro — these gestural notations would ideally be of pure, saturated color.

The daunting formal problematic which resulted was this: how to build from the independent gesture or touch some stable, over-arching structure which fulfills two essential requirements: 1) it must be constructed only from an accumulation of single touches and cannot appear to subordinate immediate sensation to another system of cognition; 2) it must at the same time effectively close off the internal system of the picture and invest each touch with consistent descriptive sense in relation to every other touch. Without the latter, painting would remain literally pre-artistic, an arbitrary slice out of an undifferentiated field of minute, equivalent, and competing stimuli. Impressionism, quite obviously, found ways around this impasse, discovered a number of improvised, ingenious devices for making its colored touches jell into readability and closure: disguised compositional grids, sophisticated play within the picture between kinds of notation and levels of descriptive specificity, selecting motifs in which the solidity of larger forms is inherently obscured, and finally, building the picture surface into a tangibly constructed wall or woven mesh of pigment. The persuasiveness of these solutions, however, depended to a great degree on the built-in orders of the places they painted. The aquatic resort or dazzling shopping street offered 'reality' as a collection of uncomposed and disconnected surface sensations. The disjunction of sensation from judgement was not the invention of artists, but had been contrived by the emerging leisure industry to appear the more natural and liberated moment of individual life. The structural demarcation of leisure within the capitalist economy provided the invisible frame which made that distracted experience cohere as the image of pleasure.

The most provocative and distinctive pictorial qualities of early modernism were not only justified by formal homologies with its subject matter as an already created image, they also served to defend that image by preserving it from inappropriate kinds of attention. So that the promises of leisure would not be tested against too much contrary visual evidence — not only dissonant features of the landscape like the famous factories of Argenteuil, but also the actual varieties of individual pleasure and unpleasure in evidence — the painters consistently fix on optical phenomena which are virtually unrepresentable: rushing shoppers glimpsed from above and far away, the disorienting confusion of the crowded *café-concert,* smoke and steam in the mottled light of the glass-roofed railway shed, wind in foliage, flickering shadows, and above all, reflections in moving water. These phenomena have become, largely thanks to Impressionism, conventional signs of the spaces of leisure and tourism, of their promised vividness and perpetual surprise, but as optical 'facts' they are so changeable or indistinct that one cannot really hold them in mind and preserve them as a mental picture; therefore one cannot securely test the painters version against remembered visual experience. The inevitably approximate and unverifiable registration of these visual ephemera in painting makes larger areas of the canvas less descriptive than celebratory of gesture, color, and shape — pictorial incidents attended to for their own sake.

The passage from deliberate evasiveness and opacity to insistence on material surface — to modernist abstraction, in short — has been best articulated, I think, in an essay on Monet by the novelist Michel Butor.[37] Speaking of "Regattas at Argenteuil" of 1872, a picture dominated by broadly rendered reflections of sailboats and shoreline villas, he states,

> It is impossible to interpret the reflected part as the simple notation of what lay before the painter's eyes. How can one suppose that Monet would have chosen any one of the millions of images that the camera might have registered? He constructed an image, animated by a certain rhythm, which we may imagine as conforming to that of the liquid surface (yet there is nothing to confirm even this), based on real objects.
>
> The semantic relation of above and below obviously works in both directions: a) the upper names the lower: this aggregate of blotches which means nothing to you is a tree, a house, a boat; b) the lower reveals the upper: this boat, this house, which may seem dull to you contain secret congruences of color, elementary images, expressive possibilities.

> The upper part corresponds to what one recognizes, the reality one is used to; the lower, which leads us toward the houses and boats, corresponds to the painter's act. The water becomes a metaphor for painting. The very broad strokes with which these reflections are indicated are vigorous assertions of material and means. The liquid surface provides an instance in nature of the painter's activity.

Monet uses the artifice of painting to make his scene better, more congruent and formally satisfying, than it could ever be in life. Impressionism's transformation of leisure into an obsessive and exclusive value, its inversion of the intended social significance of its material, necessitated special painterly means, which in turn invert the intended social significance of its medium. Nineteenth-century high culture was nothing if it did not embody the permanent, indisputable, and ideal; the avant-garde appropriates the form of high art in the name of the contingent, unstable, and material. To accept modernism's oppositional claims, we need not assume that it somehow transcends the culture of the commodity; we can see it rather as exploiting to critical purpose contradictions within and between distinct sectors of that culture. Validated fine art, the art of the museums, is that special preserve where the commodity character of modern cultural production is sealed off from apprehension. There the aggressively reiterated pretense is that traditional forms have survived unaltered and remain available as an experience outside history. Marginal leisure-time subcultures perform more or less the same denial of the commodity using the objects at their disposal. Lacking legitimating institutions, their transformation of the commodity must be activist and improvisatory: thus their continual inventiveness in displacing provided cultural goods into new constellations of meaning. The privileged moments of modernist negation occur, if the present argument is correct, when the two aesthetic orders, the high and the low, are forced into scandalous identity. Each of the two positions occupied by the avant-garde artist, the high-cultural and subcultural, is thereby continuously dislocated by the other. And this ceaseless switching of codes is readable as articulate protest against the double marginalization of art — and through that, against the forced marginalization of individual life in the wake of 1848 and 1871.

The instances of repeated return to mass-cultural material on the part of the avant-garde can be understood as efforts to revive and repeat this strategy — each time in a more marginal and refractory leisure location. Seurat in the 1880's, when he conceived "Sunday Afternoon on the Island of the Grande Jatte" as the outsized pendant to his "Bathers at Asnières",[38] pointedly placed an awkward and routinized bourgeois leisure in another context, that of exhausted but uncontrived working-class time off. The nearly exclusive subject of his subsequent figure painting was, as Signac has informed us, the tawdriest fringes of Parisian commercial entertainment, the proletarianization of pleasure for both consumer and performer alike. This scene was dissected according to the putatively objective and analytic system of Charles Henry. But according to the first-hand testimony of Emile Verhaeren,[39] Seurat was moved to the artifice and rigidity imposed by Henry's emotional mechanics through identifying an analogous process already at work in his subject. Art historians have long noted the appearance in Seurat's later paintings of the exaggerated angular contours which were the trademark of the poster artist Jules Chéret.[40] As much as the circus or the *café-concert,* Seurat's material was the advertisement of pleasure, the seductive face it puts on; he spoke of that face in a deferential tone, and pushed his formal means in an attempt to master it. States Verhaeren: "The poster artist Chéret, whose genius he greatly admired, had charmed him with the joy and gaiety of his designs. He had studied them, wanting to analyze their means of expression and uncover their aesthetic secrets." These last words are significant for the present argument, indicating as they do that the artist begins with an already existing aesthetic developed in the overlooked fringes of culture. In its marginality is its secret allure, one which is not so much the promise of pleasure — from the evidence Seurat was cool and critical in his attitude — but the simple existence of a corner of the city which has improvised an appropriate and vivid way to represent itself. The sophisticated and self-conscious artist, intent on controlling an artifice and abstraction which have irrevocably overtaken his art, keeping it in contact with an appropriate descriptive task, finds subject matter in which this connection has already been made.

Cubist collage stands as another step in the same direction, its critical character derived from a re-positioning of even more exotically low-brow goods and protocols within the preserve of high art. The iconography of café table and cheap cabaret mark out its milieu, and the intruder objects of Cubist collage map this territory with significant precision.[41] The correct brand name on the bottle label was as significant for Picasso and Braque as it had been to Manet in the "Bar at the Folies-Bergère".[42] The handbills, posters, packs of cigarette papers, department-store advertisements, are disposed in the pictures with conscious regard for the specific associations of each item and the interplay between them. The Cubists proceeded in the manner of mock conspirators or Poe's sedentary detective Dupin, piecing together evidence of secret pleasures and crimes hidden beneath the apparently trivial surface of the popular media. That their consumption was subversive in intent Gris indicates clearly enough in newspaper clippings that describe the 'illegality' of their manoeuvers: a discussion of artistic forgeries; a photo story on the effects of a government ban on political affiches.[43] That the Cubist scene is one of pleasure and excess is emblazoned in the continual play on the word Journal, which becomes not just the spread newspaper page, but "jouer", "jeu", "jouir" — the letters thus made to advertise familiar and prized male subcultural roles: the player, the gambler, the sexual athlete.

Collage does its work within the problematic of pictorial modernism, dramatizing the literal support while preserving representation, but it is a solution discovered in a secretly coded world describable by means of these literal surfaces. And Cubism is readable as a message from the margins not only in the graphic content of the intruder objects, but in their substance and organization as well. The printed oilcloth and wallpaper substitutes for solid bourgeois surfaces, supplied originally by Braque from his provincial decorator's repertoire, are determinedly second-rate — the equivalent in present-day terms of vinyl walnut veneers or petrochemical mimics of silk and suede. As such surfaces soon degrade, peel, flake, and fade, as newsprint and handbills turn brown and brittle, so collage disrupts the false harmonies of oil painting by reproducing the disposability of the late-capitalist commodity. The principle of collage construction itself collapses the distinction between high and low by transforming the totalizing creative practice of traditional painting into a fragmented consumption of already existing manufactured images.

VII

Today, every phenomenon of culture, even if a model of integrity, is liable to be suffocated in the cultivation of kitsch. Yet paradoxically in the same epoch it is to works of art that has fallen the

> burden of wordlessly asserting what is barred to
> politics . . . . This is not a time for political art, but
> politics has migrated into autonomous art, and
> nowhere more so than where it seems to be politi-
> cally dead.
>
> T. W. Adorno, 1962[44]

Of the surviving contributors to the theory of modernism
and mass culture that coalesced in the 1930's, Adorno alone was
able to preserve its original range of reference and intent. The
purpose of the present discussion of the avant-garde as a resistant
subculture has been to lend historical and sociological substance to
Adorno's stance as it pertains to the visual arts.[45] I have tried to
describe the formal autonomy achieved in early modernist painting
not as withdrawal into self-sufficiency, but as a mediated synthesis
of possibilities derived from both the failures of existing artistic
technique and a repertoire of potentially oppositional practices
discovered in the world outside. From the beginning the successes
of modernism have been neither to affirm nor refuse its concrete
position in the social order, but to represent that position in its
contradiction, and so act out the possibility of critical consciousness in general. Even Mallarmé, in the midst of his 1876 defense of
Impressionism as a pure art of light and air,[46] could speak of it also
as an art "which the public, with rare prescience, dubbed, from its
first appearance, intransigeant, which in political language means
radical and democratic."

We can identify, in the examples cited above, a regular
rhythm which emerges within the progress of the Paris avant-garde.
For early Impressionism, early Neo-Impressionism, and for Cubism before 1914, the provocative inclusion of materials from outside validated high culture was joined with a new rigor of formal
organization, an articulate consistency of attention within the material fact of the picture surface; joining the two permitted the fine
adjustment of this assertive abstraction to the demands of description — not description in the abstract, but of specific enclaves of
the industrial city. The avant-garde group itself enacts this engagement in an intensification of collective cooperation and interchange, individual works of art figuring in a concentrated group
dialogue over means and criteria. But in each instance, this moment is followed by retreat — from specific description, from formal rigor, from group life, and from the fringes of commodity
culture to its center. And this pattern marks for us the inherent

limitations of the resistant subculture as a solution to the problematic experience of a marginalized and disaffected group.

We can take Monet's painting after the early 1880's as emblematic of the fate of the Impressionist avant-garde. The problem of verifiable description is relaxed when the artist withdraws to remote or isolated locations to paint: the difficulty of improvising pictorial orders appropriate to a complex and sensually animated form of sociability is obviated by concentration on stable, simplified, and depopulated motifs (we *know* this is a cathedral, a stack of grain, a row of poplars — the painting does not have to work to convince). In the process, the broad and definite touch of the 1870's, held between structure and description, is replaced by a precious, culinary surface, which largely gives up the job of dramatizing constructive logic. Not coincidentally, the 1880's was the period when Monet, thanks to Durand-Ruel's conquest of the American market, achieved secure financial success. Pissarro in 1887 dismissed it all as showy eccentricity of a familiar and marketable kind:[47] "I say this: Monet plays his salesman's game, and it serves him; but it is not in my character to do likewise, nor is it in my interest, and it would be in contradiction above all to my conception of art. I am not a romantic!"

Pissarro had by this time thrown in his lot with the Neo-Impressionists, for whom Monet's "grimacing" spontaneity was precisely a point at issue. Monet had transformed Impressionism from a painting *about* play to a variety of play in itself (this is the sense in which modernist painting becomes its own subject matter in a regressive sense). Seurat and company moved back to the actual social locations of play — and again put the formal problem of individual touch/sensation versus larger governing order squarely in the foreground. The result of Seurat's laborious method was drawing and stately compositions made assertively out of color alone. But we have already read evidence of the subsequent retreat in Signac's testimony of 1894:[48] "We are emerging from the hard and useful period of analysis when all our studies resembled one another, and entering that of varied and personal creation." What that meant, as the group carried on after Seurat's death, was a repertoire of stock tourist views: sunsets, Côte d'Azur fishing villages, Mont St. Michel, Venice. And the pointillist touch had, in the process, come loose from its moorings in Seurat's system. In the later Signac and Cross, the intimate connection between pictorial vocabulary, syntax, and a precise representational task is no longer in force: the touch expands, becomes freer and expressive in itself, works with its neighbors less within finely adjusted color relationships than as part of a relaxed, rhythmic animation of flat areas. As in the Impressionism of the 1880's, making the single gesture or touch now advertises itself as a kind of play within an unproblematic playground, one provided by motif and picture surface alike.

This "varied and personal" tendency was pushed further by the younger painters soon to be called Fauves. Derain and Matisse especially, who came to artistic maturity within the late Neo-Impressionist milieu in southern France, used the liberated pointillist gesture as their point of departure. The result was a painting built from loose sprays and spreading patches of saturated color, the descriptive function of which is casually approximate and unsystematic. Conventionalized landscape motifs do much of that work and allow the free abstraction of surface effects. Derain's dealer Vollard knew his business when he dispatched the young artist to London to paint a collection of postcard views: Big Ben, Westminister Abbey, Tower Bridge (Vollard was thinking of the success of Monet's London pictures of the nineties).[49] And the Fauve 'movement' was practically appropriated even before it gained its public identity in the *Indépendants* and Autumn Salons of 1905: the major pictures were spoken for by collectors; Vollard was buying out their studios; the influential critic Vauxcelles, who supplied them with their supposedly derisive sobriquet, was in fact lyrically supportive. [50]

But with that success went the sort of indeterminacy that Pissarro had decried in Monet. Derain testifies to this himself; writing from L'Estaque in 1905, he expressed these anxious doubts to Vlaminck:[51]

> Truly, we had arrived at a very difficult stage of the problem. I am so lost I wonder what words I can use to explain it to you. If one rejects decorative applications, the only direction one can take is to purify this transposition of nature. But we have only done this so far in terms of color. There is drawing as well. There are so many things lacking in our conception of art.
>
> In short, I see the future only in terms of composition, because in working before nature I am the slave of so many trivial things that my excitement is quashed. I cannot believe that the future will follow our path: on the one hand, we seek to disengage ourselves from objective things, and on the other, we preserve them as the origin and end of our art. No, truly, taking a detached

point of view, I cannot see what I must do to be
logical.

With assimilation into a more or less official modernism
came then the felt loss of a descriptive project and a corollary
erosion of pictorial logic. The rapid collapse of Fauvism as a
shared enterprise, which followed directly on its public success,
testifies to the cost of this indeterminacy. The reaction of Braque,
who had taken liberated Fauve gesture and color the furthest toward surface abstraction, was silently eloquent: withdrawing with
Picasso from the exhibition and gallery apparatus during the crucial years and renewing the old avant-garde commitment to collective practice. Even if the collectivity was reduced to the minimum
number of two, the effacement of creative 'personality' was all the
greater. And that combined withdrawal and commitment to rea-
soned, shared experiment was tied down to specific representation
— and celebration — of a compact, marginalized form of life.[52]

Like the others, of course, this moment didn't last. After
Braque's departure for the war, Picasso retained the identification
with mass culture, but now only in the terms which the culture
industry itself dictates. The sign of manufactured culture is empty
diversity, an eclecticism resulting from market expediency, targeting
consumers, and hedging bets. Modernist practice sustains its claim
to autonomy by standing in implicit opposition to the diversity of
material glut, the evident shape of the work standing in critical
contrast to the shapelessness of human life subject to production-
rationality. My argument has been that modernism has done this
successfully when it has figured in detail the manufactured culture
it opposes, put it on display by shifting boundaries and altering
received meanings. The Berlin Dadaists were most attentive to this
side of cubist collage, and sought in their own work to make this
significance brutally explicit. Raoul Haussmann wrote in 1919,[53]
"In Dada, you will find your true state: wonderful constellations in
real materials, wire, glass, cardboard, cloth, organically matching
your own consummate, inherent unsoundness, your own shoddi-
ness." The example of Berlin Dada demonstrates, however, that to
make this meaning explicit was to collapse art into a kind of poli
tics, to end all its claims to resolve and harmonize an unendurable
social order. The cubist precedent was, in contrast, an effort to fend
off that outcome, to articulate and defend a protected aesthetic
space. And because it was so circumscribed, it was overtaken and
assimilated like each of the avant-garde subcultures which preceded
it.

Collage — the final outcome of Cubism's interleaving of high and low — was smoothly incorporated as a source of excitement and crisp simplification within an undeflected official modernism. The translation of the collage pieces into painted replications folds the noisy, heterogeneous scene of fringe leisure into the sonority of museum painting. And any critical distance from mass culture was lost the moment Picasso returned in 1915 to conventional illusionism and art-historical pastiche, while at the same time continuing to produce Cubist pictures. That move instantly drained Cubism of its claim to logical and descriptive necessity, acknowledged that it had become a portable style, one ready-to-wear variety among many on offer. Maurice Raynal, writing admiringly in 1924 of Picasso's "Three Musicians",[54] said more than he knew when he called the picture, "rather like magnificent shop windows of cubist inventions and discoveries." The subject matter of that picture and others before it tells the story as well: after 1914, as if on cue, the raffish contemporary entertainers who provide the principal subjective presence in earlier Cubist figure painting give way to Harlequins, Pierrots, Punchinellos — sad clowns out of Watteau and the pre-industrial past, the tritest possible metaphors for an alienated artistic vocation.[55]

VIII

The basic argument of this essay has been that modernist negation proceeds from a productive confusion within the 'normal' hierarchy of cultural legitimacy. Modernism repeatedly makes subversive equations between high and low which dislocate the apparently fixed terms of that hierarchy into new and persuasive configurations, thus calling it into question from within. But this pattern of alternating provocation and retreat indicates that these equations are, in the end, as productive for affirmative culture as they are for the articulation of critical consciousness. While traditionalists can be depended on to bewail the break-down of past artistic authority, there will be significant elite fractions which will welcome new values, new varieties and techniques of feeling. On the surface, this is easy to comprehend as an attraction to the glamour of marginality, to undangerous poses of risk and singularity. But there is a deeper, more systematic rationale for this acceptance, which ends in the domestication of every modernist movement.

The context of subcultural life is the shift within a capitalist economy toward consumption as its own justification. The success of this shift — which is inseparably bound up with the developing management of political consent — depends on expanded desires and sensibilities, that is, the skills required for an ever more intense marketing of sensual gratification. In our image-saturated present, the culture industry has demonstrated the ability to package and sell nearly every variety of desire imaginable, but because its ultimate logic is the strictly rational and utilitarian one of profit maximization, it is not able to invent the desires and sensibilities it exploits. In fact, the emphasis on continual novelty basic to that industry runs counter to the need of every large enterprise for product standardization and economies of scale. This difficulty is solved by the very defensive and resistant subcultures which come into being as negotiated breathing space on the margins of controlled social life. These are the groups most committed to leisure, its pioneers, who for that reason come up with the richest, most surprising, inventive, and effective ways of using it. Their improvised forms are usually first made saleable by the artisan-level entrepreneurs who spring up in and around any active subculture. Through their efforts, a wider circle of consumers gains access to an alluring subcultural pose, but in a more detached and shallow form as the elements of the original style are removed from the context of subtle ritual which had first informed them. At this point, it appears to the large fashion and entertainment concerns as a promising trend. Components of an already diluted stylistic complex are selected out, adapted to the demands of mass manufacture, and pushed to the last job-lot and bargain counter.

The translation of style from margin to center evacuates the form of its original vividness and subtlety, but a sufficient residue of those qualities remains such that audience sensibilities expand roughly at the rate the various sectors of the culture industry require and can accommodate. What is more, the success of this translation guarantees its cyclical repetition. While it is true that the apparatus of spectacular consumption makes genuine human strivings — even the resistance it meets — into reified commodities, this is no simple procedure: exploitation by the culture industry serves at the same time to stimulate and complicate those strivings in such a way that they continually outrun and surpass its programming. The expansion of the cultural economy continually creates new fringe areas, and young and more extreme members of incorporated subcultures will regroup with new recruits at still more marginal positions. So the process begins again.

Elements of this mechanism are in place by the mid-nineteenth century,[56] and the rest of the century will see its coming to maturity in sport, fashion, and entertainment. The artistic avant-garde provides an early, developed example of the process at work. In fact, because of its unique position between the upper and lower zones of commodity culture, this group performs a special and powerful function within that process.

To begin with its primary audience, the fact that the avant-garde depends on elite patronage — the "umbilical cord of gold" — cannot be written off as an inconsequential or regrettable circumstance; we need to assume that so durable a form of social interchange is not based merely on the indulgence or charity of the affluent, but that the avant-garde serves the interests of its actual consumers in a way that goes beyond purely individual attraction to 'quality' or the glamour of the forbidden. That service could be described as a necessary brokerage between high and low. In its selective appropriation from fringe mass culture, the avant-garde searches out areas of social practice which retain some vivid life in an increasingly administered and rationalized society. These it refines and packages, directing them to an elite, self-conscious audience. Certain played-out procedures within established high art are forcibly refused, but the form itself, in this case easel painting, is preserved and renewed — renewed with the aesthetic discoveries of non-elite groups. The survival of high art as an irreplaceable status indicator would otherwise be very much in doubt. Nor, clearly, does the process of selective incorporation end there. Legitimated modernism is re-packaged in turn for consumption as chic and kitsch commodities. The work of the avant-garde is returned to the sphere of culture where much of its substantial material originated. In the process, outmoded or under-utilized products of the capitalist economy — or even just the disorder and brutality thrown up in its wake — are refurbished and glamourized to be sold as new.

Functionally then, the avant-garde serves as a kind of research and development arm of the culture industry: it searches out areas of social practice not yet completely available to efficient manipulation and makes them discrete and visible. For example, it was only a matter of a few years before the Impressionist vision of the spaces of commercial diversion became the advertisement of the thing itself, a functioning part of the imaginary enticement directed toward tourists and residents alike. The work of Toulouse-Lautrec as a designer and illustrator can be taken as emblematic of this shift. His cultivated irony, perversity and compositional extremism continued previously established kinds of avant-garde attention to low-life spectacle. In his commercial work, however, certain patented modernist devices became the preferred vocabulary of an emerging sector of the entertainment industry; and thereby erased was that crucial distance which allowed a Seurat to work *on* the art of a Chéret. The collapse of art into its subject was displayed as concretely as possible in 1895, when the Folies-Bergère entertainer La Goulue went out on her own at the Foire du Trône, setting up her act in a structure which appeared from the outside to be literally constructed out of two large painted panels by Lautrec.[57]

In the twentieth century, this process of mass-cultural recuperation has operated on an ever-increasing scale. The Cubist vision of sensory flux and isolation in the city became in Art Deco a portable vocabulary for a whole modern 'look' in fashion and design. Cubism's geometricization of organic form and its rendering of three-dimensional illusion into animated patterns of overlapping planes were a principal means by which modernist architecture and interior design were transformed into a refined and precious high style. Advertised as such, now through the powerful medium of film costume and set decoration — the 'white telephone' school of cinema — the Art-Deco stamp was put on the whole range of twenties and Depression-era commodities: office buildings, fabric, home appliances, furniture, crockery. (The Art-Deco style was also easily drawn into the imagery of the mechanized body characteristic of protofascist and fascist utopianism.) The case of Surrealism is perhaps the most notorious instance of this process. Breton and company had discovered in the sedimentary layers of earlier capitalist forms of life in Paris something like the material unconscious of the city, the residue of earlier repressions. But in retrieving marginal forms of consumption, in making that latent text manifest, they provided modern advertising with one of its most powerful visual tools — that now familiar terrain in which commodities behave autonomously and create an alluring dreamscape of their own.[58]

This brokerage between high and low, between legitimate and illegitimate, thus makes the avant-garde an important mechanism in a manipulative cultural economy. It mediates between three publics really: 1) its immediate initiated clientele; 2) the much larger middle-class public for validated high culture with which it is in fairly constant negotiation; and 3) those publics excluded from or indifferent to high culture which, after Courbet and outside of a few occasions of overt political revolution, the avant-garde never attempts to address directly. Though the experience of people whose horizons are closed by 'low' culture is repeatedly used to lend shape and substance to powerfully self-conscious and revelatory art, we assume no audience *there* for the qualities of negation, allusiveness, willed moral transgression, refusal of closure, formal rigor, and self-criticism which variously characterize modernist practice — however much such people might 'innocently' act out these qualities for the benefit of the artist. The cycle of exchange which modernism sets in motion moves only in one direction: appropriation of oppositional practices upward, the return of evacuated cultural goods downward. When some piece of avant-garde invention does re-enter the lower zone of mass culture, it is in a form drained of its original force and integrity. It is this one-directional exchange cycle, predicated on the purely legitimating character of museum culture and the entrenchment of the culture industry, which has made the class bias of modernism immoveable. And as long as the cycle remains in place, modernist negation becomes, paradoxically, an instrument of cultural domination.

X

> In 1868 I painted a good deal at La Grenouillère. I remember an amusing restaurant called Four-naise's, where life was a perpetual holiday . . . . The world knew how to laugh in those days! Machinery had not yet absorbed all of life; you had leisure for enjoyment and no one was the worse for it.
>
> Renoir, late in life[59]

This essay is not meant as a verdict on modernism in the visual arts. Recent discussion of the issue has suffered from a surplus of verdicts. Typically, one moment of the series of transformations described above is chosen as the definitive one. The social iconographers of modernism (the most recent trend in art history) limit themselves to its raw material.[60] The aesthetic dialecticians, Adorno holding out until the end, concentrate on the moment of negativity crystallized in form.[61] Modernist triumphalism, the later Greenberg and his followers for example, celebrate the intial recuperation of that form into a continuous canon of value.[62] Finally, that recuperation is the object of attack from two directions: from the Left, who see in this moment a revelation that modernist negation was always a sham, never more than a way to refurbish elite commodities; and from the Right, the advocates of a relaxed and eclectic pluralism, who see this recuperation as insufficient and resent the retention of any negativity even if it is sublimated entirely into formal criteria — this is the 'post-modernist' stance.[63]

Each of these positions has its own 'modernism', and takes that as the essence of the thing. The purpose of the present essay has been to widen discussion to include, or rather re-include, all the elements present in the original formulation of modernist theory. One of my motivations for writing came from reflection on the fact that the founding moments for subsequent discourse on both modernist art and mass culture were one and the same. Current debates over both topics invariably begin with the same names — Adorno, Benjamin, Greenberg (less often Schapiro, but I hope I have done something to change that). Very seldom, however, are these debates about both topics together, though at the beginning they always were: the theory of the one *was* the theory of the other. And in that identity was the realization, occasionally manifest and always latent, that the two were in no fundamental way separable. Mass culture, which is just another way of saying culture under developed capitalism, displays both moments of negation and an ultimately overwhelming recuperative inertia. Modernism exists in the tension between these two opposed movements. The avant-garde, the bearer of modernism, has been successful when it has found for itself a social location where this tension is visible and can be acted on.

Notes

[1]The source is an article entitled "The Impressionists and Edouard Manet," *Art Monthly Review,* (September 30, 1876), which survives only in an English translation. For a description of the circumstances of publication and some (inadequate) excerpts, see Jean C. Harris, "A Little-Known Essay on Manet by Stéphane Mallarmé," *Art Bulletin,* 46, (December, 1964), pp.559-63. The special power and importance of this text has been pointed out by T. J. Clark, "The Bar at the Folies-Bergère," in J. Beauroy, M. Bertrand, and E. Gargan, eds., *The Wolf and the Lamb: Popular Culture in France,* Saratoga, CA, 1977, p.234 n.5.

[2][Paul Signac], "Impressionistes et Révolutionnaires," *La Révolte,* 4:40, (June 13-19, 1891), p.4 (quoted in R. and E. Herbert, "Artists and Anarchism: Unpublished letters of Pissarro, Signac, and Others," *Burlington Magazine,* 102, (November, 1960), p.692.

[3]On Corvi and the connection to Seurat, see R. Herbert, " 'Parade du Cirque' de Seurat et l'esthétique scientifique de Charles Henry," *Revue de l'Art,*

no.50, (1980), pp.9-23. A monumental and maudlin depiction of the same dispi-
rited location by Fernand Pelez was exhibited in the Salon of 1888; see R. Rosenblum, "Fernand Pelez, or the Other Side of the Post-Impressionist Coin", in *Art
the Ape of Nature,* M. Barasch and L. Sandler eds., New York, 1981, pp.710-12.
For a contemporary description of the spectator in "Le Chahut", see Gustave
Kahn, "Seurat," *L'Art Moderne,* (April 5, 1891), pp.109-10 (selection translated in
N. Broude, *Seurat in Perspective,* Englewood Cliffs, NJ, 1978): "As a synthetic
image of the public, observe the pig's snout of the spectator, archetype of the fat
reveler *(noceur gras),* placed up close to and below the female dance, vulgarly
enjoying *(jouissant canaillement)* the moment of pleasure that has been prepared
for him, with no thought for anything but a laugh and a lewd desire. If you are
looking at costs for a 'symbol', you will find it in the contrast between the beauty
of the dancer, an elegant and modest sprite, and the ugliness of her admirer;
between the hieratic structure of the canvas and its subject, a contemporary
ignominy." That last phrase seems to me particularly astute.

[4]The lecture was given on March 27, 1890 and published in 1891 under the
title *Harmonie des formes et des couleurs;* in April 1889, Signac wrote to Van Gogh
expressing his desire to equip workers with Neo-Impressionist theory *(Complete
Letters of Vincent Van Gogh,* III, Greenwich, 1948, no.584a); on these texts, see R.
and E. Herbert, "Artist and Anarchism," p.481 n.48.

[5]"Extraits du journal inédit de Paul Signac," J. Rewald ed., *Gazette des
Beaux-Arts,* 6th per., XXXVI, (July-September, 1949), p.126 (entry of September
1, 1895).

[6]Daniel Henry [Kahnweiler], *Der Weg zum Kubismus,* Munich, 1920, p.27;
for Apollinaire, see texts in E. Fry ed., *Cubism,* New York, 1966, pp.113, 118.

[7]C. Greenberg, "Collage," in *Art and Culture,* Boston, 1962, p.70.

[8]See, for example, C. Owens, "The Allegorical Impulse: Toward a Theory
of Postmodernism," *October,* no. 13, (October, 1980), p.79: "Modernist theory
presupposes that mimesis, the adequation of an image to a referent, can be
bracketed or suspended, and that the art object itself can be substituted (metaphorically) for its referent. This is the rhetorical strategy of self-reference on which
modernism is based, and from Kant onwards is identified as the source of artistic
pleasure. . . . When the postmodernist work speaks of itself, it is no longer to
proclaim its autonomy, its self-sufficieny, its transcendence; rather, it is to narrate
its own contingency, insufficiency, lack of transcendence." As I will be arguing,
this view is based on a retrospective caricature of both modernist theory and
practice based almost entirely on Greenberg's late pronouncements — and his
unfortunate reduction of Kant (see "Modernist Painting," in G. Battcock ed., *The
New Art,* New York, 1966). Owens' argument is interesting and symptomatic in
that his struggle to articulate the position he calls post-modernist — with all the
usual tortured reconstructions of early Walter Benjamin — is no more than an
effort to find his way back to the best achievements of historical modernism,
which his theoretical blockage prevents him from recognizing as such. The success
of modernism has been precisely the narration of its contingency, insufficiency,
and lack of transcendence; but this narration only makes sense in and through the
effort to reach closure and sufficiency, even if that effort is endlessly defeated.
Without that, the late modernist or postmodernist work, whatever one chooses to
call it, lapses into a complacent nihilism, passively celebrating the insufficiency
and absence of autonomy which are the pervasive conditions of the everyday
social nightmare.

[9]Originally published in *Partisan Review,* VI, (Fall 1939), pp.34-39; reprinted in *Art and Culture,* pp.3-21.

[10]*Partisan Review,* VII, (Fall 1940), pp.296-310.

[11]"Avant-Garde and Kitsch," p.9.

[12]The historical account contained in this paragraph is based partly on my own research concerning David's pre-Revolutionary painting, the Salon audience, and the intense politicization of culture in Paris during the final crisis of the Old Regime; see T. Crow, "The 'Oath of the Horatii' in 1785: Painting and Pre-Revolutionary Radicalism in France," *Art History,* I, (December, 1978), pp.424-71. For Courbet in the Salon of 1851, the authoritative interpretation is T. J. Clark *The Image of the People,* passim and especially pp.130-54. My use of the terms "emergent" and "residual" is derived from that of Raymond Williams: see his *Marxism and Literature,* Oxford, 1977, pp.121-7.

[13]"The Social Bases of Art," proceedings of the First Artists' Congress against War and Fascism, New York, 1936, pp.31-37; "The Nature of Abstract Art," *The Marxist Quarterly,* I, (January, 1937), pp.77-98; reprinted in Schapiro, *Modern Art: the Nineteenth and Twentieth Centuries,* New York, pp.185-211.

[14]*Modern Art,* p.192-3.

[15]"Social Bases," p.33.

[16]"Social Bases," p.37.

[17]"Avant-Garde and Kitsch" concludes (p.21): "Here, as in every other question today, it becomes necessary to quote Marx word for word. Today we no longer look toward socialism for a new culture — as inevitably as one will appear, once we do have socialism. Today we look to socialism for the preservation of whatever living culture we have right now."

[18]"Avant-Garde and Kitsch," p.11.

[19]See E. Weber, "Gymnastics and Sports in *Fin-de-Siècle* France: Opium of the Classes?", *American Historical Review,* LXXVI, (February, 1971), pp.70-98; also R. Holt, *Sport and Society in Modern France,* London, 1981.

[20]See the recent study by Michael Miller, *The Bon Marché: Bourgeois Culture and the Department Store, 1869-1920,* Princeton, 1981.

[21]See K. Thomas, "Work and Leisure in Pre-Industrial Society," *Past and Present,* no.29, (December, 1964), pp.50-66; E. P. Thompson, "Time, Work, and Industrial Capitalism," *Past and Present,* no.38, (December, 1967), pp.56-97; especially suggestive for the present account is G. Stedman Jones, "Working-Class Culture and Working-Class Politics in London, 1870-1900; Notes on the Remaking of a Working Class," *Journal of Social History,* VII, (Summer 1974), pp.460-508.

[22]Karl Marx, *The Eighteenth Brumaire of Louis Bonaparte,* New York, 1963, p.104. Recent historical research has documented the virulence of the official campaign against all republican institutions and values during Bonaparte's presidency and following the coup, an ideological scorched-earth policy, driven by fears of a Montagnard electoral victory in 1852; see T. Forstenzer, *French Provincial Police and the Fall of the Second Republic,* Princeton, 1981, which concludes (p.247), "The police bureaucrats' support for Louis Napoleon's imperial pretensions even before the coup, their support for a suspension of parliament and courts, and their work on the Mixed Commissions were all part of a single radical dynamic: the defense of a threatened future by a total social prophylaxis that secured the present and effaced the recent past. In the interest of maintaining a hierarchy and avoiding an uninhabitable future, the insecurities of the Second Republic were swept away: liberalism, constitutional government, civil court procedure, and of course any form of democracy with any real political meaning for the voter. The *New Age of Caesar,* preached by Romieu, the Elysée's propagandist, expressed more than the political opportunism of the president's personal côterie. It was a radical counterrevolutionary program enforced with genuine conviction by the prefects and attorneys general. The institutionalized extremism of January to March 1852 would not be seen again until the Commune. And perhaps Caesarism's combination of mock populism and repressive ferocity in 1852 would not be fully realized until our own century." For a discussion of

Marx's interpretation of the aftermath of 1848 in light of the developing logic of mass culture, see J. Brenkman, "Mass Media: From Collective Experience to the Culture of Privatization," *Social Text*, no.1, (Winter 1979), pp.94-109.

[23]The terminology of this paragraph derives from recent work in the sociology of leisure-based subcultures in post-war Britain. The approach was initially formulated by Philip Cohen in: "Sub-Cultural Conflict and Working-Class Community," *Working Papers in Cultural Studies*, no.2, (Spring 1972) and has been continued by Stuart Hall and others associated with the Centre for Contemporary Culture Studies at the University of Birmingham. For a collection of their theoretical work and case studies, see S. Hall and T. Jefferson eds., *Resistance through Rituals*, London, 1976. A brief aside in that volume made the first connection between the subcultural response and the historical avant-garde (p.13): "The bohemian sub-culture of the *avant-garde* which has arisen from time to time in the modern city, is both distinct from its 'parent' culture (the urban culture of the middle class intelligentsia) and yet also part of it (sharing with it a modernising outlook, standards of education, a privileged position vis-a-vis productive labour, and so on.)" The link was first made specific for Second-Empire Paris and pictorial modernism by T. J. Clark in "The Place of Pleasure: Paris in the Painting of the Avant-Garde, 1860-1890," New York, William James Lecture, March 1978.

[24]Walter Benjamin, *Charles Baudelaire: A Lyric Poet in the Age of High Capitalism*, H. Zohn trans., London 1973, p.59 (this is from the first, 1938 version of the Baudelaire essay.)

[25]Benjamin, *Baudelaire*, p.106.

[26]See Jules Michelet, *L'Etudiant, cours de 1847-8*, Paris, 1877, pp.129-30. M. Fried has pointed out the importance of Michelet's references to Géricault: see "Thomas Couture and the Theatricalization of Action in 19th-Century French Painting," *Artforum*, VIII, (June, 1970), p.38. On the uses of Delacroix's "Liberty" in 1848, see T. J. Clark, *The Absolute Bourgeois*, New York, 1972, pp.16-20. The end of the revolutionary rationale in painting was the subject of recorded reflections by the aging Renoir (A. Vollard, *La Vie et l'oeuvre de P. A. Renoir*, Paris, 1919, p.42; translated as *Renoir, An Intimate Record*, New York, 1934, p.47): "But Manet and our group came along when the destructive forces deriving from the Revolution (of 1789) were exhausted. To be sure, certain among the newcomers would have liked to link themselves with tradition, the immense benefits of which they felt, unconsciously; but to do that, they would first of all have had to learn the traditional technique of painting, but when you are left to your own resources, you necessarily begin with the simple before attempting the complex, just as, to be able to read, you must first learn the letters of the alphabet. You realize, then, that for us the great task has been to paint as simply as possible; but you also realize how much the inheritors of tradition — from such men as Abel de Pujol, Gérôme, Cabanel, etc., with whom these traditions, which they did not comprehend, were lost in the commonplace and the vulgar, up to painters like Courbet, Delacroix, Ingres — were bewildered by what seemed to them merely the naive efforts of an *imagier d'Epinal*. Daumier is said to have remarked at the Manet exhibition: 'I'm not a very great admirer of Manet's work, but I find it has this important quality: it is helping to bring art back to the simplicity of playing cards." Much of the present argument is anticipated in these remarks.

[27]See D. Silverman, "The 1889 Exhibition: The Crisis of Bourgeois Individualism," *Oppositions*, no.8, (Spring 1977), pp.71-91.

[28]*Modern Art*, p.192.

[29]S. Guilbaut, "The New Adventures of the Avant-Garde in America: Greenberg, Pollock, or from Trotskyism to the New Liberalism of the 'Vital Center'," *October*, no.15, (Winter 1980), p.63-4; a brief but unsurpassed overview of the trajectory of Schapiro's career can be found in O.K. Werckmeister, review

of Schapiro's *Romanesque Art, Art Quarterly,* new series II, (Spring 1979), pp.211-18.

[30]See "Recent Abstract Painting" originally published as "The Liberating Quality of Abstract Art" (1957) and "On the Humanity of Abstract Art (1960)," in *Modern Art,* pp.213-32.

[31]See note 23 for relevant literature.

[32]Hall et al., *Rituals of Resistance,* p.47.

[33]See notes 23 and 32.

[34]See P. Mainardi, "Courbet's Second Scandal, 'Les Demoiselles de Village'," *Arts,* LIII, (January, 1979), pp.96-103.

[35]A. Proust, *Edouard Manet, Souvenirs,* Paris, 1913, p.15: "Quelque effort qu'il fît en exagérant ce déhanchement et en affectant le parler trainant du gamin de Paris, il ne pouvait parvenir à être vulgaire."

[36]The most important critical reading of "Olympia" in 1865, that of "Jean Ravenel" (Alfred Sensier), stressed this clash of cultural signifiers in a great deal of detail; see the exposition and interpretation of this text by Clark, "Preliminaries to a Possible Treatment of 'Olympia' in 1865," *Screen,* XXI, (Spring 1980), pp.18-42; Clark's argument, relevant for our purposes, is that the formal flattening and precision, the material opacity of facture, are generated out of the unresolved superimposition of two sets of ideological signs: one indicating the proletarian status of the common prostitute, the other the euphemistic conventions of courtesan imagery in both art and contemporary social practice.

[37]M. Butor, "Monet, or the World Turned Upside-Down," *Art News Annual,* XXXIV, (1968), pp.21-33. I should mention here that the foregoing discussion of modernist aesthetics is indebted to Charles Rosen's analysis of the origins of modernism in music: see C. Rosen, *Arnold Schoenberg,* New York, 1975, pp.17-22 and passim.

[38]For a summary of the evidence concerning the deliberate pairing of the pictures, see J. House, "Meaning in Seurat's Figure Painting," *Art History,* III, (September, 1980), pp.346-9.

[39]"Georges Seurat," *La Société Nouvelle,* (April, 1891); in Broude, p.28.

[40]See R. Herbert, "Seurat and Jules Chéret," *Art Bulletin,* XL, (March, 1958), pp.156-8.

[41]See R. Rosenblum, "Picasso and the Typography of Cubism," in R. Penrose ed., *Picasso in Retrospect,* New York, 1973, pp.49-75.

[42]See Clark, "Bar," p.235.

[43]The pictures are "Figure Seated in a Café" and "Teacups" (both 1914). In "Figure," a clipping from *Le Matin* describes a new system invented by the criminologist Alphonse Bertillon to prevent the forgery of works of art; one of his suggestions was that artists authenticate their works with their fingerprints. (See Rosenblum, pp.64-5.)

[44]T. W. Adorno, "On Commitment," in A. Arato and E. Gebhardt eds., *The Essential Frankfurt School Reader,* New York, 1978, p.318.

[45]The invocation of Adorno here calls, I think, for explication at some length. As Greenberg does in the American critical tradition, so Adorno stands in his as the preeminent defender of removed, inward, self-critical and self-referential artistic practice. Where Greenberg would find visual art answering his criteria in the New York abstract painting of the later 1940's and after, Adorno already had the example of the Vienna school — the liberated dissonance of the work of Schoenberg and his pupils around 1910 and its later codification in twelve-tone technique; his writing, in its thorny style and substance, was in part an effort to make thought adequate to that formal achievement. The parallels between Adorno and Greenberg continue to the present day in the attacks to which the former's account of modernist music has been subjected. His critics in West Germany, who come primarily from the Left, dismiss as a "dialectic of stagnation" his contention that

the truth of an alienated social totality can find form only in the artist's concentration on the inmost cells of enclosed technical problems (see W. V. Blomster, "Sociology of Music: Adorno and Beyond," *Telos,* no.28, (Summer 1976), pp.81-112); this they regard as a disguised and unsupportable affirmation of the frozen art-commodity beloved by bourgeois aesthetics. And these attacks have predictably undermined the authority of Schoenberg's modernist practice as well.

Adorno's position is summed up in his essay "On the Fetish Character of Music and the Regression of Listening" (included in Arato and Gebhardt, *The Essential Frankfurt School Reader,* pp.270-99) published just one year before "Avant-Garde and Kitsch". Like the latter, its defense of modernism is bound up with a critique of mass culture. The austerity and difficulty of modern music is not an internal necessity but one imposed from the outside. "Asceticism," he states ("Fetish" p.274), "has today become the sign of advanced art: not, to be sure, by an archaizing parsimony of means in which deficiency and poverty are manifested, but by the strict exclusion of all culinary delights which seek to be consumed immediately for their own sake, as if in art the sensory were not the bearer of something intellectual which shows itself only in the whole rather than in isolated topical moments." The culinary has been irretrieveably appropriated by the culture industry (that last term is his and Horkheimer's coinage), by the logic of the commodity. Later, he would condense the logic of the autonomous work of art to one line: ". . . in the future, no type of composition is expected to be 'proto' for the purposes of mass production." ("Modern Music is Growing Old," *The Score,* no.18, (December, 1956) pp.18-29.) That could stand precisely for Greenberg's original argument as well.

But if both begin from a derivation of modernism in the pervasive conditions of mass-cultural production, Adorno parts company from Greenberg's kind of analysis by keeping the larger cultural landscape continually in view, by according it equal status as an object of inquiry. Greenberg, by taking up the subject of kitsch only at the outset and then bracketing it off, tacitly re-establishes the old opposition between a high culture with all the virtues and a bereft, impoverished low culture. His implication is that modernist art, apart from its reduction in scope, is otherwise unaffected by its origins in the late-capitalist crucible: the line of 'culture' from past to present is, thanks to modernism, unbroken and high art is not implicated in a continuing way with the general culture it evades. Adorno is under no such illusion. In 1936, as he was finishing his essay "Über Jazz," he wrote to Walter Benjamin: "Both bear the stigmata of capitalism, both contain elements of change (naturally never in no way the middle term between Schoenberg and the American film). Both are torn halves of an integral freedom, to which however they do not add up." (in R. Taylor, ed., *Aesthetics and Politics,* London, 1977, p.123.)

Adorno has come down to us as the dour opponent of all Benjamin's optimism over the technology of mass art (exemplified in the famous essay "The Work of Art in the Age of Mechanical Reproduction). Though Benjamin himself saw no incompatability between their positions, Adorno's relentless refusal of all forms of the 'popular' has made him seem the distilled essence of rationalized snobbery on the Left. His at times extreme and emotional denunciations of jazz as a typically specious commodity of the culture industry are now widely regarded as embarrassing. Susan Buck-Morss, however, in her excellent study of the Adorno-Benjamin axis (*The Origin of Negative Dialectics,* New York, 1977), has provided a timely defense of his account of jazz, one which is directly relevant to our inquiry here. The notorious vehemence of his polemic is directed less against the music itself than against the way it was being heard: there was, first, the perception that the improvised breaks and loose ensemble structure were occasions for free individual expression and thus provided a progressive alternative to academic rigidity and control. There was in this — as there still is — a romantic perception of an upwelling of underclass spontaneity. A second and related reading sought to affiliate jazz with aspects of contemporary modernism, particularly in its constructivist tendencies: as he put it in (*Aesthetics and Politics,* p.125), "the appearance of montage, collective work, the primacy of reproduction over production." Adorno was intent on unmasking the 'progressive' appearance of jazz and revealing its actual conformist character, "the rigid, almost timeless immobility in the movement, the mask-like stereotype of a fusion between wild agitation which appears to be dynamic and an inflexibility of process which rules over such agitation. Above all, the law which is one of the market as much as myth: it must always be the same and simultaneously feign being always new." ("Über Jazz," in *Moments Musicaux,* Frankfurt, 1964, p.95; quoted in Buck-Morss, p.109)

For Adorno, jazz and the collective experience of mass culture in general represent a return of an archaic ritual life in the midst of a disenchanted secular modernity. Like the festive rites in preliterate societies, the apparent release of the individual from normal constraints is automatic and unreflective; in truth it effects a renewed sacrifice of individual life to the overwhelming demands of the collective. And one could not even hope that the return of the primitive might re-ground shattered, deracinated subjectivity in some more elemental strata of experience, because these rituals were thoroughly modern in character — the moments indeed when the individual was most in accord with the demands of capitalism; he ranges himself on the side of the dominating market apparatus best when he does so in postures of enjoyment and undirected leisure. Though the promise of mass culture is one of ever-expanding sensual happiness, what is delivered is always the same — the commodity, infinite in its beckoning guises, but cold and unchanging in its essence, a mockery of desire that the consumer secretly recognizes and is resigned to. It is a realm of fantasy which at the same time enforces the most disabused realism on its participants.

Adorno chooses jazz to stand for this historical development in the realm of music; but it is a mistake to say that he dismisses it. In fact, he treats it with the same seriousness and attention that he extends to music from the high-art tradition. The social contradiction which the players and audience of jazz magically resolve — that between helpless individuality and an immoveable social totality — is not resolved in the music itself: jazz is a configuration of opposites, of Salon-music virtuosity and military regimentation, which remain held in contradiction and are therefore apprehendable as such: "If jazz were really listened to, it would lose its power. Then people would no longer identify with it, but identify it itself." ("Oxforder Nachträge" (1937), in *Moments,* p.120; quoted in Buck-Morss, p.110.) In that the mass-cultural form offers a static configuration of the social antinomy its actual consumption suppresses, it offers a potential moment of revelation — or "redemption" — as well. Adorno, however, does not imagine this happening within the confines of mass-cultural practice, that is, for its own audience, but only through an outside intervention like his own. Not so with high culture, where Schoenberg's modernism constitutes an immanent critique of the decayed classicism of the nineteenth century, while preserving and extending that tradition.

But to see this, as many have, as a recuperation of a sterile high-culture/low-culture opposition would be a mistake. The best way to demonstrate this would be to bring in his contemporaneous essay on Wagner, written between 1937 and 1938 in London during his first years of exile. Like many others since, Adorno locates Schoenberg's liberated dissonance as latent in Wagner's compositional practice — in its atomization of musical material and tonal indeterminacy, the pressure of an independent expressive polyphony against the strict four-part harmonic scheme, the contextualization of the dissonance-consonance or antecedent-consequent relationship, the displacement of that relationship away from tonality into the unsystematic realm of orchestral color. Given that much of musical modernism develops directly from problems posed by Wagner, it is striking to read Adorno summing up his argument midway through the essays in this way *(In Search of Wagner,* R. Livingstone, trans., London, 1981. p.62): "The contradictions underlying the formal and melodic structure of Wagner's music — the necessary precondition of the failure at the level of technique — may be generally located in the fact that eternal sameness presents itself as the eternally new, the static as the dynamic, or that conversely, intrinsically dynamic categories are projected onto unhistorical, pre-subjective characters." We could substitute the word "jazz" for "Wagner's music" and the resulting statement would be fully consistent with Adorno's analysis. The last clause refers to the emptied mythological ciphers who inhabit the Wagnerian stage, but could just as well be interpreted to mean the modern archaic man, the jazz "subject". The seedbed of modernism is describable in the same terms as mass music. "For this reason," he states, "the really productive moment in Wagner is seen at the moments when the individual abandons sovereignty and passively abandons itself to the archaic, the instinctual . . . ." Near the end of his life, he would make the same point in more general terms ("On Commitment," p.315): "Works of art which by their existence take the side of the victims of a rationality that subjugates nature are even in their protest constitutively implicated in the process of rationalization itself. Were they to try to disown it, they would become both esthetically and socially powerless: mere clay. The organizing, unifying principle of each and every work of art is borrowed from that very rationality whose claim to totality it seeks to defy." Quite obviously, the present essay takes issue with Adorno's undifferentiated view of mass culture, but that last quotation could stand as a three-sentence summation of its central argument.

[46]"The Impressionists and Edouard Manet."

[47]C. Pissarro, *Letters to his Son Lucien,* T. Rewald ed., New York, 1943: entry of January 9, 1887.

[48]"Extraits du journal inédit de Paul Signac," p.126; Signac wrote on July 5, 1895 (p.124), "Toujours à la recherche d'une facture plus libre, tout en conservant les bénéfices de la division et du contraste." Those two aims were to prove largely incompatible.

[49]See J. P. Crespelle, *The Fauves,* New York, 1962, p.112.

[50]See Ellen C. Oppler, *Fauvism Reexamined,* New York, 1976, p.13-38.

[51]A. Derain, *Lettres à Vlaminck,* Paris, 1955, pp.146-7. Certain pictures by Vlaminck are, I might mention, conspicuous exceptions to the main tendency of Fauvism outlined here — that tendency which culminates in Matisse's "Luxe, Calme, et Volupté". Vlaminck, in pictures like "Houses at Chatou" (1905, Chicago Art Institute), remains in the bypassed, semi-industrialized *banlieue* of Paris, and employs his violent color and handling in order to convey the bleakness of the place. Fauve color and gesture work against their expected connotations of exuberance and ease; the deliberate instability of the technique is made instead to represent the raw, unsettled quality of this particular landscape. In strictly formal terms as well, it is one of the most uncompromising and unified Fauve works. We might recall that Vlaminck, a child of the suburban working class, was here no tourist, but was painting his home town.

[52]From within the group, the artist could also look outward with acuity and wit. Standing in pointed contrast to the idyllic south of France painted by the established avant-garde is the provincial and chauvinist Midi displayed in Picasso's "Aficionado" of 1912. Given the associations of French bullfighting, we have to read the figure as an enemy pleasure-seeker: the stuffed-shirt in a Nîmes cafe, arrayed in his shoddy enthusiasm for the second-rate local bullring — surely comical to the Spanish artist. There is a likely political subtext to this, the *corrida* being traditionally associated with the parties of the extreme Right and having served as a rallying point for anti-Dreyfusard agitation in the south. See Holt, *Sport and Society,* pp.115-20.

53"Synthetisches Cino der Malerei," 1918, quoted in R. Haussmann, *Courrier Dada,* Paris, 1948, p.40; also in H. Wescher, *Collage,* New York, 1968, p.136. For a Dada reading of Cubist collage in specific terms, see R. Huelsenbeck, "En Avant Dada," in R. Motherwell ed., *Dada Painters and Poets,* New York, 1951, p.36.

54M. Raynal, "Quelques intentions du cubisme," *Bulletin de l'effort moderne,* no.4, p.4, quoted in B. Buchloh, "Figures of Authority, Ciphers of Regression," *October,* no. 16, (Spring 1981), p.44.

55For the frequency of this imagery in regressed modernism and the reified notion of style which accompanied it, see Buchloh, pp.39-68.

56W. Weber *(Music and the Middle Class,* New York, 1975, pp.105-6) describes how artisan-class, radical choral groups emerged from the Revolution of 1830 and in 1832 were sufficiently organized to give a massed concert which included twenty singing clubs and 600 singers. Subsequently, several of the clubs began to perform at commercial theaters and promenade concerts. This improvised form of communal artistic life was suppressed by the state in the political crack-down of 1833-5, but the form was resurrected by an entrepreneur named William Wilhem who began receiving state subsidies for his singing classes in 1836. Called the Orphéon societies, they remained primarily lower-class in their membership, but the audience at the well-attended and fairly expensive concerts was middle-class and aristocratic. The climax of this development occurred in 1859 when the Orphéon societies were called on to perform in the new Palace of Industry of Napoleon III.

57For a photograph of the booth, see P. Huisman and M. G. Dortu, *Lautrec by Lautrec,* New York, 1964, p.84.

58For a discussion of Surrealism in these terms, see F. Jameson, *Marxism and Form,* Princeton, 1971, pp.96-106.

59Quoted in Vollard, pp.45-6.

60See, for example, R. Herbert, "Method and Meaning in Monet," *Art in America,* LXVII, (September, 1979), pp.103-106. To be fair, the first part of Herbert's article is a lengthy examination of the technical complexity displayed in Monet's later painting: this is the "method" section. But the subsequent discussion of "meaning" limits itself almost entirely to subject matter, describing the pictures of the 1870's as an "optimistic rendering of the new forces" which were changing the visible face of the city and the forms of bourgeois urbanity. This kind of social history of modernism is one determined to domesticate its object by tying its every feature to an empirical referent. In the case of Impressionism, it collapses the modernist work into the already existing arrangements of one commercial sector; it reproduces the simple position Schapiro abandoned after 1936, and by stripping Schapiro's insights of their polemical purpose, arrives at straightforward affirmation: we value Impressionism because it reproduces an ideal image of technical progress and middle-class sociability. This reading, Herbert claims, has been suppressed by a narrow "twentieth-century formalism" which ignored Monet's symbolic iconography. But if we are not to leave Impressionism as an anodyne official art of the future, mass culture's best advertisement, the contribution of twentieth-century formalism is the only corrective available — for only there do we find recognized the negation and refusal at the core of any modernism worth the name.

61See note 39 for some discussion of the complexity of Adorno's position.

62M. Fried, ". . . within the modernist arts nothing short of *conviction* — specifically, the conviction that a particular painting or sculpture or poem or piece of music can or cannot support comparison with past work within that art whose quality is not in doubt — matters at all." "Art and Objecthood," in G. Battcock ed., *Minimal Art,* New York, 1968 p.142.

63For a vulgar but perfectly representative example, see Kim Levin, "Farewell to Modernism," *Arts,* LIV, (March 1979), pp. 90-2.

Concluding Panel Discussion:

Serge Guilbaut:
We have to start the discussion somehow, and maybe I can start by asking a set of simple questions — "Do you think that the title that we chose for the symposium was adequate, do you think that we answered that question, and do you think that we should think more about the issue of modernism?"

Panel:
Yes, yes, and yes.

(laughter)

T. J. Clark:
I don't know, one of the things that seemed to emerge today was the defense of modernism from varying points of view, but anyway a defence of modernism against the idea of its death, and against the idea of its replacement by something called post-modernism. And, while obviously that is my position, I wondered whether there was something a bit illusionary in the unanimity from the platform about that. Anyway, whoever is defending the concept, it certainly has its defenders in the culture. So to that extent the degree of agreement here that post-modernism is not a serious category, and that the kind of weightless eclecticism of contemporary art is not a serious way out from the crisis of modernism perhaps needs discussing.

Is there anyone in the audience who wants to question us about this or feels very dissatisfied, with the kind of degree of dismissal here on the part of many of us of the kind of artistic practices in which many of you must be involved?

Audience:
I am interested in the concept of post-modernism just for my own teaching which is basically the study of Contemporary Art, and when you use a word like modern or post-modern, you have to be very specific and very limited about your use of them, otherwise it becomes very vagrant in its discussion. I felt that the symposium was attempting to define two directions of modernism itself, but that the term 'modernism' has been used to cover both of those aspects (modernism and modernity) without really defining what was consistent in modernism itself that might create a term that

was considered post-modernism.

So I feel that in a sense the questions of post-modernism have been coming from the rafters, so to speak, without being answered in terms of what modernism really was. Various talks brought up conditions of modernism, but never talked about it as a consistent unity. The term was used very loosely on the whole, except by Greenberg, who actually spoke of the term modernism, in a very limited and specific sense actually defined that in his early essays. I think that post-modernism really is a response to the very limited sense of modernism that Greenberg defined. But there is a political sense of modernism which I think is coming up in the other discussions, but which was never brought into focus in relationship to the formal concept of modernism.

Clement Greenberg:
I think Madame Blondin spoke of post-modernism as something quite definite, as something that was here, and that had recognizable features. Now I feel that maybe she should be asked to elaborate or justify the confidence with which she used the term.

Nicole Dubreuil-Blondin:
I don't know if I sounded confident, but I did use it in a very specific way. More, I would say, I am just beginning to inquire into the concept, because for many, many years, I have been a formalist, in the Greenbergian sense. It helped me in teaching modern American and European art; it gave me tools. And then I started to find that maybe something was wrong with it.

At the end of the sixties there was in the political atmosphere, in French Canada and everywhere, a need to go beyond strict formal analysis and say that this was linked with the dominant ideology — to challenge it from the outside. For example, I saw art being produced and discussed in such new forms as video, performance, etc., as well as the return of figuration in painting. I felt that in the new works inside the modern tradition itself, there was some kind of a more open critical situation asking questions not strictly in line with "what is the specificity of a medium," but also "what is the social function of the spectator?" "What is the role of the institution?"

Clement Greenberg:
Madam, you seem to equate modernism with formalism (or with what you call formalism). Now, I would say that that is unhistori-

cal. I don't see the foundation for that kind of equivalence.

T. J. Clark:
I think that probably the resistance one has to the label post-modernism is the resistance to a certain kind of familiar art-packaging operation. You know, combined with that, a resistance to a kind of sort of sloppy afflatus right, you know about the modernist problems being over and here we are, we have free access to the world of historical forms, and so on. I really find that so bankrupt. On the other hand, I tend to agree with you that in the 60's and early 70's there were striking signs of the unproductivity of the modernist paradigm of our artistic practice.

Clement Greenberg:
What is that paradigm, please?

T. J. Clark:
Well, I think it is an artistic practice which takes the primary arena of artistic meaning to be an ongoing work on the media of art itself. I take it to involve a kind of limiting or bracketing of the question of social place and public. I agree very much with Tom Crow that this is a restricted definition of modernism. This is the modernism of, if you like, the 1960's.

Clement Greenberg:
In the presence of pop art?

T. J. Clark:
Well yes, because I think the presence of pop art as Tom Crow, I think, tried to describe, involved a kind of openness to a range of iconography. But what occurred was a fast assimilation of that iconography into the status of near icon, as an essentially formal manoeuvre. I would agree very much with you, Nicole, that there were real signs; I think you can talk about crisis sometimes. Go beyond the lingo of crisis to some kind of serious attention to the unproductivity of a certain practice, it meeting its limits, it meeting fundamental problems. And I think the late 60's and early 70's were such a time. I think the kind of multiplication of media and false media, you know around the fringes of minimalism and con-ceptualism and so on, were a sign of that range of difficulty. And I also think that within that multiplication were serious efforts to raise again as problems intrinsic to the practice of modern art, these

problems of place, of social place, of the limits of the paradigm of artistic production, and so on.

In other words, my allegiance is with the hard textual side of conceptual art at its most serious, and with its subsequent evolution in some cases towards an art practice which tried explicitly to realize within practice the problems of the spectator's place, the problems of the gallery situation, the problems of the social engineering of art. But it is part of post-modernism that it has self-satisfiedly proclaimed that conceptual art is no longer interesting — that, thank God, it was just the end gasp of modernism. And that we can go back happily to a nice rich, fat, full range of media and reference, and it is that side of post modernism which I would reject, not the identification of fundamental problems in the results of modernist art practices.

Clement Greenberg:
I have revised my notion of modernism since I wrote a piece called 'Modernist Painting' that was taken as a prise de position and it was nothing but a description. As I said this morning, modernism in my view, represents a rescue attempt, an attempt to rescue and maintain the best standards of the past, and it has been able to do so only by innovation. Beyond that, I attempt no further definition.

The formalist business, as I heard it from Madame Blondin and Monsieur Payant, was that I have a system, that I believe only in approaching art in a certain way, and that there are artists who follow this system. Nothing of the sort. When it comes to art, the first thing, is how good it is, let's start with that. And good art can come from anywhere. You can't say in advance, you can't have a system or a theory that says that good art has to come from here, or come from there. And the idea that I have such a system or theory has always appalled me, but it has been no use pointing out in public or even adding postscripts to republications of that damn article, that I was describing something. I don't believe in the purity of art. I think it chanced, or maybe it didn't chance, it was a useful fiction, a point of orientation. I don't believe in the purity of art. I don't believe art is only a question of form. What experience has shown me is that the people who write most relevantly about art usually start, in the case of pictorial art at any rate, in the case of music, with what it looks like, or what it sounds like, and proceed from there. And they usually in my experience, show their competence by their judgments in taste. And I come back to that again.

The question is not the theoretical framework or the notion of history, the question is as, let's say, as between modernism and postmodernism, where is good art still coming from? Where is major art still coming from? And all other questions retreat before that. And so much for formalism. Let me say, formalism is a vulgar term, adopted by a certain group of very good Russian writers before the First World War, it became an epithet for the Bolsheviks. The Bolsheviks rendered it irredeemably vulgar.

Audience:
I just wondered, that sounds that you are arguing that good art is a question of personal taste then.

Clement Greenberg:
Good art always starts by being a question of personal taste. And do I have to come back to what the philosopher said, personal taste is not so personal when it is good. Good taste transcends personality.

Audience:
Is this an absolute aesthetics, then?

Clement Greenberg:
Now, no the question of the objectivity of taste has been wrestled with by better minds than mine and it hasn't been wrestled to a fall yet. But let me say, the past shows that a consensus of taste emerges, that there are what Matthew Arnold calls "touchstones", but I mean something different. And that consensus of taste agrees that Shakespeare was the greatest poet in the English language, and that Homer was the greatest poet in the Greek language. It agrees that Michelangelo, at least in the Sistine Ceiling, was one of the greatest painters, in our tradition. And it goes on that way. All the big names are there, and taste agrees in generation after generation, not because it is cowed by these names. It is not. Those who care, those who have the leisure and comfort, to apply themselves to art, end up by agreeing very largely with the past. Of course there are revisions, there are peripheral disagreements, but the consensus of taste is there and it is there in exotic civilisations, too, to show that taste somehow does work out objectively. As empirical as that. And I postulate nothing. Ok that is it.

Audience:
It is a ridiculous position, I think. It seems to me that taste is

defined by a body of critics in power and that is what creates the canon of good works.

Clement Greenberg:
Let me interrupt, you mean contemporary art or art of the past?

Audience:
We are addressing ourselves to modernism.

Clement Greenberg:
No, no I just told you I was talking about art of the past. You didn't hear that. I was talking about art of the past. About contemporary art, there has been great disagreement for the past 150 years, and the disagreements get ironed out in the course of time. The consensus of taste finally makes itself felt. Now, if you don't think Picasso was a great painter when he was great, I would say, (. . . laughter . . .) let me, I don't want to be misunderstood again. (. . . laughter . . .) Picasso is far away enough from us in the past for us to see that between 1909 and 1925 he was an extremely great painter. If you can't see that yourself, you aren't able to see painting.

Audience:
Except, can I just make one more point, it seems to me that again this rises and falls on the notion of taste. This great art. And that is not my concern. My great concern is to understand the painting where it comes from, what its intentions are, how it is received. Those things are things that you don't address and you are not interested in, clearly.

Clement Greenberg:
No, I am not interested in those questions primarily. That is true.

Benjamin Buchloh:
I thought it had been clarified a little more in Timothy Clark's paper today, that the criteria for Greenberg's normative aesthetics based on the critique of taste were historically proven to be invalid and disfunctional. I wanted to add (. . . laughter . . .) but . . .

Clement Greenberg:
I have no criteria.

Benjamin Buchloh:
But you have them in very apodictic manner, which you just performed in a very strong way.

Clement Greenberg:
No criteria were mentioned.

Benjamin Buchloh:
The question is from an historical point of view.

Clement Greenberg:
Tell me of one criterion I mentioned.

Benjamin Buchloh:
You do not mention the criteria, you say good art and you have to see it, and that is the only decision and the only capacity that you have to prove.

Clement Greenberg:
Right, but where are criteria involved in what I am saying?

Benjamin Buchloh:
What I am trying to say, and I want to give some historical information on that problem, is how then is it possible that your own judgment, which was so extremely important, omitted the two major movements in twentieth-century art history that by now not everybody, but quite a few people would agree, were the crucial movements since Cubism? How was it possible that your normative aesthetics omitted the development of Russian Constructivism and Productivism, and omitted or deleted from history the relevance of the paradigm of Duchamp's ready-made and related Dada aesthetics?

Clement Greenberg:
In the first place as I told you, I hadn't seen enough Russian Constructivist art. That was the reason I admitted. As far as Duchamp is concerned, as an artist, he is second-rate. He is minor. As a cultural event, he is very important, however. (. . . turbulence in audience . . .)

Benjamin Buchloh:
So we have to revise the criteria.

Clement Greenberg:
No we don't, I still haven't employed criteria. I have just said my taste tells me that he is a second-rate artist, and that is all.

Benjamin Buchloh:
It proves that taste as an instrument to understand history is no longer valid as a tool.

Clement Greenberg:
I am not understanding history, I am understanding art.

T. J. Clark:
I would like to say that the main drift, or one of the main drifts of my talk was to suggest that if we are addressing this question, taste seems to me a category which always disguises under its generality and appearance of an immediacy of intuition, a complex construction of understanding — of the place and significance of objects in a certain sometimes very impoverished and sometimes very rich, notion of history. And what I was trying to say was that the prescience of Greenberg's taste, as well as its omissions and "faillite" (failure) can be tied rather vividly to the elaborateness and also the limits of a certain notion of the place of art in a complex historical order. And that leads me to say with some relish, I must say, that it interests me very much that Marcelin Pleynet in the end is the spokesman here for post-modernism, and his spokesmanship has to do with a disposing of the concept of history. It is interesting that a tradition of thought with which I have been deeply sympathetic and involved over the past 15 years, the tradition of thought of French structuralism and after, has really declined now into an overt anti-historicism, into an extraordinary threadbare opposition to the basic language of historical explanation, and into a system of alibis for a played-out and banal formalism and a complacence to the kind of eclecticism to which present-day formalism has given rise. (. . turbulence . . .)

Marcelin Pleynet:
It seems to me that this symposium and the term modernism are a little bit of a tree that covers a forest. Or some kind of Trojan horse that exists only to make a certain vision of history pass by, which in a certain way is true, since the term never served any other purpose anyway. I think we have seen this morning in the discussion between Clement Greenberg and T. J. Clark that the term Moder-

nism helped Greenberg to parade one vision of history and it helped Clark to parade another one.

What surprises me in this case in particular, that these discussions can go on forever. What surprises me and what I think is utterly repetitive and very typical of art historians is the fact that they discuss on the basis of a concept of history without discussing the concept itself. Certainly they do not explain the analysis of a detail, which would only make sense if at the same time they would explain and justify the concept that is imposed on the detail.

We have heard the word 'bourgeoisie' quite frequently today, which presumably means that somehow one is convinced that there is a valid idea that believes in the organisation of society in terms of social classes. Well, these are very old concepts indeed, these are the marxist concepts, that have become entirely questionable by now as we know. One cannot simply extract them from the works of Marx and transplant them into art history without questioning them very carefully. This is just one problem. The question that has to be asked therefore is the question of the historical discourse at the moment when it actually affects history.

As much as I have been able to understand it one has examined a great number of details today, one has dealt with a considerable amount of dates and information, but one still does not know on which theoretical and historical basis these concepts that have been proposed, are actually dependent upon, and moreover, on which critical bases and historical position they have advanced. I think that is all that I had to say.

T. J. Clark:
There are several things to say to that. First of all, that is a reassurance to me, that you have not dispensed with the concept of history, but open it to question. Secondly, the notion of an openness to questioning, as opposed to the predisposition of the already made concepts is, as you know, one of the basic tactics of liberal discourse. And there seems to me a real distinction, to be made between questioning and a questioning approach to history and what are the concepts with which one best describes it, and a kind of empty eclecticism and historicism in which each age suggests its own histories, its own historicity of categories, its own sort of weightless discourse appropriate to it. Now, I am perfectly well aware that the Marxist discourse is a discourse marked at all points by all kinds of difficulty, negligence, dogmatism, etc. I still find it workable, however.

Audience:

I would like to make an observation and ask a question. This has
been for me an extraordinary conference, and I have been extraordinarily impressed with the quality of the papers given. One of the
characteristics of the papers was, however, a certain authoritarianism, dare I say. Characterized in the mind, by an intellectuality, a
forcefulness, a one-directionality, a rationality, and empiricism, a
masculinity, power. Now, I mean this as a compliment, (laughter
. . .) . . . It is a suggestive compliment, nevertheless. The question I
have has to do with the thin line that perhaps is to be observed as a
result of listening to the papers, between notions of authoritarianism and of resistance and negation. That is to say, it seemed to me
that the defense, such as it is, that has emerged regarding modernism, has to do with the negations that it has posed with regard to
the culture. And I think that in many instances, not necessarily
given during this conference, the force and energy of modernism to
pose negations against the culture has been characterized indeed as
authoritarian. Rightly or wrongly, from one, shall we say, Marxist
angle, maybe vulgar Marxist angle, that characterizes Abstract Expressionism as authoritarian because it is used for the purposes of
foreign policy. Also, descriptions of abstract painting that have
been looked at in terms of adjectives, such as energy, power, etc.

The question I have then, is that modernism has been effective,
it's been said, by its ability to pose negations. In asking what is the
ideology of modernism, one is also asking what values shall we say
modernism has to pose? The question that is in my mind perhaps
should be thought of that sticky area of late modernism, that sticky
area of abstraction. What I am curious about is, are there qualities
in that art that are more than negations? That are more than
resistances? What I am interesed in is the notion of whether those
aspects of the art, shall we say, that have to do with openness of
structure, do they carry a value? Can we take what Tim Clark said
this morning about Cézanne and the flat canvas, and transport that
notion through to later abstraction? They have to do with the
admission of context into one's response to late abstract work.

I would just like to come back to the present and I would like to
address myself first to Buchloh and to Clark. I have been trying to
extricate from the conference some understanding of what you are
presenting as a modernist art, what the characteristics of it are. So
far it seems to be that it's work which negates, it has flatness and it
could be subsumed. What about the work that is being produced
by artists right now that cannot be subsumed under any of those

categories? Is it impoverished, as Mr. Clark says? Is it something which we are temporarily putting under the definition of post-modern? What happens to the work of female artists, as Nicole described them today — autobiographical, personal, emotional, marginal? What about performance? What about video? To what extent can either Mr. Clark or Mr. Buchloh address this question?

(Clapping)

Benjamin Buchloh:
I thought I had attempted to point to one particular practice yesterday that I consider inadequate in both perspectives — the perspective of the formalist rigidity that we have inherited from Greenberg's criticism, as well as the historical claims and the historical necessities that art production under contemporary conditions faces. So when I was rejecting this particular practice of neofiguration — neofigurative art — I was not implying that other practices such as — well, I would not want to use the term video art because that doesn't really say anything — but practices that do result, for example, in conceptual art in a very systematic and very relevant analysis of the particular conditions under which the work of art is produced — under which the work of art is received — under which the work of art is distributed.

One obvious case in point would be the work of Daniel Buren. As far as the question for feminist art is concerned, I would say obviously there are feminist art that do fulfill the historical requests — that do fulfill the historical formal necessities that we have inherited, as far as the development of the aesthetic language itself is concerned. At the same time because of the precision with which they inscribe themselves in the tradition of the discourse, they do also relate to the particular historical and political condition within which they operate. So the two merge very well in certain aesthetic practices of the present day.

One example that I would like to mention would be the work of Martha Rosler. So I think there is a wide range of current activities, coming out of the late 60's conceptual art, that have in fact successfully merged those various elements of the discourse, and that can be considered as an activist political formal investigation into the production of art under the very conditions of this present decade. Whether you want to call this a modernist tradition, I would say yes, that is the continuation of the modernist practice. That is the continuation of the avant-garde implications. And I would say, to go along with what Tom Crow said, that there is no reason why the reflection on the very historic activity itself would have to be abandoned, or would have to be considered as invalid or inadequate or impossible.

T. J. Clark:

Well, I think that is an answer with which I agree in very large measure, and I won't bore you by adding to it much. For reasons to do with one's unease with Clement Greenberg's posing of the question in terms of taste, I wish to avoid a listing of heroes. But I do think there are various individuals, various groups, within this plethora of disintegrating modernist art practices . . .

Audience:

You are using constantly negative terms, like disintegration and impoverished, and yet you yourself said, "I see this as an unprecedented art risking its own destruction — a bourgeois art in the absence of a bourgeois culture." Now, if it is an unprecedented art, then why do you have such problems with it being an unprecedented situation. Why do you have to continually redescribe everything as being under the modernist condition?

T. J. Clark:

What you are saying again goes back to the notion that there is a new history appropriate in every new appearance within capitalism. This is nihilism.

Audience:

From what I've been getting from the conference is a repetition of precedents. See this is what I am trying to understand. What can I take with me from this discussion in order to analyse consider and reflect upon contemporary work?

T. J. Clark:

I can give you a straight answer to that. I have said that I think that the 70's are a period in which, very graphically, problems appeared in the kind of ability to reproduce itself of a certain classic central modernist practice. What I am saying is that this produced a plethora — I'll use the word again — a plethora of kinds of material, kinds of spread and expansion of practice, kinds of attempts at new reference, and so on. We are living in that situation. But I think to call that post-modernism is obstructive because it seems to me that what those practices still address is the fundamental problem which modernism addressed —which I tried to describe in historical terms this morning. I do think there are certain — plenty in fact, well not plenty, but there are certain practices within that spectacle of art at the present time which live up to these minimum demands. That we have an art now which poses to itself the problems of modernism's place, limits, historical situation and responsibilities, and which tries to integrate those limits within its formal practice. Tries to include a sense of limits, place, purpose, function, within its practice. We have, in my opinion, those practices if you want me to name them — I think that again with Benjamin Buchloh, really, that the practice of Art and Language — for all its erratic, strange, and at times sort of mannerist proceedings in the 70's I see as a serious practice, directed to the problems of modernism. As Terry Atkinson is constantly fond of reiterating — there is nothing dafter than all this stuff about modernism going away. Modernism is our resource. We may have problems with it. We may in some sense be, or feel ourselves to be moving towards the outside of it, but it's our resource. We cannot do without it. We are not somewhere else.

Contributors

Benjamin H. D. Buchloh is Assistant Professor of Art History at the State University of New York at Old Westbury and the Editor of the Nova Scotia Series.

T. J. Clark is Professor of Art History at Harvard University, Cambridge, Mass.

Hollis Clayson is currently Assistant Professor of Art History at Northwestern University, Chicago, Ill.

Thomas Crow is Assistant Professor of Art History at Princeton University, Princeton, N.J.

Nicole Dubreuil-Blondin is Associate Professor of Art History at the University of Montreal, Montreal, P.Q.

John Wilson Foster is Associate Professor of English Literature at the University of British Columbia in Vancouver, B.C.

Serge Guilbaut is Assistant Professor of Art History at the University of British Columbia Vancouver, B.C.

Clement Greenberg, the critic, lives in New York, N.Y.

Henri Lefèbvre, the philosopher, lives in Paris, France.

Marcelin Pleynet, an art critic and theoretician, is editor of Tel Quel Magazine in Paris, France.

David Solkin is Assistant Professor of Art History at the Unviersity of British Columbia in Vancouver, B.C.

Allan Sekula is an artist and photography critic and Assistant Professor of Photography at Ohio State University, Columbus, Ohio.

Paul Hayes Tucker is Associate Professor of Art History at the University of Massachusetts at Boston.

Sources

Original titles and sources of the essays published in this collection are as follows:

The essay by T. J. Clark was previously published in slightly different form with the title "Clement Greenberg's Theory of Art," in *Critical Inquiry,* September, 1982.

The essay by Benjamin H. D. Buchloh was previously published in an extended version in *October,* No. 16 (Spring 1981). The version in this volume was first presented at the Vancouver Conference on Modernism.

The essay by Thomas Crow is an expanded version of the paper delivered at the Vancouver Conference on Modernism. A French translation of the essay was previously published in *Parachute Magazine,* Vol. 30/31 (May-June 1983).

The essay by Marcelin Pleynet was previously published in *Tel Quel* under the title "Modernisme-modernité et philosophie de l'histoire."

The excerpts from Henri Lefebvre's *Introduction a la modernité* are published by kind permission of Les Editions de Minuit, Paris.

The translations of the essays by Nicole Dubreuil-Blondin, Henri Lefebvre and Marcelin Pleynet were provided by Paul Smith.